W61.

THE ESSENCE OF EXMOOR

The story of Exmoor since the Second World War

by

Victor Bonham-Carter

Sally
with best love from
Victor

THE EXMOOR PRESS

THE EXMOOR PRESS
Dulverton, Somerset

British Library Cataloguing in Publication Data
Bonham-Carter, Victor
The Essence of Exmoor
l. Somerset (England). National parks, history
I. Title
942.385085

ISBN 0 900131 69 1

Printed in Great Britain by G.P. Printers, South Molton, Devon

Contents

Illustrations

Dedication

To Cynthia, my wife
with much love

Preface

No book of this kind could possibly be written without a great deal of help. I have been given that help most generously by a number of friends and acquaintances – people in the know on a variety of subjects, who not only supplied me with information and comment, but who also read through portions of the text. Indeed each chapter has been checked for accuracy by one or more persons. Without that precaution I would not have dared hand the typescript over to my publisher, Steven Pugsley, whose patience and advice has been a strong support from the beginning. The opinions are of course my own. I should add that, unless otherwise stated, prices and statistics quoted in the text apply to the year 1990; and that, throughout the text I refer to Exmoor National Park as ENP and the Authority as ENPA.

I wish therefore to acknowledge my deep gratitude, first to Roger Miles, who has been an unfailing source of advice, who read through the entire typescript, and with whom I discussed a host of problems: also to Noel Allen and Caroline Giddens, experts in natural history, who did much reading and gave me valuable assistance. I wish also to thank – in alphabetical order – the following:

Harold and Margaret Bale, Tim Davey, The Rt. Hon. Sir Robin Dunn PC, Graham Floyd, David and Jane Hill, Mansel Jaquet, David Knowles, John Leech and his Hobby Horse team at Minehead, E.R. (Dick) Lloyd, Col. Walter Luttrell, Janet McCarthy, David Mansell, Hugh Maund, John Milton, Lance Nicholson, the organisers of the Hunting of the Earl of Rone festival at Combe Martin, the late Laurie Pidgeon, Jan Ross and other members of the Community Education Service, Diana and Maurice Scott, Christopher Shapland, John Whitcutt, Tom Yandle, and several members of the staff of the Exmoor National Park Authority and of the the Rural Development Commission. The assistance of others, not mentioned here, is duly acknowledged in the text.

Victor Bonham-Carter
Milverton
Winter 1990

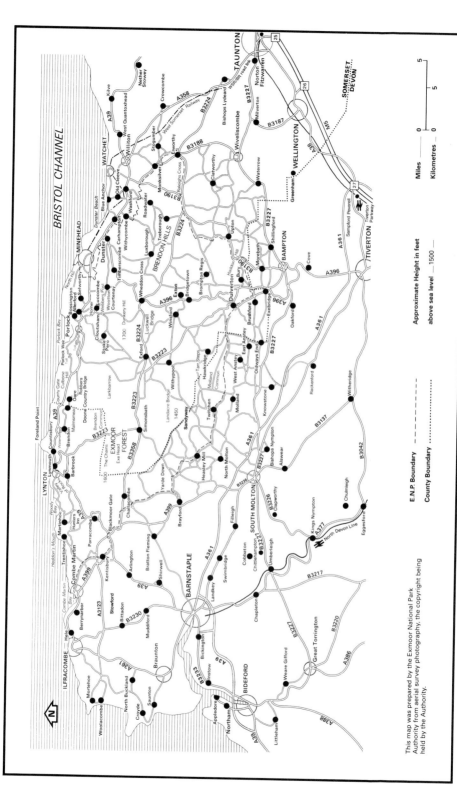

This map was prepared by the Exmoor National Park
Authority from aerial survey photography, the copyright being
held by the Authority.

Approximate Height in feet

above sea level ___1500 ___

E.N.P. Boundary   — — — — —

County Boundary   ·················

Miles   0   5

Kilometres 0   5

A Question of Identity

According to my dictionary, identity is defined as the 'state of being some specific person or thing'. Add to that, recognition. You recognise a 'specific person' in two ways: by his or her appearance – face, figure, hair (or lack of it), colour of skin, and so on, the body in other words; and also by the spirit that animates that body – the character. This dual test enables you to recognise the identity of any person. How can you apply it to a 'thing' – to Exmoor, for example? I believe you can do it in the same way, by body and character.

The body of Exmoor is its landscape. As described in a later chapter, it has a complicated geological foundation and a series of soils characterised by peat in parts of the higher moorland, and loams in the lower hills and valleys. It is the latter that have encouraged reclamation for farming and forestry over a long period of time. Exmoor is therefore fragmented – a patchwork of browns and greens according to the season, with farmsteads and fields, bounded by hedges, stitched between stretches of moorland; or, as in the Brendons, mainly devoted to arable, pasture and trees. The moorland proper survives in several blocks of land, the main one or 'heartland' running westward from Dunkery Beacon to beyond The Chains (the watershed of the principal rivers running north and south) with smaller blocks along the coast and inland at Molland Moor, West Anstey Common, Winsford Hill, Withypool Common, Brendon Common, and elsewhere. Fragmentation means variety – ancient native hardwoods, a blanket of conifers on Croydon Hill, trickling streams, the Barle in spate, a stupendous coast, the barley lands of Porlock Vale, and an abundant wild life inhabiting the whole area. A mosaic that delights in a hundred ways, emanating from the landscape which is the body of Exmoor.

How then does one define the character of Exmoor, bearing in mind that its body makes such a powerful impression on the senses? The answer, I believe, lies in the history, the people, and the literature.

The history has been recorded in a number of books. Two that cover the canvas and are both in print are *Exmoor* by S. H. Burton (Hodder & Stoughton) and *Yesterday's Exmoor* by Hazel Eardley-Wilmot (Exmoor Books). Apart from making good reading, they repay serious study if you want to know more, not only about what has happened on Exmoor over the past thousand years – and much more has happened than you would guess – but how this once wild and isolated area has contributed to the social history of England. I do not propose to delve deeply into details described by these and other books, but briefly to recall that Exmoor was originally a wilderness, punctuated by a handful of small settlements and composed of great stretches of moorland, collectively established by the Normans as a Royal Forest – not trees, but 'simply a district in which the deer and certain other wild animals were reserved to the king and protected by forest law' – to quote E.T. MacDermot, author of the classic, *A History of the Forest of Exmoor* (Barnicott & Pearce). For all practical purposes the Royal Forest *was* Exmoor, administered by a Warden assisted by Foresters, who acted as gamekeepers and enforced the law against poaching with cruel severity – at least until the end of the 13th century. In 1301, however, the boundaries were contracted and penalties reduced, until finally in 1508 the Royal Forest was in effect 'privatised'. Thereafter it was leased for a fixed rent to the Warden, who was free to make what money he could out of grazing and other uses of the Moor, and enjoy the hunting – all this consistent with obligations due to and observed by certain rights-holders bordering the Forest, known as the 'Free Suitors' of Hawkridge and Withypool, and other 'Suitors at Large'.

No one took Exmoor seriously for the purposes of intensive farming or forestry until the Napoleonic Wars, when sudden thoughts were given to growing timber for the Royal Navy. To that end the Royal Forest was 'disafforested' by Act of Parliament in 1815, enclosed, and the land divided between the Crown and neighbouring landowners and Suitors. Almost at once the timber proposals were abandoned and the Crown Allotment offered for sale. In the event it was bought by a Midland industrialist, John Knight, who also acquired other parcels of land, totalling altogether some 20,000 acres – roughly the same acreage as the old Royal Forest of which he bought about four-fifths.

The story of the immense efforts and outlay invested by John Knight and his son, Frederic, over some eighty years in their reclamation of several thousand acres of high moor, creation of individual farms and farmsteads, maintenance of sheep herdings on the unimproved lands, construction of roads and boundaries, ventures in mining, and the resultant growth of the community based on Simonsbath – all this has been placed on record by C.S. Orwin in *The Reclamation of Exmoor Forest* (OUP), revised and expanded by R. J. Sellick in a reprint by David & Charles in 1970. Moreover, further information, not available to either MacDermot or Orwin and Sellick, has recently come to light through the researches of Roger A. Burton in his privately published book, *The Heritage of Exmoor*.

The significance of the Knight enterprise reposed in the fact that it ended, once and for all, the medieval practices of the Forest and introduced radical methods of husbandry and estate management that, after many trials and errors, left a permanent mark on the landscape – in striking contrast to the Acland regime at Holnicote which, notwithstanding the magnificent legacy of the Horner woods and strict stewardship of the pure-bred Anchor herd of Exmoor ponies, was patriarchal and traditional. Modern Exmoor began with the Knights.

The Knight lands passed to the Fortescues of Castle Hill in 1897, but the system of stock raising on the tenant farms and sheep ranching (with Cheviots) on the open moor continued, surviving the depressed years of the 1920s and 1930s. During that time, the Fortescue estate (which had totalled around 25,000 acres in 1900) was slimmed down by the sale of the Brendon and Honeymead properties, without altering the familiar pattern of moor and in-bye fields, characteristic of hill farming on Exmoor. The second world war wrought great changes thanks to the Government drive for food production. At Honeymead, purchased by Sir Robert Waley Cohen in 1927, a thousand acres of old pasture were broken up and, by 1945, a pedigree herd of British Friesians had been introduced, while 2,455 sheep and 158 beef cattle were being carried on 1,175 acres. Elsewhere the Honeymead example was followed on a much more modest scale, but – by the end of the war – the nation was receiving two-thirds of its total food requirements from home sources and – in contrast to the abandonment of agriculture after the first world war – legislation was passed, underpinning British farming with a system of subsidies and guaranteed prices for the next forty years.

Strangely not all hill and marginal land farmers on Exmoor benefited by wartime prosperity, due mainly to an anomaly in the hill farming legislation as explained later; for it was thanks to the initiative of a group of Exmoor farmers, who commissioned a survey and report from Bristol University, that the true situation was revealed and ultimately corrected by the Livestock Rearing Act 1951 – a move that led, in turn, to the establishment by the Ministry of Agriculture of Liscombe Experimental Farm, near Tarr Steps, in 1954, the year when Exmoor was designated a National Park.

I have concentrated thus far in these notes on hill and moorland farming because, without livestock grazing, the uplands would be choked with thicket and scrub, so that Exmoor would possess neither its fine and open landscape, nor its farming families. Hill farming and the people engaged in it at every level form the foundation of the history of Exmoor; and that is still true today. Landowners, tenants, freeholders, shepherds, cattlemen, labourers, mechanics, agents, vets, hauliers, dealers, auctioneers, and a host of craftsmen and contractors engaged, year in year out, in work on and for the land.

A few names taken at random from church and estate records, and gravestones in village churchyards, over the past 200 years would include, among the landowners, Acland, Fortescue, Halliday, Herbert, Knight, Luttrell, Notley, Sydenham, Snow, Trevelyan, Wyndham; among the farmers and those who worked for them, Bawden, Blackmore, Buckingham, Chidgey, Court, Dascombe, Fry, Greenslade, Hayes, Huxtable, Lock, Milton, Nancekivell, Peppin, Pugsley, Quartly, Rawle, Richards, Ridd, Ridler, Shapland, Steer, Thorne, Tout, Vellacott, Webber, Westcott, Winzer, Yandle. Then there are those remembered for their life style, interests, eccentricities, or participation in some notable event. Men such as Dr Charles Palk Collyns, Dulverton doctor, who saved staghunting when it was at a low ebb in the middle of the last century, and wrote a classic account of the subject; Fred Goss, the harbourer and gamekeeper at Pixton; Fenwick Bisset who in effect founded the Devon and Somerset Staghounds and built the kennels at Exford; Ernest Bevin, a village boy born out of wedlock who rose to

become Foreign Secretary, and William Dicker, headmaster of the
village school for 35 years, both of Winsford; Alfred Pool, inventor,
who built oil engines and farm machinery at Chipstable; Parson
Jack Russell, who kept his own pack of hounds at Swimbridge;
Parson Froude, a 'rough customer' at Knowstone; Parson Boyse of
Hawkridge who wrote an historic hunting diary; Parson Thornton,
the first incumbent of Simonsbath in the 1850s, and author of a
valuable, though unorganised, volume of reminiscences; George
Williams, founder of the YMCA, born at Ashway, near Dulverton;
Edmund Wood, village carpenter, Bible Christian preacher, known
as the 'Boanerges of the Pulpit', who travelled the Kingsbrompton
circuit; Arthur Heal, huntsman, present when the Prince of Wales
hunted with the 'D & S' in 1879 and gave the stag the *coup de grâce*;
Arthur's son, Fred, piloted the naturalist, Richard Jefferies, over
Exmoor in 1883 and briefed him for his book, *Red Deer*; John
Fortescue, historian of the British Army; Lionel Edwards and
Alfred Munnings, artists of Exmoor; the Scottish shepherds who
came south to serve the Knights and settle on Exmoor – Little,
Gourdie, Johnstone (among others); and of course R. D. Blackmore
who quarrelled with Nicholas Snow, or rather vice versa, over
the comic character, Farmer Snowe, in *Lorna Doone*. Blackmore
apologised and sent Snow a loving cup, but they never really made
it up.

It is of course impossible to make a tidy list of names and events,
and I make no apology for mine; but that is the fascination of
probing into local history, and anyone who loves Exmoor will make
up his or her own. Nor do I apologise for the prominence of hunting in my version. The plain fact is that the sport has been a passion
among Exmoor countrymen, from the lord in his castle to the poor
man in his hovel, from far far back in time; and, translated into the
circumstances of today, it still is.

The third ingredient in the character of Exmoor, as I conceive it,
is literature, but that is too wide and diverse a subject to encompass
in a paragraph here. I shall attempt an assessment of it in the last
chapter of the book which, however, is not intended as a history of
the past – though obviously no history can do without the past –
but as an interpretation of Exmoor as it has moved on in time since
the Second World War, and as it is today.

PART ONE

Why a National Park?

CHAPTER ONE

The Birth of the National Park

When I came out of the Army in 1946, I was determined to get into farming, convinced that producing food was a vital job essential to our very survival as a nation. That may sound dramatic nowadays in a period of food surpluses, but it was only too evident during the Second World War when German U Boats nearly brought us to our knees – as they had done in the First – and which prompted Parliament to pour money into the land. By contrast with 1921 when all support for home farming was withdrawn, the Government elected in 1945 continued to subsidise agriculture as a practical move towards economic recovery – to save currency and to go on making good use of the 30 million or so acres of fertile farmland in the U.K. Moreover there was real fear of a world food shortage, which would have hit Britain particularly hard if the food was no longer there to be imported.

At all events this is what brought me and my family to the West Country and, after a long search, to Langaller Farm, Brushford, a run-down hilly farm of 135 acres on the edge of Exmoor: where, for nine years, we applied for every subsidy available, took the plough round the farm, ripped out redundant hedges (several fields were three acres or less) and useless scrub, laid miles of land drains, found water and installed drinking troughs in all the fields, adapted buildings, pioneered silage in the area, and raised output tenfold on what had once been an indifferent beef and sheep holding to one producing milk from a high-yielding herd of Guernseys, and bacon from numerous litters of Wessex and Landrace pigs.

That was the practical part, but I was keen to put my ideas down on paper and, having served a short apprenticeship on *The Countryman* magazine before the war, I wanted to see these ideas in print. My opportunity came when entering for an essay competition organised by the Association of Agriculture in 1952 with the subject, *The Towns know too little about the Country – how may this be remedied?* In my essay I re-deployed the argument just outlined, that – thanks to the war – home agriculture had already come back into its own, and that it must be kept going to enable us as a nation to pay our way and live; further, that economics were the foundation upon which country life and work was built. This meant that, in addition to the primary employments of farming, forestry, etc, small-scale industry would have to be established in rural areas to absorb surplus labour and provide the means for social life. Happily my essay came first out of some 1300 entries and I collected the then substantial sum of £100, the only prize I have ever won in my life – I never won anything at school – and worth at least twenty times as much now!

Of course, I was not the only farmer breaking old pasture. Other 'up-country' incomers were working on similar lines as regards ploughing and re-seeding; but, more importantly, so were numerous farmers on Exmoor proper, who were taking the plough ever further 'up the hill': to the extent that, within a few years, it became clear that an alarming amount of moorland, including some of the finest stretches of landscape, was being rapidly eroded; but few of us worried about that in the early 1950s, nor did the Government. More and more food, please, was the order of the day. I and most other farmers were happy to go along with that.

Then came the designation of Exmoor as a National Park in 1954 under the National Parks and Access to the Countryside Act 1949, followed within a few years by a crisis that detonated the long battle between farmers and foresters on the one side and their opponents on the other over the conservation of moorland on Exmoor. To understand why that happened and how it developed, it is necessary to look behind the 1949 Act and much of the other legislation, enacted immediately after the war, that affected land use including access to and enjoyment of the countryside by the public.

*   *   *   *   *   *   *   *   *   *   *

The story starts early in the 19th century when the Romantic movement was generating a passion for the wild in Nature: in literature expressed, for example, in the works of poets such as Byron, Coleridge and Wordsworth. The latter is often quoted as the first man to propound the concept of National Parks for, in his

Guide to the Lake District (1810), he wrote that it should become 'a sort of national property, in which every man has a right and an interest,who has an eye to perceive and a heart to enjoy'. He might well have said something similar about Exmoor a dozen years earlier when he and his sister spent a year (1797-8) at Alfoxden House near Holford in West Somerset. Together with their friend, Samuel Taylor Coleridge, they engaged in long (often nocturnal) walks along the coast to Lynton, which aroused local suspicions as to their being French spies. However, Wordsworth was a snob, for he wanted 'national property' reserved for the enjoyment of those with 'pure taste', certainly not rude artisans and vulgar shopkeepers.

As the 19th century advanced, pressures – additional to the aesthetic – built up, piecemeal, with different motives and sources of energy, deriving principally from reaction against the Industrial Revolution, which was rapidly ridding the country of the last vestiges of feudalism and digging away at the foundations of rural society. Open fields had long been enclosed and bounded with hedges, while common land – those uncultivated open spaces as large as Brendon Common and as small as Exford village green – was shrinking fast, from a total of 3.2 million acres in 1800 to 2.6 million in 1873. Exmoor lost no fewer than 30 commons between 1841 and 1872. At the same time the population of Britain was rising fast and changing in character. According to the Census of 1851 it was almost equally divided between country and town, but the latter was moving rapidly ahead. An industrial economy and the urban society it supported generated living and working conditions that, in the circumstances of Victorian Britain, were bound sooner or later to burst their bonds.

Amenity – the Reaction Against Industrialism

Social unrest normally expresses itself in politics, and politics was indeed inherent in most of the amenity movements after 1850. In any event, at some stage early or late, Parliament had to be invoked to protect existing rights or create new ones; and that was evident when an early amenity organisation, the Commons Preservation Society, was founded in 1865. This was a typically English institution, in that a handful of altruistic persons, fortunately in positions of influence, undertook what Parliament should have dealt with earlier: namely to prevent the enclosure of commons round London. As it was it fell to the Society to defend the rights of the commoners in the courts; and it was this action, taken at the eleventh hour, that prompted the Government to pass the Metropolitan Commons Act 1866 and the Commons Act ten years later. It would have been unthinkable for London to be deprived of Hampstead Heath, Wandsworth, Wimbledon and other open spaces and, further afield, Epping Forest as well.

Meanwhile the Society was extending its scope from urban to rural commons, and then to footpaths and bridleways, a logical step explained in its change of title, first to the cumbersome one of Commons, Open Spaces and Footpaths Preservation Society, now shortened to The Open Spaces Society. The record of its progress compares to the pattern of advance and retreat experienced by the British Army in the Peninsula War in Spain, 1808-14, a campaign won by skilful leadership and sheer dogged persistence, notwithstanding – in the Society's case – an outright defeat in 1901 over access to Stonehenge, where at one point the owner threatened to sell the stones to America! It is heartening to know that today the Society is as active as ever, and that its work in defence of commons and rights-of-way is just as vigorous as in the 1860s.

The interplay of access, conservation and recreation – three components of amenity – filled a whole century of time between 1850 and 1950, with plenty going on before and after those dates. Exmoor was no exception, although change was relatively restricted. The Royal Forest had been, as explained, a wild waste of moorland grasses, heather and gorse, roamed by the red deer and other wild creatures, and summer-grazed by sheep and cattle, but otherwise little troubled by man until John and Frederic Knight began draining and deep-ploughing portions of it and creating hill farms around Simonsbath in the 19th century. The area of common land was also reduced. Even so the many habitats of fauna and flora all over the moorland, then well over 100,000 acres in extent, cannot have been seriously disturbed; while recreation, in the form of field sports, detracted very little from the abundance of Nature. Indeed it was thanks to hunting under the regime of Fenwick Bisset, Master of the Devon and Somerset Staghounds, that the deer population markedly increased. To judge from the memoirs of the Rev. W.H. Thornton, keen fisherman and vigorous horseman who rode all over the Moor, discharging his duties as the first parish priest of Exmoor, 1856-60 – by which time the Knights had completed most of their reclamations and were consolidating their new farms – wild life was as abundant as ever. Tourism and other intrusions came later.

Interest in Landscape and Wildlife

Educated interest in Nature owed much to the amateurs. The later Victorians were avid 'bug-hunters', to use the term generically, but earlier they had had to contend with a legacy of cruelty to animals, or at best with indifference to their suffering, also with traditional practices of trapping for food, and – almost universally – with sheer ignorance of the importance of Nature in the scheme of things, other than the countryman's instinctive wisdom. As always in Britain, advances were hesitant and piecemeal. The Society for the Prevention of Cruelty to Animals (SPCA) was founded in 1824 (Royal in 1840), primarily to stop the ill-treatment of horses and cattle in markets, and to eradicate bear-baiting and cock-fighting, still covertly carried on. The RSPCA then turned to the protection of wild birds, vivisection, and 'blood sports' – causes which also became the concern of other organisations later. In 1885 the Selborne Society was founded to promote the aims of the great naturalist Gilbert White, followed, four years later, by the Society for the Protection of Birds (Royal in 1904), which soon became a powerful national body, campaigning at first against the slaughter of game birds, the use of plumage in the fashion trade, and the obsessive collection of eggs.

It was due to consistent lobbying by these and other organisations that a sequence of Acts for the protection of wild life was passed in Parliament, an early example being the Sea Birds Protection Act 1869: though differentiation between predators, rare species, and those common in one area and not in another, always presented difficulties, and enforcement a very problematic business indeed. Publication and education, however, proved effective in the long run, and in this the RSPB led the field: with the issue of leaflets, posters, articles, and letters to the press; and, later on, broadcasting. It created close contacts with schools, and in W. H. Hudson, the writer, had an eminent and popular protagonist who was the author of several RSPB titles. He died in 1922 and left nearly £6,000 to the education account of the Society.

The success of the Commons Preservation Society and of the RSPB proved that private initiative was as likely to bring about changes in public opinion and legislation as head-on pressure in Parliament. It was Robert Hunter, hon. solicitor to the Commons Society, who first proposed the idea of an organisation empowered to purchase and manage land and buildings for the benefit of the nation. Soon joined by Octavia Hill, housing reformer, and Canon H.D. Rawnsley, defender of the Lake District, these three set up The National Trust for Places of Historic Interest or Natural Beauty in 1895, and duly registered it as a charitable body. The three founders were fundamentally concerned with the aesthetics of environment, man-made as well as natural beauty; and so in addition to acquiring suitable properties, they proposed to permit public access, encourage an atmosphere of appreciation, and ensure that the organisation had the means and the standing to pursue these aims in perpetuity. So rapid was their progress that, in 1907, barely twelve years after foundation, Parliament conferred upon the Trust the unique power to declare its properties inalienable: which meant that they could not be sold or mortgaged, nor compulsorily acquired, except by permission of Parliament. The relevance of these events for Exmoor will be described in due course.

By 1910 the National Trust had acquired several sites of high ecological value, notably parts of Wicken Fen in Cambridgeshire. It was felt by certain naturalists, however, that the Trust was not, at that date, adequately equipped to manage these places (in contrast to its architectural and archaeological properties), or, more importantly, to take charge of the many other sites about the country that might qualify as Nature Reserves. Accordingly a new body, the Society for the Promotion of Nature Reserves, was founded in 1912, inspired and largely financed by the Hon. Nathaniel Charles Rothschild (familiarly known as N.C.R.), a pioneer of great vision. The main object of the SPNR was not to acquire reserves, but to survey the country for sites, persuade or otherwise induce owners to part with them and hand them over to the National Trust, and generally educate the public about Nature and the interaction of fauna and flora – ecology, in fact. By 1915 a list of 284 possible sites had been drawn up, but already the First World War was putting a brake on activities, which were virtually brought to a stop by the untimely death of N.C.R. in 1923. The next sizeable step forward had to wait for nearly thirty years.

Meanwhile progress of a sort was sustained by stealth. Nature Reserves were created in effect in some of the properties of the Forestry Commission, established by Parliament in 1919, also in private woodlands, and in the gathering grounds of water undertakings. A far more significant event was the formation of the Norfolk Naturalists' Trust in 1926, the first of its kind, with powers to own and hold land for the purpose of Reserves. No similar body was created until after the Second World War, Yorkshire setting up in 1946; and now County Trusts exist all over the country, associated under the umbrella of the Royal Society for Nature Conservation, the eventual successor to SPNR. Exmoor, lying as it does across the two counties, comes within the purview of Devon Wildlife Trust and Somerset Trust for Nature Conservation. Nature studies have also been undertaken by the Natural History section of the Somerset Archaeological and Natural History Society, founded in 1849. Since 1974, however, Exmoor has had its own Natural History Society, formed by a group of local enthusiasts with headquarters at Minehead.

Recreation

As regards recreation in the countryside, it was again mainly private initiative that set the pace, once working hours in factories had been reduced, however slightly, Saturday half-day introduced, and four bank holidays a year enacted, thanks to Sir John Lubbock, in 1871. Leisure was beginning at last to be regarded as a right for all working people. As to means, the railways were the first in the field with cheap fares and excursions that took the ordinary man and his family to the seaside. Inland it was difficult to travel far outside the railway line, especially on a day's outing, but the possibilities were greatly extended by the 'safety' bicycle, introduced c.1885-6, a cheap and handy form of transport as you could put your machine in the guard's van and start out from any station. It was also a pleasant way of exploring the countryside, companionable, and carried few social distinctions. Moreover the Cyclists' Touring Club, founded in 1878, gave cycling holidays a great impetus by supplying its members with maps and a list of recommended accommodation. The bicycle was at the height of its popularity in the Edwardian era, before cars became common.

Other open air organisations soon proliferated – for walking, camping, rock climbing, sailing, etc. The Ramblers' Association – to take one example – is recognised today as the national organisation for walkers, and is powerful and respected. Although adopting its present title as late as 1935, its origins lay in the Federation of Rambling Clubs founded in 1905 to unite the activities of the many individual clubs that had by then come into being. Young towns-people, from school age upwards, had acute problems wanting to get away from the smoke and noise of the streets and over-crowded homes, and go out into the countryside and fend for themselves. The Boy Scouts (1908) and later the Girl Guides, provided part of the solution; also the extraordinary energy of T. A. Leonard who founded the Co-operative Holidays Association in 1891 and the Holiday Fellowship in 1913. The Trade Union movement was also active in the field. But the most important contribution came from Germany, where Richard Schirrmann, an enlightened schoolmaster, established Youth Hostels before the first war, and where they blossomed after 1918 in response to the special circumstances of German life – poverty induced by inflation of the mark, and the national characteristic of romanticising the simple life. Britain followed suit with the launch of the Youth Hostels Association in 1930, which grew fast, but even faster after 1945 when, in company with other open air organisations, it was faced by a massive demand for recreation in the countryside in an age of affluence.

Access

We must return to the matter of access for, without a solution to that problem, the pressure for leisure would have been stifled. As it was, it built up a dangerous head of steam over a long period of effort in and out of Parliament. As far back as 1884, James Bryce had introduced the first of a series of Private Bills to permit access to mountains and moorland. All Bryce's exertions were in vain, as were those of Charles Trevelyan who introduced Bills in 1908, 1926, 1927 and 1928; of Ellen Wilkinson in 1931, and of Geoffrey Mander in 1937 and 1938. In April 1932 the campaign was given an edge by militant action. Hikers organised mass trespass in the Peak District, a huge area of open moorland sandwiched between Manchester and Sheffield; and it was here that Tom Stephenson conceived the idea of a long-distance footpath through disputed land over the Pennines. The Pennine Way became a rallying cry for the open air movement, and Tom Stephenson himself – he later became Secretary of the Ramblers' Association – played a leading part in the fight for public access. However the opposition was powerful, and preparations for war provided the Government with a ready-made excuse to do nothing. Eventually in 1939 Arthur Creech Jones presented a Bill that passed its Second Reading but was so mutilated in Committee that many of its supporters withdrew their backing. Although the Access to Mountains Act 1939 reached the statute book, it was rendered inoperative by the Second World War, and was duly repealed by post-war legislation.

National Parks

The idea of National Parks, as places of wilderness and landscape beauty to which people had access as of right, is historically closely integrated with that of land use and land planning. It was the lack of effective legislation to control housing and industrial development after the first war, when farm land was cheap, that led to aberrations only too familiar today – the by-pass villa and pretentious bungalow, ribbon-built to save the cost of service roads and public utilities, drab council house estates socially segregated from the rest of the community, long stretches of coastline submerged in spoliation. The prospect of subtopia was unlimited, against which a mixed bag of amenity organisations was powerless. Public opinion, however, was not yet ready for effective public planning, hence the foundation in 1926 of the Council for the Preservation (later Protection) of Rural England, due to the initiative of Guy Dawber and Patrick Abercrombie, both architects. Its aims, in brief, were to organise concerted action against the disfigurement of the countryside, co-ordinate effort among its members, and ensure that amenity attain a standing which Government departments, and private and public developers alike, could not with impunity brush aside. It meant that, until the countryside came under effective planning, the CPRE was forced to assume a quasi-planning role which should have been played by a Ministry. This is exactly what happened over National Parks, for the CPRE invited the Labour Government of 1929 to investigate the possibility of establishing special areas of fine landscape, rich in natural resources and wild life, i.e. National Parks, where conservation and recreation and other apparently conflicting uses of land might nonetheless be successfully combined. The Government responded by appointing a Committee, under the chairmanship of Dr Christopher Addison, Parliamentary Secretary to the Ministry of Agriculture, which reported in 1931. Interestingly it revealed the inherent dilemma of conservation and recreation, for the Committee recommended two types of Park: 'national reserves' of landscape and wild life, which needed an element of protection against public use or over-use; and 'regional reserves' near towns for uncomplicated public enjoyment. This problem was to recur in post-war legislation. In the event the Addison Report was not implemented owing to the economic recession then becoming acute and to the fall of the Labour Government, although the concept of National Parks was not allowed to die.

In 1935 the CPRE set up a Standing Committee on National Parks, with a wide representation of interests, chaired by Norman Birkett, eminent barrister (later one of the two British judges at the Nuremberg trial of Nazi war criminals) and having, as drafting secretary, John Dower, architect, and son-in-law of Charles Trevelyan who had introduced four of the earlier Bills on access. The Government resisted pressure from the Standing Committee on the grounds that, following the Town and Country Planning Act 1932 (a paper tiger), the new legislation would be capable of protecting the countryside. The Standing Committee categorically disagreed and, in his booklet, *The Case for National Parks*, Dower asserted that local planning authorities had neither the finance nor the competence to look after National Parks, which posed particular problems of access and protection requiring special powers.

Then, in September 1939, came the outbreak of the Second World War, a temporary halt to all peacetime planning, and the beginning of a new era for Exmoor, whither we must now return.

*   *   *   *   *   *   *   *   *   *   *

Exmoor in Wartime

The new era was not characterised simply by the destruction and disruption of wartime, which affected Exmoor, as a region, far less than many other parts of the country: but by the fact that the war acted as a catalyst for farming and land use, and indirectly prepared the way for the designation of Exmoor as a National Park. Meanwhile it is fortunate that Jack Hurley, late editor of the *West Somerset Free Press* and local historian, succeeded in recording in his book, *Exmoor in Wartime* (Exmoor Press) a wealth of information, some serious, some not, about life on Exmoor 1939-45, which does not deserve to be forgotten.

Once Hitler had occupied Prague in March 1939, almost all doubts about the inevitability of an European war were dissolved, and preparations were put in hand at once, or re-started from the stage they had reached at the Munich crisis in the autumn of 1938 – ARP, gas drill, reception of evacuees, territorial training, etc, all sandwiched into the routine of ordinary summer holidays and seasonal events – village fetes and flower shows, gymkhanas, polo at

Dunster, annual races at Bradley Ham. Then, on the first Friday in September, the Dunster Show opened and Hitler marched into Poland; and, in the afternoon, the first trainload of 800 children arrived from London for billeting in Minehead and Watchet. Several similar convoys followed, some of them misdirected when, for instance, instead of school children, a train full of expectant mothers (some very near their time) and babies arrived unannounced; the school party came later. However, by the end of the first week almost all the arrivals had been found homes in Minehead, in the Dulverton and Williton rural areas, and elsewhere in the hinterland of Exmoor. Locals complained of 'children verminous, raggedly clad, thinly shod, ignorant of elementary hygiene, bedwetters by long habit . . . children who could not even comprehend the purpose of knives and forks at table. Some of the adults were little better.' For their part Londoners missed the noise of traffic and bustle of the streets, and the quick-fire neighbourliness of Cockney life. It was disgusting to have to drink milk out of a cow, and the silence of the countryside was frightening. Husbands demanded their wives return, and within three weeks over a hundred mothers did so, taking their children with them, from the Dulverton area alone. 'The original intake there was 750. By Christmas fewer than 100 remained.'

Two events put a stop to the receding human tide. One was the unprecedented severity of the winter that broke over Exmoor in January 1940. Huge drifts of snow blocked the moorland roads, ice stripped the branches off the trees and pulled down power and telephone lines; and when the thaw set in, young icebergs sailed down the river Barle and tore the centre out of Tarr Steps. The second event was the sudden demise of the 'phoney war' when, in April, Hitler invaded Denmark and Norway and, in May, the Low Countries and France. The war had begun in earnest, but by July was already almost over. Invasion for the first time since 1066 was an astonishing possibility, and as Dr Johnson said 'when a man knows he is to be hanged in a fortnight, it concentrates his mind wonderfully'. Boredom, the curse of inaction, was banished at a blow. As the news got worse and worse, one emergency order followed another, many of them issued by Ernest Bevin, then Minister of Labour and National Service and, as noted, illegitimate offspring of a family in Winsford. There is a plaque to his memory in the village now! Signposts were dumped, salvage drives and savings weeks organised, church bells silenced, and national treasures secreted in such places as the cellars and outhouses of St.

Audries Girls' School, West Quantoxhead, and the crypt of St. Andrew's parish church, Wiveliscombe.

As to defence, pillboxes peppered the coastline and at key locations inland – some survive as eyesores to this day – and Minehead lost its pier. Anti-aircraft batteries had trained in peacetime at Doniford near Watchet, and the possibility of a German attack up the Bristol Channel had converted the environs of Exmoor into an important area for artillery and searchlight units. In fact, by 1941, the invasion scare was over, but the Home Guard had sprung to life (known at first as Local Defence Volunteers), and over a thousand men in Exmoor and West Somerset had registered in the first 24 hours. There was a comic side to some of this. The most popular unit was the horse patrol recruited from the followers of the Devon and Somerset Staghounds, and in which Ernest Bawden, the huntsman, was a section commander. Homely anecdotes are still remembered, such as:

Sentry at road block: 'Halt. Who goes there?'
Male Voice: 'Only me and Muriel'.

But the lonely hills and combes of Exmoor were seriously watched and guarded, rifles replaced shot guns, and a regular company and battalion organisation evolved out of the early amateur patrols. Class distinction was at a discount. One elderly private, former Equerry to the King and chairman of Baring's Bank, preferred the obscurity of the ranks to the eminence of a commission. He was allowed to remain where he was.

Some of the most vivid memories concern the nightly drumming of German planes on their way to bomb Bristol and South Wales. Sarah Fuller, then evacuated with her family to a cottage near the Valley of Rocks, recalled:

> It was scarcely dark before the raids on South Wales began. We were directly opposite Swansea, and lying in bed at night I used to dread the droning, throbbing er-er-er-er- sound of the German bombers coming up the Channel – then the explosions of bombs falling and the heavy staccato rattle of anti-aircraft guns. Each kept it up until the very ground on our side of the Channel was shuddering like a minor earthquake. Then the fires burning endlessly and the searchlights crossing and criss-crossing like frantic Northern Lights. My mother used to stand outside for hours, hypnotised night after night watching that terrible drama – till told to come in, or she'd get a chill.[1]

1. *Exmoor Review*, 1990.

What went over sometimes came back. Helmut Ackenhausen, member of a crew of a Junkers 88, crashed on Porlock beach in September 1940. He returned on a friendly visit thirty years later, and had himself photographed in the police cell where he was first taken. Bombs were ditched in numerous spots in open country – one 500-pounder landed within 200 yards of the newly completed Nutscale reservoir that supplied Minehead, a real disaster had it destroyed or even cracked the dam. Several Allied planes crashed on the Moor. Geraldine I'Anson, at school at Simonsbath House, remembered a Wellington bomber that fell in the fields above the village. 'The crew were killed, and debris scattered over a wide area. We were of course forbidden to go near, but in a very short space of time, an astonishing arsenal of items found its way, oblivious of danger, into our bedrooms'.

In the second half of the war, Exmoor was invaded at last – by the Americans. Camps were pitched in 1943-4, and the moorland fully used for infantry, tank and artillery training. This was when Larkbarrow and Tom's Hill farmsteads were destroyed by gunfire, and never rebuilt; but the military roads built over North Hill proved a tremendous asset to Minehead. In the spring of 1944 General Eisenhower arrived by special train at Dulverton to inspect his troops training on the Moor. Afterwards he rode a horse over to Winsford, and thence to the Royal Oak at Withypool for a beer, before returning to the train to say goodbye to Arthur Saunders, the stationmaster, and his wife. Dulverton was a busy station then. On one day in May it received 15 troop trains, each carrying a thousand men and quantities of stores.

Return to Peace

The European war came to an end in May 1945, and the Japanese one soon after. The Home Guard stood down, and Exmoor was gradually cleared of unexploded shells and bombs, and tidied of wartime debris. Nature re-asserted herself wherever man had intruded, but what had never stopped was the husbandry of the Moor. Over Somerset and Devon, as in other counties, farming was controlled by the Government for the whole of the war through the War Agricultural Executive Committees ('the War Ags'). Prices for products were guaranteed, pools of labour and machinery organised, feeding stuffs, petrol and a host of other supplies rationed or otherwise strictly administered, demonstrations and farm tours made available, and directions issued as to cropping.

In her history, *The NFU in Somerset* (NFU Taunton), Olive Hallam records that the 'War Ag'

> had control over cropping and every other form of production from the land, and power to dispossess those who fell short of a fair standard of husbandry. Quotas for the tillage area were set by the Ministry of Agriculture. While the growing of corn, and particularly wheat, was vitally important, the nutritional value of milk gave its production a high priority, particularly in the West Country.
>
> Somerset farmers were, generally speaking, slow to adapt themselves to changing conditions . . . The agricultural statistics for 1945 show that, out of approximately 12,000 holdings in Somerset, 57 per cent were under fifty acres, 38 per cent under twenty acres. The smaller the holding, the poorer the farmer, was probably a truer saying at the beginning of the war than at the end. These small farmers had been struggling for years for their existence, a way of life that left them little opportunity or will to learn new methods or to take advantage of the latest scientific discoveries.

As a whole, the response to the drive for more food was remarkably good, especially in milk, arable crops, and the adoption of leys in place of old worn-out permanent pastures; and the farmers concerned prospered accordingly. Wartime prosperity did not, however, benefit hill and marginal land farmers on Exmoor, producing beef and sheep, in the same degree. Early in the war a hill sheep subsidy scheme aimed at hill farms in other parts of the country carrying sheep that 'ran free', was not applied to Exmoor on the grounds that, as the sheep were sometimes folded, the area did not come within the meaning of the Act. The problem was not solved until after the war, and then by the initiative of Exmoor hill farmers themselves. First came the Hill Farming Act 1946, which met half the cost of improvements and paid subsidies on sheep and cattle, but still failed to improve conditions for those who farmed wholly or partly on enclosed land on Exmoor and the Brendon Hills. As mentioned earlier, something radical had to be done. The first move, inspired by a group of Exmoor farmers, was to commission Dr C.V. Dawe of Bristol University to undertake a survey. 386 farms were investigated, located roughly on the 800-foot contour, the returns analysed over the winter 1947-8, and published early in 1949 as *Exmoor, an Economic Review*. It encompassed a wealth of information about profitability, livestock, labour, weed infestation etc, but also public services and the state of buildings and farm roads, some of which were so full of potholes that no tradesman would drive up them. It revealed inter alia that only two farms were connected to main electricity and that, in general, only holdings over 250 acres (about one in six) earned anything beyond the value of family labour.

The survey was followed by a report, *Meat from Marginal Land*, which drew on the findings and advanced a policy to restore profitability and thus induce capital investment; provide aid by means of short-term loans and grants; demonstrate and extend modern husbandry as applicable to the hills; and so to create a real prospect for livestock rearing on high land and marginal farms 'lower down the hill'. It was principally due to these efforts by Exmoor farmers that the Livestock Rearing Act was passed in 1951, and a sum of £20 million allotted for grant aid. On Exmoor it led also to the establishment in 1954 of Liscombe experimental farm by the Ministry of Agriculture, and progressively to the installation of road grids at the approaches to Dunkery, Winsford Hill, Anstey Common, and other areas of open moorland, hitherto understocked.

*   *   *   *   *   *   *   *   *   *   *

Land Use

In Britain, apart from the drive for more food and higher industrial production, and meeting the demands for land needed for defence, all activity about the future of land use ceased in 1939 – apparently – overnight. However, as the war dragged on, and as service men and women had time on their hands to think and dream about a better Britain, a ground swell of opinion revived and became the force, ultimately expressed in the Labour landslide in the General Election of 1945. Meanwhile, at Ministerial level, research into the future of land use was revived, once the coalition Government under Winston Churchill had taken charge in the summer of 1940 – a highly creditable fact in view of the crushing pressures exerted by the war.

In that year, Sir John Reith, former Director-General of the BBC, was appointed Minister of Works, and commissioned to devise a national plan for land use and for procedures for controlling and directing development. Reith drew on the work of pioneers, such as

Dudley Stamp, who had conducted a Land Utilisation Survey as far back as 1931-3, which recorded 'with the help of thousands of volunteers, the then existing use (or non-use) of every acre of England, Wales and Scotland'. This Survey made possible three historic Government Reports which, in their turn, fathered much of the post-war planning legislation.

The first of these was the Barlow Report 1940, from which emerged the general conclusion that there must be 'forward planning in the location of industry and that the days of *laissez-faire* producing a satisfactory answer were over'. In other words development should be controlled and concentrated in urban areas, and the countryside conserved: otherwise we should be shutting our eyes to the lessons left by the sporadic building and other spoliation of the 1920s and 1930s, and heedlessly throwing away an irreplaceable heritage, the land itself. The second was the Scott Report on Land Utilisation in Rural Areas, and the third the Uthwatt Report which dealt with the development value of land, both published in 1942.

So far as the countryside was concerned, it was the Scott Report that set the pace, a wide-ranging document that not only reinforced Barlow as regards rural planning, but tackled the contingent subjects of Nature conservation, National Parks, recreation and access. For example, Section 178 outlined the need for National Parks and other open spaces, the preservation of the coast, and the registration of common lands, their upkeep and use. Section 179 recommended that Nature Reserves should be defined and established as separate entities, including areas of geological interest. Another part of the Report referred to rights-of-way. By any standard the Report was an immense step forward. It is a sad fact, however, (though one member of the Scott Committee, Professor S. R. Dennison, foresaw the possibility) that Scott's assumption that prosperous farming would of itself protect and enhance the landscape, i.e. that use equalled beauty, was disastrously disproved in the post-war years: farming became progressively more mechanised and intensive and all at the expense of its manpower (which declined sharply) and of the landscape which it systematically destroyed by bulldozing hedges, ploughing up moorland, and damaging habitats.

The follow-up to the Scott Report was prompt, and John Dower – by now a wartime civil servant and already surveying potential sites for National Parks – was commissioned to write a full report, published in April 1945 as *National Parks in England and Wales*. This was a masterly document, imaginatively conceived and expertly

presented, defining the scope and nature of National Parks, suggest-
ing suitable areas, outlining the administration, and examining
problems – so that, together with Scott, it has been rightly accepted
as the basic blueprint for conservational planning in the countryside. Shortly after its publication, the Labour Party was swept into
power in the General Election, and the future brightened by the fact
that two of the newly appointed Ministers – Lewis Silkin at Town
and Country Planning, and Hugh Dalton as Chancellor of the
Exchequer – were keen ramblers and sympathetic to Dower's work.
Action soon followed. Silkin appointed a Committee under Sir
Arthur Hobhouse, chairman of the County Councils' Association,
to consider the implementation of Dower, and hammer out procedures for rights-of-way and access. A separate Committee on
Wildlife Conservation was set up under the chairmanship of Sir
Julian Huxley.

The Hobhouse findings were published in 1947 and crystallised
most of what Dower had proposed, including the appointment of a
National Parks Commission as an executive body, the selection of
National Park areas, each to be administered by a Committee with
planning powers, and a series of supporting suggestions as to scenic
areas outside the Parks, publicity and finance. By 1947, however, the
implementation of these proposals was being pre-empted or undermined by other post-war legislation. For instance, farming and
forestry were exempted from the constraints of planning, while the
Town and Country Planning Act 1947 awarded development control
to the county councils – all of which seemed, at one moment, to
dispose of the need to legislate separately for National Parks. Since
however important matters such as access and Nature conservation
were either omitted or inadequately covered by the Act, further
legislation was finally agreed and embodied in the National Parks
and Access to the Countryside Act 1949.

Alas, the 1949 Act proved a poor thing for reasons pithily
summarised by Ann and Malcolm MacEwen as 'lack of powers,
gross underfinancing and confused or divided authority'.[1] Thus the
National Parks Commission was made advisory, not executive, so
that at the very outset it was denied the status and ability to stand
up to Ministries and other statutory agencies, which sought to make
use of National Park land. Ten Parks were designated between 1951
and 1957, and in eight of them the administration was virtually

1. *Greenprints for the Countryside* (Allen & Unwin).

surrendered to their constituent county councils. Only two (the Peak and the Lake Districts) operated under Joint Boards and enjoyed any semblance of independence, and only the Peak had its own planning officer and staff. The Commission was given no power or money to acquire land, except through the Minister, otherwise Government finance was confined to percentage grants in respect of approved expenditure only. In short, National Parks were absorbed into local government which, from the start, had regarded them as intruders. It took a long time and much bickering and lobbying to instil a sense of 'national' responsibility into their administration, in which those 'national' members appointed by the Minister were always in the minority.

Access fared little better. Under the Act access to open country was only permissible under an access agreement with a landowner, or where an access order had been made by the local authority, which was a very rare occurrence. Only in the Peak was access, on any scale, a legal reality. As to rights-of-way, county councils were required to prepare maps and, after a period for objection etc., convert them into definitive documents, a process never properly completed in some counties. Although the councils had powers to close, divert, and create new paths, progress was painfully slow; so, as time went on, a way round to avoid long-drawn-out negotiations and compensation and other costs, was discovered in the use of the definition 'permissive', which means what it says. Any path so defined can be lost at any time, if the owner of the land so wishes.

Whilst the 1949 Act converted National Parks into Cinderellas, Nature conservation became, by comparison, the belle of the ball. In 1945 Sir Julian Huxley was appointed chairman of the Wild Life Conservation Committee, created to advise on the implementation of that part of the Dower Report. Huxley was supported by a bevy of high-powered scientists, all of whom – individually or through the various voluntary societies – had already done much to educate the public and lobby the Government about conservation. Among them was Professor A.G. Tansley, noted ecologist and author, who succeeded Huxley when the latter was appointed to UNESCO in 1946. The WLCC profited particularly from all the preparatory work on Nature reserves, which included the issue of a memorandum, *Nature Conservation in Great Britain* (1943), thanks to the initiative of the Society for the Promotion of Nature Reserves in harnessing the efforts of the British Ecological Society and others, and in keeping on good terms with the Forestry Commission which, with its

National Forest Parks, had already blazed a trail in combining conservation with recreation. The publication of WLCC's own report, *Conservation in England and Wales* (1947) was paramount in persuading the Government to set up a separate agency, the Nature Conservancy, first as a Research Council, and then reconstituted by Royal Charter in 1949 as a legal entity on its own, equipped not only to provide scientific advice on the conservation of wild life and conduct research, but with powers to establish and maintain Nature Reserves, and designate Sites of Special Scientific Interest, and all that that implied.

In short, conservation was to be detached and given effective independence, while National Parks were to be left on the shelf to look after the aesthetics of the environment. It meant that Dower's vision of a single organisation in charge of protecting the landscape, conserving wild life, and providing access for public enjoyment, all three to to be inter-active and mutually dependent, was blurred beyond recognition.

CHAPTER TWO

The Battles for Exmoor, 1954-1977

With Britain recovering from the war, the 1950s were a hectic
decade, whatever one's trade. New farmers like me were reclaiming
scrub and rough pasture, and in addition at Langaller I was
employing prisoners-of-war to dig trenches for land drains, in an
effort to make even the boggy bottoms grow short-term leys of
clover and Italian ryegrass. The prisoners were a rough lot of
Soldaten, Germans mostly with a handful of dissident Ukrainians,
housed at Baronsdown near Dulverton, whence they were trans-
ported every day by lorry. A mixed homesick lot, under discipline of
sorts, with a Feldwebel in charge who had to use his fists on
occasions to keep order, which suited me; but when he knew that I
spoke some German, he became cheeky and tried to make trouble
with the Polish couple who worked for and lived with us in the
farmhouse. However, Konrad had fought with the Polish Armoured
Division in Normandy, having earlier – I believe – been captured by
the Russians after serving on the 'wrong' side at Stalingrad; so he
was not the sort with whom to try conclusions, though fortunately it
never came to that.

Langaller was 'dirty-boot' farming with a vengeance, because we
were attempting the almost-impossible, i.e. reclaiming poor land for
cropping and re-seeding, while trying to make a living with a dairy
herd of non-pedigree Guernseys and a pack of Wessex pigs, that
rootled on the cleeves too steep to plough. Even though the
Government was generous with grants, guaranteed prices and
plenty of advice, I found I had to start a second career as a writer to
make ends meet; notwithstanding the fact that twelve hours a day
were often insufficient for all the work that had to be done on the

farm, and that one had to sleep sometime! Writing was done early in the morning, or after carting the milk churns to Dulverton station and scrubbing out the cowshed, or at any old time on wet days. I was in my early thirties and still young enough to cope with it all.

I have mentioned my good luck in winning the prize essay competition organised by the Association of Agriculture, and so it seemed natural to chance my hand further in the same direction. My luck held and I plunged into journalism and broadcasting, with always a book on the stocks. It was a good time to plunge, for new weeklies abounded and these were the high days of radio, when the West of England Home Service at Bristol was acknowledged the best of the BBC regions, with Frank Gillard as head of programmes. My alliance at Bristol with the producer, Robert Waller, an active author himself, was rewarded with ten or more years writing and presenting programmes on a wide variety of subjects. They included straight talks on village life, past and present; farming subjects such as 'Cutting costs on a small farm', 'Farming to beat the climate', 'Silorating hay'; also 'Paths and commons', 'Rogation', 'Parish Government'; features on Alfred Pool, the Chipstable village engineer, Glastonbury (with Geoffrey Sale, headmaster of King's School, Bruton), the St. Ives and Taw and Torridge Festivals, and – most important of all – an hour-long programme about the Dartington Hall estate at Totnes. This led to a commission by the DH Trustees to write a comprehensive history of the estate since its purchase in 1925 by Leonard and Dorothy Elmhirst. It was a mammoth job that took me fifteen years, during which time I completed a *magnum opus* (of about $\frac{1}{4}$ million words), recording the progress of the dozen or so departments, ranging from farming and forestry to adult education and the arts, together with staff lists and annual accounts, more of a reference work than one to read through from the first page to the last, and limited to twelve privately published copies. In addition I wrote a shortened version for the general public, *Dartington Hall. The History of an Experiment*, with a separate chapter on the School contributed by the headmaster, W. B. Curry, published by Phoenix House in 1958. Finally, as a necessary concomitant, helped by two members of the estate staff, Robin Johnston and Eric MacNally, together we sorted and assembled the mass of documents, photographs, publications, and tapes, without which it would have been impossible to do the work, and set up a Records Office, which today has become a treasure house of information about this unique enterprise.

The connection with Exmoor may seem slender; in fact, Dartington vastly broadened my understanding of the economics of country life, especially with regard to the development of workshops and small industries in or near villages – in my view an essential component in the future economy of Exmoor, at present over-dependent on the seasonal nature of tourism.

Exmoor in the 1950s

After protracted political bargaining, Exmoor was designated a National Park in 1954, to be administered not by a Joint Board representative of the two counties, Devon and Somerset, (who had opposed designation and within whose boundaries the Park lay) but by three separate committees, one for Devon, one for Somerset, and a Joint Advisory Committee. This made for muddle and procrastination and, apart from routine planning matters, rendered the new Authority powerless to deal with the main issue that bedevilled Exmoor for the next 25 years – land use. In 1956, when the Authority started work, I was appointed a member of the Somerset and Joint Advisory Committees by the Minister of Housing and Local Government (predecessor of the Department of the Environment) and served for six years, 1956-62. Business was slack at first, as pressure upon the moorland had not yet become a problem, nor was tourism regarded as anything but a useful cash crop for farmers willing to offer accommodation. One of the early members of the Joint Advisory was S.H. (Tim) Burton, a master at Blundell's School, Tiverton, and a successful writer of educational textbooks, who later became a vigorous chairman of the Exmoor Society and a splendid fighter for Exmoor. Tim also wrote the first full-length history of the subject, *Exmoor* (Hodder & Stoughton), in which he recalls the appearance and atmospherics of the area:

> In the far-off days of 1952 . . . the world – the moorland world, that is – seemed a simple place. Not for us the car-borne hordes already threatening the peace of better-known holiday areas. Most of the comparatively few visitors to heartland Exmoor came to ride, hunt, walk, fish. They were solitary figures in an unchanging landscape. For, incredible as it now seems, the landscape then was largely unchanged from the days when the last of the Knight farms had been made and Exmoor's own way of sheep-ranching had been established as 'a proper job'.

And in those halcyon times, as memory now presents them, there was no obvious threat to our peace. The walker could spend a whole summer day in solitude, entering the open moorland and leaving it where he chose. Or call at a lonely farmhouse and receive in exchange for his news that characteristic manifestation of Exmoor people's friendliness, a cream tea – unpriced and uncommercialised.

At that time no inroads of consequence into the moorland were being made by the hill farmers, who were busy reviving their land and buildings and increasing their stock, assisted by the provisions of the Livestock Rearing Act and other Government support. However there was not long to wait, and when the threat came, it did so from an unexpected quarter. First, however, it is appropriate to recall the two prime aims of the National Parks Act 1949: which were to protect and enhance the landscape of the designated area, and to promote its enjoyment by the public. There was also a qualifying clause to the effect that these aims should be pursued with 'due regard to the needs of agriculture and forestry', which seemed sensible at first sight, no damaging intent anticipated.

The First Battle

Early in 1958, however, information was leaked to Dr Richard Harper, respected medical practitioner in Barnstaple, and his wife, Margery, both of them enthusiasts of Exmoor, that the Forestry Commission and the Fortescue estate were negotiating for the planting of The Chains and part of Furzehill Common, some 1200 acres in all, with conifers, and to build roads capable of bearing up to ten tons. Such a plan, if carried out, would fundamentally alter a wild open tract of great natural beauty and ecological value – supporting the largest stretch of deer sedge in southern England and, at 1500 feet, the gathering ground of the principal rivers running north and south: an area uniquely characteristic of Exmoor. The Harpers were horrified and, with a handful of helpers, set about organising a public petition of protest to be sent up to Whitehall, collecting over 3,000 signatures from supporters all over the Moor. They also generated plenty of publicity in the local and national press (including a leader in *The Times*) and mounted a highly effective campaign. Meanwhile the authorities had made a move. Representatives of the National Park Authority (ENPA) met those from the Forestry Commission at Brendon Two Gates on a cold day in March, but made no progress. In April George Wyndham, chairman of ENPA, Peter Hutton (a Committee member) and I spent the best part of a day walking over the ground, starting from the Edgerley Stone. Then came a series of dramatic events in June: first, a full-scale meeting in the area between the principals of the interested parties, including Lord Strang for the National Parks Commission and Lord Radnor for the Forestry Commission. At the end of a long hot afternoon, Lord Radnor announced that, in view of the intensity of local feeling, he would not pursue the plan – a generous as well as a wise move, because neither the NPC nor the ENPA had the power to stop him, since both forestry and agriculture were exempt from planning control. The final act of the drama closed with the untimely death of both Lord and Lady Fortescue, within a week of each other, shortly after the meeting.

The Exmoor Society

I am told that The Chains affair was the only 'victory' ever won by any National Park against a Government agency for the first twenty years of their existence. However, the events of 1958 were not the end of the story which contained several morals: that the next assault upon the moorland was only a matter of time, that the ENPA had no teeth, and that the only alternative was to found a voluntary society to act as a watchdog for the future and tell the public what was happening. Thanks to the initiative of John Coleman-Cooke, naturalist and author, a steering committee was formed from some of the protesters, meeting at Simonsbath House (now a hotel) which John was renting from the Fortescue estate. By early 1959 the new body had been formally constituted as a branch of the Council for the Protection of Rural England (CPRE), with John as chairman, Peter Hutton and Harry Sutton (of Lynton) as Secretaries, and Sir Gonne Pilcher as President.

Since its main aim was to watch and communicate, publication became a prime activity of the new Society. This quite soon it was issuing a *Newsletter* in April, an *Annual Report* in August, and a magazine in the autumn, the *Exmoor Review*. John Goodland launched the first issue (probably with his own money) in 1959, and thereafter it became the official journal and flagship of the Society: evolving into a well-produced, wide ranging annual, with contributions about many aspects of Exmoor – archaeology, history, the coast, local life and work, natural history, and so on; also for many years, vigorous and factual expositions of the extent and condition of the moorland under threat. Latterly the *Review*, with a circulation of over 3,000 copies, has established itself as one of the best regional magazines in the country, and unique among National Parks. From time to time, too, the Society has published reports on specific problems; it has also organised seminars and public meetings – all in support of its role as a pressure group and communicator. This was difficult in the early days when cash was short; even so it managed to make ends meet and, in addition, raise money for new National Trust properties on Exmoor – £5,000 for Heddon's Mouth, and just under £1,000 towards the endowment of the fund for Woody Bay.

The Vanishing Moorland

Between 1960 and 1965 the pace of moorland loss was moving so fast that the ENPA, keenly aware of its weakness, asked the Minister of Housing and Local Government for amending legislation to put some teeth into the 1949 Act but to no avail. During this time several thousand acres of heather and grass moorland were lost to the plough and to fencing in areas such as Countisbury, Fyldon Ridge, Porlock Common and Porlock Allotment, all valuable for their flora, birds and mammals, and enjoyed by walkers and riders. The Minister took no action because food production was still the priority policy, dictated by the Minister of Agriculture, and willingly supported by farmers and landowners, to whom most of the National Park belonged. There was the rub. Contrary to the view then widely held – and still extant now – that National Park land was 'nationalised' land, comparable with the great Parks in North America, most of Exmoor was – and still is – private property belonging to owners or farmed by tenants who asserted, with some justification, that they had the right to 'do what they liked' with their own acres, particularly if reclaiming moorland added to their income. Moreover, as an ex-farmer myself I sympathised with anyone who wanted to make two blades of grass grow where one grew before; it was a creative as well as an economic thing to do. It was, on the other hand, a very different matter to invade ancient swards of heather, gorse, whortleberry, molinia, sphagnum moss, etc., and even relatively recent pasture, laid down in the last century which had long reverted to a semi-wild state and become a natural habitat: and all within the boundaries of the National Park which had been designated for purposes other than cultivation. The Government refused to admit that as the legislation was ambiguous, and that as the prime purpose of the 1949 Act was for the benefit of landscape, wildlife and access, then a farmer should be compensated for not ploughing or otherwise radically altering the sward on his own property – a policy always advocated by the Exmoor Society. By doing nothing Whitehall simply left it to those on the spot to fight it out: which is what happened without reaching a solution, but generating long and bitter controversy.

The Survey of Land Use

Whereas the hubbub over The Chains in 1958 had united many people of varying interests and persuasions about Exmoor, the new situation polarised opinion into two opposing sides – the right to cultivate on one side, and the duty to conserve on the other. What was to be done?

The first step, obvious to the Exmoor Society though not apparently to the ENPA, was to define the area of moorland on a map, supported by statistics as to the type and extent of the vegetation; secondly to estimate how much moorland had been lost and where, over the past eight years (i.e. since the Ordnance Survey revision of 1957-8); and thirdly to present a case based on this technical assessment for preserving the essential areas of moorland 'as a firm guide to such action as ought to be taken'.

Early in 1965, the Society approached Miss Alice Coleman, FRGS, of the Geography Department, King's College, London, then in charge of the Second Land Utilisation Survey of Great Britain, and engaged in completing a scientific record of land use over the whole country. Miss Coleman agreed to place Exmoor at the head of her list – the work to take the form of O.S. $2\frac{1}{2}$ inch maps, displaying the precise extent of types of agriculture, forestry, and natural vegetation (moorland) by a system of colours and symbols. A start was made at once and the Land Use Map (in draft form) exhibited at South Molton Town Hall on 9 October 1965 at the Exmoor Society's Annual General Meeting. Not long afterwards, Geoffrey Sinclair, the surveyor, completed the Map and agreed to keep it up to date each year. It was then loaned to the National Parks Commission in London, and subsequently shown both to the planning staffs of Devon and Somerset County Councils, and to an informal gathering of the National Park Committees of the two counties. Finally another copy was ordered, incorporating the latest information as at June 1966.

Sinclair then extracted a variety of statistics from the Map, dividing the whole area into five regions, and defining the acreage and ground cover (types of moorland, heather and grass). He was then able to estimate that, whereas in 1957-8 the moorland had totalled 58,745 acres, by 1965 it had fallen to 50,665, i.e. a loss of 8,080 acres or an average of over a thousand acres a year. By June 1966 the total acreage had fallen to below 50,000 acres. These statistics and Sinclair's detailed exposition of the findings were published by the Exmoor Society as a booklet, *Can Exmoor Survive?*, which also contained further comments on the need to keep the moorland in good heart by means of the traditional system of sheep and cattle grazing, else the sward would revert to scrub; and emphasised the delicate balance of vegetation, woodland and scenery in an area (only 170,000 acres) as small as Exmoor National Park. As Burton wrote in his book:

> Not only is Exmoor small and fragmented, it is hybrid. By that I mean that it consists of varied types of scenery: wooded valleys; bare combes; little waters; grass plateaux; heather stretches; a stupendous coast; and many farms where land has been cultivated for a century or more. It is in short a fine patchwork of wildness and cultivation constituting a delicate balance that is easily upset.

and he added:

> Time and again ENPA showed itself insensitive to this fragile beauty. It reacted complacently to a succession of ploughing proposals. 'After all it's only a hundred acres', or 'It's an extension of the existing improvements'. A moorland 'take' of only fifty acres is more damaging to Exmoor than a stranger can comprehend; but a National Park Authority consisting very largely of local councillors, who claim to know the moor and who base their 'moral' right as arbiters on their intimate knowledge and their elected status, should have a far better record.

The booklet also assessed the ownership of the moorland at 15,000 acres (plus) in 'public hands' (i.e. National Trust and Somerset County Council , but exclusive of some common land, due to be registered under the Commons Registration Act 1965) hence reasonably safe; the balance of c. 35,000 acres in private hands, far from safe. Fencing was not considered a reliable guide to areas of open moorland, notwithstanding some 'guesstimates' by ENPA and CPRE: nor was it practicable to try to add such information to the Land Use Map, as the speed at which new or rehabilitated fencing was being erected would soon overtake any map work. Finally it was possible only to broach ideas about methods of restricting reclamation and enclosure, whether by purchase or by some other form of compensation. A solution to that ultimate problem had to wait another fifteen years. Meanwhile – facts had to come first.

The Lynton Conference

Can Exmoor Survive? was published in time for the National Parks Conference held in the Valley of Rocks Hotel at Lynton on 27-28 September 1966. Over 100 delegates attended, including representatives of the nine other National Parks, nearly all the National Park Commissioners and their new chairman, Baroness Wootton of Abinger. F.T. Willey, Minister of Land and Natural Resources, was also present. An excellent display of photographs, diagrams and maps, including one based on the Land Use Map commissioned by the Exmoor Society, was provided by the planning department of Somerset County Council, where the Society's ideas were strongly supported by Roger Miles, forestry officer and landscape architect. The Society was officially complimented by Baroness Wootton in her speech and, on the second day, by Miles himself in a highly professional exposition, entitled 'Looking after Landscape'. In this he referred specifically to the Land Use Map as 'a fundamental piece of equipment for landscape planning', and wished he had had access to it before undertaking his Survey of Afforestation and Existing Woods on Exmoor, a task that fell to him immediately after the row over The Chains in 1958.

Any euphoria generated by the Lynton Conference quickly evaporated. Although Sinclair's statistics of moorland loss were accepted by officers of the Ministry of Agriculture (MAFF) and the two county councils as being accurate to within plus or minus three per cent, the NFU and CLA rejected the whole exercise and countered with a questionable statement to the effect that the loss had averaged less than 100 acres a year, and asserted the farmers' right to continue ploughing as they thought fit. In July 1968 a new Countryside Act was passed that converted the National Parks Commission into the Countryside Commission and, at the last moment, adopted a few clauses that tied no-ploughing to access, and required farmers to give six months' notice of intention to plough. If by then no deal was reached, then the National Park Authority could fall back on compulsory purchase. None of this worked on Exmoor. Instead ENPA came to a 'gentleman's agreement' with the NFU whereby voluntary notification would be followed by negotiation over any plan to plough within what was termed the 'Critical Amenity Area', i.e. ENPA's distillation of Sinclair, estimated at c.43,000 acres. The NFU made much of this, saying that negotiations 'ran exceptionally smoothly with constructive debate and without rancour or bitterness'. All very fine, but the net result as regards moorland protection was almost nil. The extent of Critical Amenity was ultimately agreed, but no compensation was offered for not ploughing – indeed in a test case at Exe Cleave, dragged out over three years, the ENPA Committee refused to find the money for an Access Agreement – and so moorland loss galloped on.

*   *   *   *   *   *   *   *   *   *   *

A Fresh Start?

In 1974 ENPA was -reorganised as a single Committee of Somerset County Council with Devon representation. It was given a unified staff, more money, and a headquarters at Exmoor House, Dulverton – a great improvement, anyway in terms of structure. A retired Army Officer and local landowner, Major-General R. D. Wilson, who had studied National Parks abroad, was appointed National Parks Officer. Any hope, however, that the new regime would restrain invasion of the remaining moorland in the interests of conservation was doomed from the start. The Committee was dominated by farming and landowning interests, their whole tenor being one of not interfering with the status quo. Naturally the conservation lobby did not accept the situation lying down, with the result that the next three years were a period of all-out, at times abusive, struggle between the two sides, culminating in the appointment by the Government of Lord Porchester in 1977 to conduct an official enquiry.

Since the sequence of events is clearly and factually set out on pp.177-181 of Ann and Malcolm MacEwen's book, *National Parks: Conservation or Cosmetics?* (Allen & Unwin), I do not propose to go into detail here, except briefly to record the following.

Firstly, had it not been for Malcolm MacEwen's service on the ENPA Committee (as a Ministerial appointee), and for his vigorous and sustained defence of conservation issues, nothing would have changed. The Committee set its face from the first against one opportunity after another to make sensible progress, especially as its primary task was to prepare the National Park plan. For instance, it disregarded a report on heather management by John Phillips, recommended by the Institute of Terrestrial Ecology; it appointed Geoffrey Sinclair as a consultant – consulted him once – and then sacked him; while in the Park plan it merely expressed pious sentiments for the encouragement of conservation, but not at the expense of profitable agriculture.

Then, in 1976, the fundamental issue burst into conflagration with two major proposals to reclaim moorland in particularly sensitive areas. One was submitted by Ben Halliday, owner of the Glenthorne estate that lies between the Oare valley and the sea: a spectacular property of heath and woodland, part of which had earlier come into the hands of the National Trust; but due to its ground cover and Alpine contours difficult to manage profitably. For economic reasons Halliday wanted to plough 250 acres of moorland at Yenworthy and North Commons (not common land in law), and offset the loss of moorland (in a Critical Amenity Area) by negotiating a management plan with ENPA, embracing forestry, nature conservation, access and rights-of-way. This was an imaginative concept in terms of multiple land use, and in principle it seemed to point the way forward. In the event Halliday had his way as to ploughing at East Yenworthy, but agreed to spare the western part running up to County Gate, also North Common, which lay south of the A.39, under an Access Agreement, still the only means whereby ENPA could compensate the landowner, short of outright purchase.

The other proposal was more critical and, in what happened, more damaging, since it did present ENPA with a golden opportunity to acquire a key property: namely 374 acres at Stowey Allotment, south-west of North Common, well within the heartland of the Moor and offered for sale in the summer of 1976. ENPA put in for it, bid too little, lost it, whereupon the young farmer who bought it promptly notified his intention to plough. Then followed s sorry and discreditable tale of mishandling. Briefly, ENPA did virtually nothing until shortly before the farmer's notice ran out, when John Cripps, chairman of the Countryside Commission, wrote expressing his concern and released his letter to the press. This was the first time that the proposal became widely known, as ENPA had shrouded the subject in silence. A site meeting eventually took place on 25 March

1977, after which the County Valuer advised against the offer of a management agreement costing £9,000 p.a., even though the Commission subsequently agreed to advance nearly 90 per cent of the sum for one year, to allow time to think again. But ENPA had made up its mind and allowed the reclamation of the entire property: all this despite protests by a vociferous minority on the Committee, and violent objections by the amenity lobby, notably the Exmoor Society and the Ramblers' Association.

Although the battle for Stowey Allotment was over, the implications were not. An adverse report was submitted by the Countryside Commission to the Department of the Environment, while the chairman of Somerset County Council had already approached the Secretary of State and asked him to intervene. This led immediately to the appointment of Lord Porchester by the DoE and MAFF acting together (joint action for the first time), to conduct a 'study' of land use on Exmoor. Porchester, a leading landowner and former chairman of the Association of County Councils, started work at once in early summer, 1977.

CHAPTER THREE

Hill Farming and Conservation

Lord Porchester called for written evidence by 18 June, and then held a series of public hearings at which all interested organisations and individuals were able to give evidence and be questioned by him. The main meeting was held at the Shire Hall, Taunton, at which all the parties were represented, including ENPA officers and Committee members, and the various landed and conservation interests. No holds were barred and, during a long tough day's discussion, Porchester proved a formidable inquisitor – firm, fair, dismissive of woolly statements, with a keen eye for weak points in whatever quarter; nonetheless a true judge, not a prosecutor. On 18 July he toured the Moor, and by the time they left he and his assistants had heard a wide range of views, gathered numerous statistics and publications (including the Land Use Map and *Can Exmoor Survive?*), and were thus aware of all the issues, necessary for the preparation of his Report.

A Study of Exmoor was published by HMSO in November 1977. It was an exhaustive and important document which, in the light of subsequent events, proved a turning-point in the battles for Exmoor. It certainly justified all the efforts of the Exmoor Society, and confirmed most of Sinclair's calculations. First, it settled the statistics. Between 1947 (when aerial surveys were made) and 1976, the area of moorland had fallen from 59,000 to 47,000 acres – a loss of 12,000 acres, of which 9,500 had been taken into agriculture. Secondly, more than half the remaining hill land within the Critical Amenity Area was improvable; hence it was extremely vulnerable and, if ploughed or otherwise altered, would reduce the moorland to a fraction of its then, let alone

2   Moorland reclaimed: South Hill

3   Stowey Allotment from the air

4   The mine chimney at Burrow Farm, on the Brendon Hills

5   The farmstead

Burrow Farm

6   The sheep barn

7   *Shearing*

Hill Farming

8   *Dipping*

former, extent. The remoteness and ecological character of Exmoor would inevitably be destroyed. Porchester therefore recommended, as a first step, a new version of the Land Use Map – Map 1 to record all the areas of moor and heath; Map 2 to define 'those particular tracts of land whose traditional appearance the Authority would want to see conserved, so far as possible, for all time'. This meant no ploughing or interference with the sward in any of the moorland running, roughly, from Dunkery westward to Chapman Barrows, other moorland stretches north of this and along the coast, the southern heather moors at East and West Anstey, also Winsford Hill, Withypool and Brendon Commons, and certain other areas: amounting to c.81 per cent of all the moorland recorded on Map 1.

Porchester criticised the Ministry of Agriculture (MAFF) for failing to consider conservation in grant-aiding schemes for reclamation, and for keeping ENPA in the dark about such schemes. He recommended therefore that no further grants be given in support of proposals for reclamation within Map 2. He was doubtful, however, of the efficiency of management agreements which had not worked hitherto: so long as MAFF encouraged reclamation as described, or in the absence of compensation to the farmer, or most important, because there were no accepted 'ground' rules for determining compensation. He therefore recommended that all arrangements regarding moorland should have the force of law: specifically notification by farmers; and the making of Moorland Conservation Orders by ENPA whereby agricultural operations, other than traditional grazing, were banned in those Map 2 areas capable of improvement. Compensation would take the form of a lump sum equal to the loss of value caused by the Order.

Porchester appeared to be a magician. Within a matter of months, he had produced a workable solution, that pleased most people. It even seemed to please the ENPA Committee, which accepted the recommendations almost unanimously, though with reservations about compensation. Nonetheless it allowed the Glenthorne compromise to go through – for Stowey it was already too late. The Labour Government then prepared a Bill embodying most of Porchester, but when voted out of power in the spring of 1979, the Bill fell with it. However, Porchester's work was not all thrown away. The mapping of the moorland went ahead and when finally agreed, the revised total in Map 2 amounted to just under 40,000 acres or about one quarter of the Park. Meanwhile, discussions proceeded for a new statute passed in 1981 as The Wildlife and Countryside Act. This abandoned Moorland Conservation Orders in favour of voluntary notification and management agreements – still the rule today – and offered a farmer two forms of compensation, either a lump sum or an annual payment representing loss of profit had he resorted to intensive husbandry in the sensitive area, such agreement to last 20 years. The guidelines for this financial settlement were worked out between CLA, NFU, and ENPA, with the help of the agricultural economics department of Exeter University.

The Act was subjected to a lot of criticism, especially in regard to Nature conservation (only partly corrected by the Amending Act of 1985), for the area of moorland in Map 2 was a good deal less than that desired by the Nature Conservancy Council, which wanted to protect all those areas where moorland and other sorts of wildness were dominant. This is a subject for a later chapter, but it means that moorland protection is not only incomplete, but contains one obvious weakness. Should a farmer want to plough in a sensitive area (Map 2 and part of Map 1 are now redrawn as the Conservation Map), disregard any potential grant from MAFF, and refuse to negotiate a management agreement with ENPA, then there is nothing to prevent him doing so – and there have been some narrow squeaks. In short the farmer still holds the cards. He does not have to negotiate, but if he does then the ENPA has to pay. In the end it is goodwill that holds the edifice erect.

However, the voluntary system has worked better than expected By the end of 1990, 4,078 acres/1,651 ha. were protected by management agreements at an annual cost of £93,000, of which 90 per cent is met by the Treasury. Moorland loss has been halted, though the risk remains. One consequence has been the readiness of ENPA to purchase properties, when opportunity offered and funds were available. By 1990 it owned 6,244 acres/2,528 ha. of moorland including 1,741 acres/705 ha. at Warren Farm, bought with the help of the Heritage Memorial Fund, re-selling a portion of the holding and leasing back the moorland to the new owner under restrictive covenant. 'Nationalisation by the back door' say some critics: may be, but had, say, 50,000 acres of moorland been bought by the National Park in 1954 at, say, £100 per acre, costing the tax payer a sum in the region of £5 million, then a great deal of money and human stress would have been saved. Just a speculation!

Decade of Change

The 1980s will go down in history as the period in which the policy of subsidising and supporting food production at all costs was progressively abandoned – some forty years after the Agriculture Act 1947, the anchor of post-war farm revival. In an effort to reduce the cost of its Common Agricultural Policy (CAP), the European Economic Community (EEC) engaged in frantic efforts to lower the mountains of grain, butter and meat, and the levels of the wine and milk lakes. To that end quotas were introduced and price supports cut, while various options were advanced to help compensate for the consequent loss of farm income, but all contributing towards reducing food production by 20 per cent. Although hill farming escaped the worst, the increase in food surpluses proved the clinching factor in saving the moorland, at any rate as regards further ploughing etc, for which there was no longer any economic justification without grant-aid.

So much confusion has arisen out of the number and variety of schemes launched or proposed to keep farmers in business without adding to farm surpluses, and to encourage them to enhance the environment, that I can do no more than comment on some of them. In general there are two levels of support – national or Ministry of Agriculture (MAFF) schemes, and ENPA schemes – let us look at MAFF first.

One scheme is the *Set-Aside*, whereby farmers are paid to leave some of their land unused – not a popular solution, since it encourages weeds, prompts the farmer to intensify yields on the remainder of his farm, while the fields so set aside might ultimately attract development. In any event Set-Aside is exceptional on Exmoor, as arable is relatively scarce in hill country. A related concept is *Extensification* – one more manufactured word! – which aims at reducing the number of animals on farms, and promotes a low input/low output system in contrast to the intensive practices of today. That means it is, by its nature, friendly to the environment. The economic equation for the farmer, however, is not easy to solve, and any shortfall arising out of adopting the system would have to be met by grant-aid until, ultimately and hopefully, the improvement in the natural fertility of the soil and health of the stock generated a satisfactory profit. This practical problem might partly be met by the *Farm Woodland Scheme*, which requires a minimum planting of 3 hectares in return for an annual payment; or by the *Farm and Conservation Grant Scheme* which offers (up to 50 per cent of cost to hill farmers) under various headings – shelter belts, hedges and walls, regeneration of heather and grass moorland, etc. – but the farmer still has to find the remaining 50 per cent to pay for environmental improvements that do not yield immediate cash returns.

The constant challenge to hill farmers, and on Exmoor in particular, is of course that of making ends meet and keeping the land in good heart in an area where climatic and soil conditions are unfavourable. Hill farming is always a struggle. For that reason the EEC has designated most uplands as *Less Favoured Areas (LFAs)*, where the farms qualify for certain livestock premiums (made annually per breeding ewe and per suckler cow), and other allowances (commonly known as 'headage' payments) which, until recently, were paid at a flat rate irrespective of numbers carried on a holding. This generated an increase in the ewe population of nearly 50 per cent between 1973 and 1988, while lambs (under one year old) rose by nearly 60 per cent. This has encouraged over-grazing by conservational standards – let alone the creation of a sheep meat surplus – and although the payment system has now been altered, it is still far from watertight, so that alternatives will have to be considered if the pastures are not to be further degraded. One possibility is to pay, not according to numbers of stock – difficult to control and calculate fairly – but on an area basis; but here again the quality of the sward has to be taken into account, and that would involve an expert botanical assessment. However, since subsidies provide up to c.40 per cent of a hill farmer's income – the balance being met by the sale of fat lambs, wool, beef calves, and 'stores', or breeding stock – they cannot be removed or severely cut without doing great financial damage. Moreover LFAs are multi-purpose. They are not intended solely as economic supports, but are social and conservational in aim as well – to halt depopulation on the hills, keep family farms together, and discourage amalgamation into large units or ranches, run by a man and a boy, in which environmental management would be at a discount.

Support by the EEC and MAFF for hill farming on Exmoor has been supplemented by several ENPA schemes – two in particular. *The Landscape Conservation Grant Scheme*, as the name implies, provides money for the preservation or enhancement of traditional features, either as an independent source of aid or as a top-up to MAFF's *Farm and Conservation Grant Scheme*, already mentioned; also the ENPA *Farm Conservation Scheme*, started in 1990 and on trial for three years, aimed at 'promoting wildlife and landscape conservation on a whole farm basis' – a deliberate move towards integrating orthodox and conservational systems of husbandry, farm by farm. This too is the target of a totally separate agency, the Farming and Wildlife Trust, a registered charity operated by the Countryside Commission and landed interests, which advises farmers outside the National Park on how to combine profitable farming with practical conservation, but does not offer finance other than paying the salaries of its field officers. Inside the Park, such advice is given by ENPA staff.

Farmers too have been exhorted to diversify in order to maintain their incomes, and all kinds of exotic activities have emerged – fish ponds, war games, clay pigeon shooting, farm shops, wildlife zoos, equestrian eventing, etc. The obvious opening on hill farms, and long the custom on Exmoor, is holiday accommodation, but even that is not always an easy option. There may be no room in the farmhouse for visitors, even if they are wanted, while converting a redundant barn into holiday flats can be a heavy investment. This is of course distinct from selling a barn for conversion into a permanent residence, acceptable only if there is no other use for a building of architectural interest, and if it is not in an isolated spot. Otherwise it is a doubtful proposition, since it merely exacerbates the problem of second homes and promotes the suburbanisation of the country. Running a riding establishment – to take another example – must of necessity be on a small scale if it is an adjunct to full-time farming. If, on the other hand, it is the principal activity, then it can hardly be defined as diversification of hill farming, unless the holding is large enough and financially capable of sustaining two main businesses.

It is obvious from all this that the present programme of economic supports and environmental inducements is too complex. It is like a patchwork quilt that constantly has to be repaired and enlarged, and this leaves out of account a variety of schemes offered by other agencies, public and private: such as English Heritage's field monument protection scheme, Nature Conservancy Council's management agreements for Sites of Special Scientific Interest, Crown Estate awards, and the Forestry Commission woodland planting grants. Recently, too, the Country Landowners' Association (CLA) has proposed an Environmental Land Management Services scheme (ELMS), whereby owners offer to look after patches of the countryside – not only in National Parks – in return for a fee, in contrast to the present trend of converting farmers, by means of grants, into 'park-keepers', as the CLA puts it.

Environmentally Sensitive Areas

To filter all that is on offer and cope with the paperwork is unreasonably time-consuming for a hill farmer on Exmoor or anywhere else, who has an all-day job to do outside. That is why a gleam of light has appeared on the horizon with the advent of *Environmentally Sensitive Areas (ESAs)* of which, so far, ten have been designated in England and two in Wales, Exmoor *not* being one. On the face of it, ESAs might well emerge as a simplification of the whole problem of making conservational farming work: in that, in such an area, farmers would receive a guaranteed income for managing their land according to an agreed programme, which would include such things as the maintenance of hedgerows, banks or walls, not overstocking the pastures, and keeping the moorland in a fit state for wildlife. As yet this is a voluntary scheme, limited in scope and very much on trial; nonetheless it is promising as it moves away from the fragmentation of grant-giving, and from the stop-gap practice on Exmoor of paying a farmer for not doing damage – a purely negative approach – towards the positive concept of whole farm planning, which is also ENPA policy. Until Exmoor becomes an ESA, if ever, the ENPA Farm Conservation Scheme, on trial 1990-3, is designed to apply similar principles; and this strengthens the claim that the ENPA itself should be empowered to co-ordinate all schemes of aid and monitor their progress on the farms concerned. Much depends. of course, on adequate Government funding.

'Wind of Change' is now a familiar phrase, but the wind has changed extraordinarily quickly on Exmoor. Farmers are now willing to look at conservation as an important source of income – indeed they have no choice – and adapt their farm practice accordingly. The ironical thing is that it really means they are reverting to traditional grazing on the hills, but if that fails to provide a satisfactory living, then the shortfall must be made good by environmental grants, which will enable them to restore and enhance the landscape as well; and this is an objective to which no tax payer would refuse to contribute; indeed it will probably cost him less than subsidising food surpluses. One word of caution. How far an Exmoor farmer will be prepared to live and work as, in effect, the paid manager of his own land, remains to be seen. His sense of independence must not be undermined, nor his skill depreciated, particularly when so many hill farmers, with long family traditions behind them, regard themselves as stewards of their portion of our national heritage. One such farm and family I now propose to describe.

BURROW FARM

We start our journey from Raleighs Cross, once a cider stop for drovers, who grazed their beasts along the verges on the way to Barnstaple and penned them overnight on the rough sward outside the inn. Go westward along the road for a mile and then fork right at Beulah Chapel built in 1861 by the Bible Christians (a break-off branch of Methodism, grafted back again seventy years later) to serve the Welsh and Cornish miners who worked down the iron mines, first opened in the 1850s along the veins of ore on either side of the road between Raleighs Cross and Heath Poult Cross. The relevance of the mines here is that, having flourished for thirty years and sustained vigorous communities – catapulted with their cottages and schools and chapels and all the clutter of industry into an isolated and silent landscape – collapse engulfed them overnight. It was a brief West Somerset Rhondda. Reminders today are few, though sometimes impressive. Among them is the Incline, a massive earthwork $\frac{3}{4}$ mile long, over whose back cables controlled the trucks carrying ore down to Comberow and thence by rail to Watchet harbour for shipment to South Wales. There are mounds of 'deads' here and there, a handful of cottages at Sminhays, a plethora of shafts and adits long sealed, sections of abandoned railway track between the head of the Incline and Gupworthy (the western terminus of the line) and – in a field by itself – a gaunt chimney, standing like a sentinel over the ruins of the engine house that once pumped water out of Burrow Farm mine. Recently it has been repaired by ENPA to remind future generations of the industrial past in this remote corner of West Somerset.

The Chimney stands near the highest part of the farm, a tableland of permanent pasture, most of it at between 1,000 and 1,200 feet. From different points you can see Withiel Florey church in the distance, a tiny historic building painted white, standing beside a farmyard – a hidden place of worship lovingly attended and supported by a handful of parishioners, who have, more than once, raised large sums of money to restore the fabric and ensure survival, where their forbears have been baptised, married and buried for the past 900 years. You can also see the gleam of Wimbleball Lake, the reservoir constructed in 1974-9, fed by the river Haddeo to the east, and by various small streams that rise on Brendon Hill and flow through Burrow Farm on their way down to the Lake near Bessom Bridge.

As you go over the land with the farmer, Harold Bale, his wife, Margaret, and their son, Colin, you will notice several things that in themselves are clues to the care of the land. One is the state of the hedges and of the banks on which they are planted. Too often about the countryside you see boundaries of this kind that have been let go – riddled with rabbit holes below, gapped and ragged or overgrown on top. Here they are in good order, trimmed regularly or brushed on either side so that they continue to grow upwards for periodic laying. Most of them are of beech, which stands up well to winter storms and keeps its brown leaves right through to the spring, when the green shoots burst through again. On the west side against a lane, father and son have laid a length of ash with expert skill that is a work of art. A good hedge is a positive asset. The whole edifice serves both as a secure fence and as a shelter for stock against the prevailing wind; likewise as a source of small timber – fence posts, bean poles, pea sticks, and firing for the Rayburn. And, as a natural extension of the fence, the gates are properly hung, and open and shut without the aid of a tangle of string. There is another remarkable feature. All the hedges-and-banks are straight, dividing the fields into regular blocks. This, it is thought, has an historical reason: namely that well over a century ago the farm was reclaimed from thicket and scrub, and a new holding carved out of what was probably common land. Thus the pioneers who did the work were free to construct straight and convenient boundaries which, today, in an era of machinery, is an added blessing.

The farm derives its entire income from beef cattle and sheep. A Charolais bull is run with a herd of Hereford X Friesian cows during the summer months to produce a calf a year. Next year the calves run out with their dams on summer grass but, over the worst of the winter, are housed in sheds and fed on silage. At 15-18 months they are sold off as 'stores', ready for fattening by farmers in the vale.

The main source of income, however, is sheep: in this case a flock of over 400 breeding ewes plus 100 ewe lambs, which works out at about two per acre over the whole farm. While the traditional hill breeds include Exmoor Horn, Devon Closewool, Scottish Blackface, and Cheviot, here Texel and Suffolk rams have been introduced to the flock to produce cross-bred ewes and good quality butchers' lambs. As the gestation period lasts five months and lambing takes place in late March and early April, when climatic conditions have begun to improve, mating will have taken place at the end of the previous October or early November. The ewes are separated into groups of 40-50 and put to the rams, grazing day and night in the fields until the end of January, or whenever the weather breaks for good. They are then brought into the capacious sheep barn and fed concentrates and hay or silage, 5-6 weeks before lambing.

Lambing is an anxious time and lasts about three weeks. It draws on all the skill and experience of the farmer and his family, helping with difficult births, coping with orphans and triplets, tailing, castrating, and injecting lambs with vaccine. By the end of April or earlier, when the spring grass is coming through, ewes and lambs are turned out to graze and suckle all through the summer months until weaning is reached. After mid-May, when the lambs are about six weeks old, they are drenched against intestinal infections at regular intervals, and a strict eye kept at all times on condition and growth. That means at least twice-daily inspection all through the year, whether it be to detect and correct troubles from worms, maggots, fly or other parasites – sheep attract most of them – or a dangerous condition such as bloat, when internal gases inflate the stomach as a result of over-indulgence in rich spring grass, or when an animal falls over and cannot get up again because of the weight of wool on its back. Attention and experience expressed in the farmer's quick eye is the key to such problems.

June is shearing time. Some farmers employ contractors who go round from farm to farm, as they do on a large scale in Australia and New Zealand. Often neighbours combine and help shear each other's flocks – indeed mutual help for all sorts of jobs is an essential feature of family farming, especially in the hills. Here, however, the farmer and his son manage the shearing themselves. It lasts about a week using clippers operated by electricity from their own generator. The fleeces are rolled up, packed 20 to a bag, and taken to South Molton, where they are graded and sold according to quality and weight. A 6lb fleece fetched, say £3-£4 (1989), but the price dropped steeply in 1990 and so the wool cheque is a useful but not major item of income, especially when 15 per cent has to be deducted for VAT, an irritating charge! Lambs – on this farm at any rate – are not sheared, to allow them to grow a better fleece next year; nor are they mated until 18 months old for a similar reason – waiting makes for bigger and better stock.

Dipping is done in July, for fly and maggot this time, and repeated in September/October for scab. The dip is, basically, a concrete bath, sloped at the far end and where the sheep scramble out after being pushed into (and under) a chemical solution designed to kill vermin that lodge in the wool. Finally, from the end of June onwards, comes the critical moment when the lambs are fat and ready for sale at about 90 lbs liveweight. Some 500-600 are sold off, but about a hundred will be kept back as replacements for breeding. With the sale of lambs and of the older 'full-mouth' ewes and other culls, the cycle of the sheep year is complete. Work does not stop however. The ewes' milk has to be dried off, teeth checked (age is calculated by the number of teeth, since the value of the animal depends on its ability to graze), and the flock given a breather before mating in the autumn as described.

We started our tour at the Chimney and we return to it and its large hump of spoil that has been dug into over the years for hard core for gateways. Harold even remembers his father ploughing out the long track up to the farm (now a smart drive), and hauling core from the mine to give it a surface. Nothing was easy in those days. His grandfather used to get up at three in the morning, swallow some cider and a hunk of fat bacon, and go off shearing; and he lived to a good age, though no one knew exactly what it was! History is always with us, not only in people's memories, but in many other clues about the past or the nature of the ground. Field names, for example: Mead (a wet meadow or just one shut up every year for hay); Splat (a small piece); Ball (a little hill or rise); Gutter Close (where surface ditches were dug for irrigation or 'drowning'); Naked Boy Field (near the boundary stone of that name) – while Barns Close, Cuckoo Field, or Square Field need no explanation. Burrow Farm cannot easily rid itself of its connection with the mining of the last century. In one field west of the Chimney, Harold had to level out the 'deads' to make a manageable pasture, now a fair sward of cocksfoot, ryegrass, timothy, and clover. To the east a hole suddenly opened up in the ground, over an old stope probably, but it had to be fenced.

The life of the hill farmer on Exmoor is neither impossibly hard nor idyllic. There are very bad times, as in the winter of 1962-3, when many farms were isolated by snow and ice, communications cut, and supplies had to be dropped by helicopter; but there are also good moments when the sun has dried the dew on the grass, campion and stitchwort are burgeoning in the hedges, and the lambs are plentiful and skipping. Let it never be forgotten that the future of Exmoor lies largely in the hands of the hill farmer. He has a clear economic role to play – to raise hardy and healthy breeding stock, as well as calves for fattening and fat lambs for the market; but he cannot do this without support from the tax payer, who has a right to insist that such support goes hand in hand with care for the land. At Burrow, which has belonged to Harold's family for close on a hundred years, care is inherent in husbandry, and the land is kept in good heart because the farmer would not think or do otherwise.

PART TWO:

Elements of Exmoor

CHAPTER FOUR

How Wild is Exmoor?

Exmoor is not so wild as Dartmoor, which overlies a bed of granite and where erosion has uncovered the tors. By contrast Exmoor has a mixed geological foundation of Devonian sandstones, slates, and occasional limestones. Although weathering has broken up the highest rocks and washed the debris downhill, it has not exposed the summits or outcrops, apart from freak formations such as the Valley of Rocks, or isolated clumps of boulders, or slopes of scree. Much of the moorland above c.1,200 feet, e.g. along the ridge westward from Dunkery towards Chapman Barrows, is clothed with a blanket of peat, virtually undisturbed since its gradual and original formation. With a rainfall in excess of 70 inches a year, such places are often waterlogged, even in high summer, fundamentally because they lie on top of a thin ($\frac{1}{4}$ inch) iron pan that prevents draining. The surface vegetation is therefore populated with mosses, rushes and cotton grass; and it was by intruding into this area, in the northern part of the Royal Forest, with grandiose ideas about growing corn, that John Knight in the 1820s-1830s found it necessary to break the pan with ox teams before ploughing for a tilth. Later in the century his son, Frederic, tried again, with a cable plough, but soon gave it up. So there are no naked Alpine heights on Exmoor, a point well made by Hilary Binding:

> Strangely, the heights of Exmoor make dull photographs . . .
> Travelling between Cloutsham and Porlock Hill recently a friend and
> I considered the question of photographing the ridges. All around us
> lay sinuous, curving hills, one ridge flowing into the next . . . We

look on the hills of Exmoor with a panoramic eye, taking in the whole surrounding sweep. The camera cuts the view into chunks which do not satisfy, at the same time reducing the subtle curves and colouring of the ridges to monochrome humps which put one in mind of the supposed images of the back of the Loch Ness monster.[1]

In short a 'humpy back' constructed of lofty long ridges and plateaux, permeated with springs, whence combes and 'goyals', coursing with water for most of the year, run out north and south like fissures in the back of a whale. The monster is an apt analogy.

Moorland and Farmland

In his book, *The Vegetation of Exmoor* (Exmoor Press), Geoffrey Sinclair described the five regions of moorland vegetation that emerged from the Land Use Map (since absorbed into the ENPA Conservation Map) which he completed in 1965. These were coastal heaths, northern heather moors, southern heather moors, central grass moors, and Brendon heaths (now mostly covered with conifers). These are, of course, generalised descriptions, no sharp boundaries, one region over-lapping another, so that you rarely find pure stands of any single species of plant unmixed with others in any of the regions. They concern rather whatever dominates a sward, and that depends partly on the type and condition of the soil, and partly on the intensity of grazing by livestock. In round terms, therefore, heathers are dominant in about half the total area, surrounding the grasses and sedges which prevail in the centre of the moorland.

Principal heathers are bell heather (*Erica cinerea*), ling (*Calluna vulgaris*), and cross-leaved heath (*Erica tetralix*). The principal grasses are purple moor grass (*Molinia caerulea*), mat grass (*Nardus stricta*), and bent grass (*Agrostis* species). Deer sedge (*Scirpus cespitosus*) flourishes over about 150 acres of The Chains where, as in other waterlogged areas, you also find cotton grass (*Eriophorum angustifolium*); rushes, soft and sharp-flowered (*Juncus effusus* and *Juncus acutiflorus*); and Sphagnum mosses. Whortleberry (*Vaccinium myrtillis*) is still common, notably on the flanks of Dunkery, where it used to be regularly harvested. Familiar, especially on dry stony soils, are common gorse (*Ulex europaeus*) and western gorse (*Ulex*

---

1. *Exmoor Review*, 1990.

gallii); while bracken (*Pteridium aquilinium*), once more or less confined to steep slopes, is now colonising many level areas as well and spreading fast. Alien elements introduced to Exmoor that have become rampant and constitute a major menace are rhododendron (*Rhododendron ponticum*) and Japanese Knotweed (*Reynoutria japonica*).

Exmoor is not wild in the absolute sense of the term. The moorland heathers and grasses inhabit only about a quarter of the Park, woodland about a tenth. For various reasons – one being the reclamation of at least 10,000 acres of moorland since the second world war – the organisers of the Duke of Edinburgh's Award Scheme decided to demote the area from their gold badge to the silver, essentially because it no longer satisfied the full qualifications of 'wildness'. That is to be regretted. Yet the very fact that Exmoor is fragmented lies at the heart of its identity. Visually and physiographically, the landscape is composed of vast views, a precipitous coastline, steep wooded combes and river valleys, narrow lanes lined with banks and beech hedges, indigenous native trees contrasting with blocks of conifers, undisturbed meadows, an exceptional stretch of cereal cropping in Porlock Vale, but principally acres of in-bye pasture and occasional arable underpinning the open moor.

Fragmentation of this kind has rendered it a haven for wildlife of great variety. It is the remaining habitat of size and significance in England of the wild red deer, and it has an abundance of smaller mammals, insects, birds, and reptiles, and a host of plant species, some of them rare: e.g. the heath fritillary and high brown fritillary butterflies; merlin among the birds; and the lesser twayblade among the flora – a fact fully recognised by the ENPA, which has a duty under the original 1949 and recent 1981/1985 Acts to protect wildlife, and to co-operate to that end with other conservation bodies, both statutory and voluntary.

Protection

One practical way in which the ENPA promotes protection is by means of the management agreements with farmers, who occupy 4,078 acres/1,651 ha. in the vital conservation areas, whereby they are compensated for not ploughing or otherwise altering the natural sward. The actual effect on wildlife exercised by these agreements is assessed at the outset and monitored at five-yearly intervals. The Authority applies the same criteria over the 6,244 acres/2,528 ha. of

moorland and over c.1,000 acres/400 ha. of woodland, which are its
own property.

Aside from the ENPA, the principal statutory organisation for
Nature conservation is the Nature Conservancy Council, which
operates through National Nature Reserves (none on Exmoor as
yet) and seven Sites of Special Scientific Interest within the Park
boundaries. In addition to four Sites – Barle Valley, Dunkery area,
Watersmeet, and West Exmoor – important for ancient woodland
and associated flora, there are two Sites – one at Glenthorne, and a
small one at Dean Steep – of geological interest; and one more at
Porlock Marsh, which lies behind a natural shingle beach and ridge
and comprises 'strandline, shingle, maritime grassland, saltmarsh
and brackish water habitats uncommon in Somerset'. A total for
SSSIs of 12,557 acres/4,960 ha. The extension of statutory protection by means of National Nature Reserves and SSSIs by the
NCC over much more of wild Exmoor is fully anticipated.

The two county wildlife trusts, Devon Wildlife Trust and
Somerset Trust for Nature Conservation, are also vitally concerned
with Exmoor, and have investigated several aspects of wildlife in
the Park. These include a survey of otters in 1979-80, red deer in
1981-2, and woodland lichens in 1987-88. The otter survey revealed
that this fascinating little animal had virtually vanished from the
area. There was only scarce evidence of breeding, and such otters as
still existed or might have come into Exmoor were too few to
perpetuate themselves. Apart from its work on ancient woodland
and maintaining two reserves, one at Hurscombe (which includes a
small plantation of hardwoods given by the London Branch of the
Exmoor Society), and the other at Mounsey, the Somerset Trust
undertook a pilot survey in 1987 of grasslands in the Upper Barle
Valley, concentrating on 99 fields of 'significant nature conservation
interest', amounting to 311 acres/126 ha. Most of these fields were
reported as being 'rushy in parts with a typical association of soft
and sharp-flowered rush, meadow sweet, marsh marigold, cuckoo
flower, ragged robin, and marsh violet'. At the time of writing the
survey is being extended to other areas of grassland, all lying
outside the ENPA Conservation Map and estimated to amount to
2,470 acres/1,000 ha.

The work done by the two county trusts, the residential courses
run by educational bodies such as the Leonard Wills Field Studies
Centre at Nettlecombe, the contributions by the Royal Society for
the Protection of Birds, the Somerset Archaeological and Natural

History Society, and the background support of the Exmoor Society – the principal watchdog among voluntary organisations dedicated to safeguarding the integrity of the Park – all this underlines the importance of the part played by the 'private sector'. And that is where one particular local organisation, the Exmoor Natural History Society, based in Minehead, fills such a valuable role in educating and informing the public about wildlife on Exmoor, in addition to research. Its members are regularly out and about observing bird and plant life, the movement of deer, the behaviour of small mammals, amphibians, reptiles, insects, moths and butterflies, indeed practically every aspect of the natural world within the Park. The information is recorded, published in the *Exmoor Naturalist*, the Society's annual journal, and ultimately finds its way into a supplement of the *Check-List of the Fauna and Flora of Exmoor National Park*, first issued in 1988. The sheer output of this small organisation of some 500 members is astonishing. The first number of the *Exmoor Naturalist*, for example, issued in 1975, ran to 16 pages, the 16th in 1990 had 84 – in total a formidable volume of facts and comments. The Society also conducts an annual heath fritillary survey and publishes occasional studies – on flowers, birds, moths and butterflies, and an atlas in diagrammatic form of the frequency of plants recorded 1974-83. It also employs other means of communication: a field centre at Malmsmead open for two afternoons a week from May to September; regular walks, excursions, and lectures; and manages a nature trail in Treborough Woods, a conservation area at Woodcock Gardens, Wootton Courtenay, and a wildflower walk at Minehead Warren. Noel Allen, the chairman and founder of the Society, and Caroline Giddens, the secretary and botanical recorder, have both published works on their own account. Together they are the joint authors of *Exmoor Wildlife* (Exmoor Press).

The Coast

One vital element in the landscape of Exmoor, and a prime reason for its designation as a National Park in 1954, is its 34-mile coastline. Its value is not only aesthetic which indeed is magnificent. It lies also in its geological and other natural characteristics – the age and hardness of its Devonian rocks that withstand the constant assault of the sea and the erosion of the climate; in the refuges it provides for nesting to seabirds, such as herring gulls, petrels,

cormorants, shags and razorbills; and resting places (preferably on
the few stretches of beach) for migrants, such as dunlins, curlews,
sandpipers and terns. Coastal vegetation is likewise both distinct
and attractive, including the feared rhododendron, but also colonies
of thrift, sea campion, thyme, and kidney vetch. Trees, especially
oaks, clothe whole sections of the coast, e.g. from Minehead to
Culver Cliffs, Porlock Weir to Glenthorne, and at Lee Bay and
Woody Bay west of Lynmouth. Another peculiarity is the conform-
ation of the cliffs, termed 'hog's-back', because at some distance
inland they start their downward slope, before reaching the ultimate
edge and sheer drop to the sea. Although landslides have occurred
here and there, the hog's-back contour promotes rain run-off and
helps prevent the penetration of static water into the crevices of the
rocks. Nonetheless the unrelenting action of the sea and weather
have, over hundreds of years, taken their toll. Explorers such as
David Webb, and Terry Cheek (who once climbed along the cliffs
from Foreland Point to Combe Martin in 4 days, 6+ hours) have
described the character of the coastline 'from the inside'. In Webb's
words:

> The extraordinary tide range of the Bristol Channel and the ceaseless
> Atlantic swell combine to attack Exmoor, leaving 'hanging valleys'
> with 100-foot waterfalls, and deep narrow 'guts' bitten between the
> more resistant crags. Even these last bastions are being reduced to
> bluffs, stacks and arches, the softer strata being eaten out to form
> complex caves, some having 'side-windows', 'skylights', and 'blow-
> holes'.[1]

Despite this long term process of erosion, there is no doubt that
the Exmoor coast – by its inaccessibility – largely protects itself.
The breaks in the cliff line are not numerous: principally at Porlock
Bay, Lynmouth and Combe Martin, at Heddon's Mouth, and at
minor curves of the coast as at Woody Bay, Lee Bay, and Wringcliff
Bay, etc. In addition there are several combes, with streams that
cascade over the cliff edge; but these are almost all concealed and
virtually inaccessible. Man however is a penetrating animal and so it
is wise not to leave protection entirely to Nature; and so the whole
coastline is recorded on the ENPA Conservation Map; while
recently it has been designated a Heritage Coast, one of 44 such
areas in England and Wales distinguished for their 'exceptional

1. *Exmoor Review*, 1971.

quality', by the Countryside Commission. This will add positive
force to existing protective measures once the practical effect of
'heritage' has been translated into a management scheme. In
addition two sections of the coast have been classified as SSSIs –
one at Porlock Marsh of 408.08 acres/165.15 ha., and the other at
Glenthorne of 32.8 acres/13.3 ha., which runs from The Caves to
the Giant's Rib.

The best means of enjoying the Exmoor coast is to walk the
coastal path, which forms part of the South West Way and runs for
over 500 miles from Minehead, right round Cornwall and along to
Poole in Dorset. The air is clean, the sky limitless, and the scenery
staggering – inward towards the line of hills that run from Dunkery
westwards, and outward (on a clear day) over the Bristol Channel to
the Welsh coast: an unique combination of landscape and seascape.
It is hard on such occasions to realise that pollution is a real and
constant danger, even in this remote area – from sewage and oil
discharges into the sea, from plastic netting, string, and cling
wrapping that lay traps for birds, and from the thoughtless disposal
of cans, cigarette packets, and glass bottles that so often betoken
man's uncaring concern for this priceless heritage.

CHAPTER FIVE

Trees

Exmoor is ancient and much of it still looks very old. Geologists tell us that, up to c.20,000 years ago, the Bristol Channel was either frozen over or teeming with icebergs that pressed up against the coast line, which extended further out than now. Inland, though not lying under the Ice Cap, Exmoor was a high plateau, barren and lifeless, covered with snow and ice in the dark winters, and bitterly cold. The ground was lashed with storms, but thawed under the summer sun to a shallow depth down to the level of the permafrost. The extremes of climate eroded the rocky hill tops. Alternate freezing and thawing split the surface of the ground, ice filling the cracks during the winter, while in the summer it became so waterlogged that the stones and soil became unstable and slipped down the slopes. Rivers gouged out ever deeper beds or overflowed to lay down broad valley bottoms, supplemented by the soil and scree washed down from the heights.

Millennia passed and the Ice Cap gradually retreated northwards. The Lyn river, once forced westwards through the Valley of Rocks, burst through into the Channel at Lynmouth. Water released by the melting ice raised the sea level round the coast, covering the 'subterranean' forests off Porlock and Minehead Bays. By then a tundra-type vegetation had stabilised the land, succeeded by dwarf shrubs and trees invading from the south, when England was still joined to the Continent. There was no orderly sequence of growth but, in all probability, birch and pine sprang up on the high ground; willow and alder in the marshes; oak, elm, lime and other familiar species took hold in the valleys; hazel proliferated. By c.5000 BC, the climate had turned mild and moist, favouring growth in great variety, by which time also Stone Age man had set about clearing the uplands for nomadic agriculture. Subsequently the use, first of bronze, then of iron for tools increased the pace of clearance; but it was not until after the Romans had left Britain in the fifth century AD, and when the Saxons were displacing the native Celts during the Dark Ages, that forests were mentioned in documents. Even so, the first true catalogue of woods on Exmoor is to be discovered in the Domesday Book 1086, which differentiated between *silva*, tall trees, and *silva minuta*, underwood, virtually all being broadleaved (or hardwood) species. The heaviest concentrations were, as might be expected, in the less accessible parts – along the coast, in the deep combes, on the flanks of some of the steeper hills, or in other areas not hitherto cleared by the Saxons, who had however penetrated far into the heart of Exmoor.

Wood was for centuries an absolutely essential raw material – for building, furniture, tool handles, tanning, charcoal, ships, and a hundred other uses; but it was a finite resource. Trees were not cultivated, except for coppicing, i.e. the system whereby a tree was cut down to its stump or stool, and the re-growth harvested every twenty years or so. Otherwise replacement depended on natural re-generation, and even that was difficult in such places as deer parks or other reserves, where the animals nibbled off the shoots and saplings. It was not until the late 17th century that the Government of the day took notice of the vanishing reserves of growing timber, due in large part to the heavy demands of shipbuilding, so vital to Britain as a naval and mercantile power. John Evelyn sounded the alarm with the publication in 1664 of his classic, *Silva, or a Discourse of Forest Trees and the propagation of Timber in his Majesty's Dominions*. Official reaction was half-hearted, but private landowners responded readily in the following century, combining patriotism with commercial instincts and the fashion of landscaping their estates under the guidance of experts such as 'Capability' Brown and Humphry Repton.

However, due to Continental and colonial wars, and the rise of industrialism, the demand for timber continued to grow, so that by the early 19th century the crisis had again become acute. In 1810 the Government of the day set up a department of 'Woods, Forests and Land Revenues' and, by 1812, was contemplating the possibility of growing trees for naval ship building in the Royal Forest of Exmoor: not, of course, a forest of trees at all, but an area originally reserved to the monarch – at least since Norman times – for hunting the wild red deer. The Royal Forest was duly reduced to an area of c.20,000 acres around Simonsbath, and after 1508 leased to the Warden at a fixed rent, a sum more than recovered by letting grazing on the moorland to neighbouring farmers during the summer. The last lease ran out in 1814 and, despite offers by the then Warden (Sir Thomas Acland, 10th baronet) to rent or buy, it was not renewed. Instead in 1815 the whole area was formally 'disafforested' and thereafter allotted to the various landowners and rights-holders, the Crown retaining 10,262 acres. Soon afterwards, in the way that Governments often do, the Crown Allotment was sold off; and this, together with most of the other allotted areas, was bought up in 1818-20 by John Knight, a Midland industrialist, who then set about his historic reclamation of several thousand acres of high moorland.

Hedge Wood

John Knight and his son, Frederic, undertook relatively little afforestation during the eighty or so years they owned the Simonsbath estate; but they did construct turf and stone-faced banks, topped by beech hedges, as field fences, and for the 29-mile boundary 'wall' (some of it dry stone walling) round the estate. Beech normally stands up well to wind and rain, makes a good shelter, and – if trimmed or laid – retains its leaves through the winter until the green buds push through in the spring. For this purpose a beech nursery was installed at Simonsbath and used to stock Birch Cleave – despite its name, a 26-acre beech wood, planted c.1840 with Scots pine as nurse crop – and at 1,100 feet one of the highest plantations of its kind in the country. Beeches were also grown as shelter belts round the farms at Warren, Emmett's Grange, Wintershead, and Horsen.

Exmoor beech hedges and banks were the subject of a National Park Study undertaken in 1977 by Barbara Salter, who found that most of them dated from the last century and were largely a legacy of the Knights, at any rate in the Forest area. By 1977, however, their condition had sadly deteriorated, due to the expense of hand labour and loss of skilled workers, and the introduction of mechanical trimmers. Nonetheless Exmoor was far better off than most other parts of the country. Out of an estimated total of c.3,500 miles of hedgerows (two-thirds beech), only 200 miles had been lost over the previous 20 years: due to the amalgamation of small fields

9 *Contrasts: moorland, woodland and in-bye land*

10   *Hoccombe Water and John Knight's wall*

11   Woods by the coast at Glenthorne

12   Regimented conifers: plantations on Croydon Hill, near Dunster

13 Traditional management in Exmoor National Park woodlands

or simply because the hedges had been let go too long. The balance had either been reasonably maintained or was capable of restoration. The function of these hedgerows had not altered, serving as stock proof fences and field boundaries and, as landscape features, valuable as habitats for wild flowers and hedge plants, and for small fauna of various kinds; also as sources of 'garden' wood and fuel for the stove. Fortunately their value has now been recognised for its long-term advantages, and the main objection of cost now qualifies for grant-aid; likewise the planting of small areas of woodland and shelter belts on farms.

Private Planting

Substantial areas of woods and park land on estates elsewhere on Exmoor had existed long before the arrival of the Knights. Dunster, for example, had two medieval deer parks; one, known as the 'Hanger' between the village and the river Avill, the other at Marshwood near Carhampton. In 1755 Henry Fownes Luttrell decided to construct a new deer park on high ground south of the castle, 348 acres in extent, fully fenced, into which the deer were transferred. He also planted the park, which already contained a few oaks of great antiquity, with mixed broadleaved trees. His descendant, Alexander Fownes Luttrell, was one of the first to introduce exotic species into his woods, notably Sitka spruce and Douglas fir some of the latter reaching up to 150 feet or more in height.

The deer park at Nettlecombe Court, home of the Trevelyan family (now the Leonard Wills Field Studies Centre) grew oaks of great size and splendour. Collinson, the county historian, wrote in 1791:

> The seat of Sir John Trevelyan stands near the church, and is a good old mansion, pleasantly situated in a fertile vale, environed with well-cultivated hills, and having to the west a beautiful grove of oak.

The Nettlecombe oaks were a constant source of wonder. Some of them marked down during the Napoleonic wars for use by the Admiralty; but after the battle of Waterloo they were not needed and so were duly spared. It is also related that, about 1847 or earlier:

> £40,000 was offered for about forty acres of oak timber on this property; and an old man at Nettlecombe said that the tools were actually brought to the place to fell them, when the owner changed his mind and they were allowed to stand.

As recently as 1951, the forester, J.D.U. Ward, in a letter to *Country Life*, reported two Nettlecombe oaks with a girth (i.e. at 4 feet 6 inches from the ground) measuring 31 feet 10 inches and 32 feet 2 inches respectively. Broadleaved trees, especially oaks, not only live long but re-establish themselves in the most unlikely circumstances. John Crothers, warden of Nettlecombe, has said:

> The old deer park was ploughed and converted to pasture in 1963. Nine years later, when the Field Studies Council acquired the lease, the land was rapidly reverting to rough grassland. In January 1972, I ran a fence across the middle. Mr Harold Scott, the local farmer, is invited to graze his sheep in one half but all stock have been excluded (save for occasional accidents!) from the other, an area of about 12 acres, for 15 years. Trees are steadily invading the ungrazed area – which is otherwise now dominated by brambles and nettles – and the various species display distinct patterns of colonisation.
>
> Oak saplings have mostly sprung up downhill from their putative parent, just outside the canopy. Distribution of the seeds is presumably by their falling to the ground and subsequent rolling (or being washed) downslope, although squirrels are doubtless involved as well. But there are also oak saplings growing just outside the canopy of copper beech and sweet chestnut trees! This suggests that jays (the only bird known to feed extensively on acorns) are also involved.[1]

Plantations clothing the Glenthorne estate, along the north coast of Exmoor, were begun by the Rev. W. Stevenson Halliday, who built his house down by the sea in the 1830s – so remote and difficult of access that most of the materials had to be brought by sea. He used Monterey cypress for shelter belts, but planted beech, larch, and varieties of pine in the combes, and re-established the Yenworthy and Stag's Head woods. Latterly, the present owner, Ben Halliday, came to a management agreement with the National Part Authority, which provides for a network of waymarked walks through the woods. Walking in Glenthorne is rewarding for its scenery and botanical interest, but calls for stamina!

The family, best known for its association with Exmoor proper, is the Aclands. At one time they owned a huge tract of land stretching from Holnicote and Selworthy in the north, over Dunkery, down to Winsford Hill and – up to the end of the 18th century – Pixton Park at Dulverton, when the latter passed by marriage to the Herbert

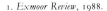

1. *Exmoor Review*, 1988.

family (earls of Carnarvon). Pixton today is well wooded but not with trees of great age. Most of the broadleaves were planted by the Carnarvons in the 1850s-1860s, while – since the last war – a substantial acreage has been planted up with softwoods, due mainly to the interest of Auberon Herbert, and his mother, Mary, widow of Aubrey, diplomat, Member of Parliament, and Balkan specialist, who died in 1923 at the early age of 43: all of them romantic, if not eccentric, figures in the life of the locality.

The Acland legacy to Exmoor is manifold. In terms of trees, the Sir Thomas already mentioned, successor to some spendthrift forbears and no great saver himself, spent a great deal of money afforesting the Holnicote estate. The following summary of his silvicultural activities is taken from page 51 of *The Trees and Woods of Exmoor* (Exmoor Press) by Roger Miles, who has contributed greatly in the writing of this chapter. He is also the author of *Forestry in the English Landscape* (Faber), and spent most of his professional career in the service of Somerset County Council and the Exmoor National Park Authority.

At the beginning of the 19th century, the hills behind Selworthy were bare of trees. Starting at the Lynch end, and influenced strongly by a belief in the value of evergreen, or ilex, oaks for pheasant cover and feed, Sir Thomas planted the great amenity woods which we can all enjoy today. He established the trees there and in other Holnicote woods, section by section, to commemorate the births of his children . . . There are entries like these:- *Selworthy Combe* Mr Acland 23,000; *Park Plantation*, Mr Arthur, 17,200; *Luckham Plantation*, Miss Acland, 28,000; *Tivington Plantation*, Mr Henry, 26,000; *Holnicote Plantation*, Mr Leopold, 25,000.

An old list revealed that some 800,000 trees were planted near Holnicote and Winsford between 1810 and 1826. Sir Thomas died in 1871. Both he and his son, another Sir Thomas (11th baronet), were Members of Parliament and active in other public work, but they also took a keen interest in their Exmoor estate and enjoyed walking through the woods. I quote again:

Many of the paths at Selworthy and in the Horner Valley are named after various friendships . . . Thus, *Katherine's Well, Walton Walk, Lady Acland's Walk, Windsor Path, Mr Hancock's* and *Mr Muller's Paths. Cabinet Walk*, in the Horner Valley, was named to celebrate the inclusion of a son, Arthur, in W.E. Gladstone's Cabinet. Both

Gladstone and his wife planted oak trees at Holnicote in 1877 – the one planted by Mrs Gladstone fell down, but that planted by her husband is growing vigorously and may be seen (with a stone marker) beside the public path south of Holnicote House.[1]

The Acland connection with Exmoor continued until 1944 when the 15th baronet, Sir Richard and his wife, Anne, decided to make over all the land on the Holnicote and Killerton estates to the National Trust – 'partly as a matter of principle, and partly in order to preserve them intact for future generations'. Since then the Trust has had to wrestle with the complex problem of keeping the woods in good heart, while balancing the needs of commerce and amenity. Geoffrey Hordley, chief forester at Holnicote, has outlined the programme conceived in 1973, pointing out that replacements – especially on the farms – were long overdue, and the 'open grown' hardwoods needed almost a lifetime to 'attain the shape and character that is so much a part of the English countryside'.

> Of all the rules which govern the landscape planting of trees, by far the most important is 'the 360 degree rule'. Every planting site at Holnicote was viewed from all points of the compass and from as far away as possible. Only from long range can the whole be seen in perspective. It is virtually impossible to replace trees on a one-for-one basis even if that is desirable, which it rarely is.
>
> The Holnicote Landscape Planting Scheme took off in the autumn of 1977 in the vale between Piles Mill, near Allerford, and Ebbshill. The following year the higher end of the vale around Blackford and Tivington was planted. It had by then become apparent that, although the original idea of choosing native hardwood species for open sites remained valid, there was scope for a greater variety on certain sites.[2]

He then listed, in appropriate situations, field maple, lime, crab apple, Scots pine, and Monterey pine, hornbeam (between Allerford and Bossington), black poplar: with horse chestnut, wild cherry and red oak above Selworthy Farm and adjacent cottages and elsewhere. By 1981 the main lowland areas had been adequately re-stocked and attention turned to the upland farms . . . where beech, ash and holly were more suitable. He added that the hill farms were perhaps the most difficult to deal with, 'the balance between understocking and

---

1. Roger Miles: *Trees and Woods of Exmoor* (Exmoor Press).
2. *Exmoor Review*, 1985.

overstocking being very fine'. By the end of 1983 the original seven-year plan was complete: 875 trees had been planted, 27 species used, the great majority being oak, sweet chestnut, beech and ash; some 500 of the trees required individual cages to guard against stock. Sir Thomas the 10th, and all the Aclands would have approved.

The Twilight of Trees

While the 18th century was a period when landowners, for a variety of reasons, planted a large quantity of trees, yet demand kept ahead of supply so that inroads still had to be made into the reserves of timber inherited from the past. By the middle of the 19th century, however, the situation had changed. Iron, then steel, replaced wood in the construction of ships, while the market for coppice products, tanbark, and charcoal was being extinguished by new industrial processes and materials. Hardwoods, especially oak, planted in the 1700s and maturing in the late 1800s and early 1900s were no longer needed for commercial purposes on the same scale as before, and lost value as capital assets on estates. Instead, woodland came to be appreciated as a habitat for game and its aesthetic attractions. Timber was still in great demand, not hardwood but softwood, for building, paper making, and a hundred other uses: an economic fact either overlooked by landowners too conservative to change – though there were exceptions – among them on Exmoor, Sir Thomas Acland (the 10th) and A. F. Luttrell at Dunster, who experimented with spruces, pines, larch and Douglas fir – or because the terms of trade encouraged the import of cheap food and raw materials (including softwood timber) in exchange for coal and manufactured'goods. The State, represented by a mere 70,000 acres of Crown Forests, made no move until 1901-2 when it acquired a further 3,000 acres of woods at Tintern in the Wye Valley, and in 1904 opened a school for foresters in the Forest of Dean. Meanwhile Parliament sat on a series of Reports until 1909, when the Liberal Government founded the Development Commission to promote – among other duties – the afforestation of nine million acres over the following half-century; but all this was at the eleventh hour. The war intervened, and not one of the nine million acres was planted.

When war broke out with Germany in August 1914, Britain was importing over 90 per cent of its softwood requirements, while only c.5 per cent of its land surface was devoted to woodland, mostly hardwood. Moreover since both food and timber – essential for our war effort and very survival – were bulk cargoes, the depredations of German U Boats struck at the very heart of our national existence. The Government, however, seemed in no hurry and it was not until July 1916 that the Prime Minister, Mr Asquith, appointed a Forestry Sub-Committee of the Ministry of Recon- struction 'to consider and report upon the best means of conserving and developing the woodland and forestry resources of the United Kingdom, having regard to the experience gained during the war'. The chairman of the Sub-Committee was Francis Acland (later the 14th baronet), yet another family and Exmoor connection. The Acland Report was presented in 1917, when U Boat sinkings were at their height, accepted by the Cabinet in 1918, and translated into action by the passage of the Forestry Act 1919, which established the Forestry Commission and to whom the historic forests of the Crown Commission were transferred.

The new measures for forestry had, therefore, no influence on the emergencies of the First World War which absorbed, in volume, about one-third of all the timber standing in 1914. Felling took place on all the estates on and around Exmoor, labour being supplied by Canadians, Portugese, prisoners-of-war, and the Womens' Forestry Corps. Haulage rather than felling was the more serious problem. Horses did most of the work, supplemented by a few tractors and steam lorries, most logs being loaded on to trucks on the handful of single-track railways (Barnstaple-Ilfracombe, Taunton-Barnstaple, and Taunton-Minehead) or on to ships at Watchet. The West Somerset Mineral Railway (Watchet-Brendon Hill), which might have proved useful, had already been abandoned. Exmoor roads suffered severely.

The Forestry Commission quickly made its mark on the British countryside, in several senses. By 1939 it had acquired over a million acres of land and planted (or was planting) nearly three-quarters of its first 20-year target, becoming the largest landowner in the country. However it came in for criticism, both due to lack of experience and pressure placed upon it to plant up as much land as quickly as possible, and with softwoods at that.

The appearance of many of the new softwood plantations antagonized public opinion for aesthetic reasons, and the restrictions imposed upon access through planted land aroused added opposition.

Large rectangular blocks of conifers, often of one species unrelieved by mixture with another, an apparent exclusion of hardwoods and a grid-iron pattern of fire breaks and rides intersecting newly afforested areas, seemed typical of the Commission's work . . . The large scale of many plantations and the obliteration of subtle natural contours by their rigid patterns, the sombre colours and the sharp outlines of the young trees, all conflicted with popular conceptions of woodland beauty. The even age, dense planting, suppression of undergrowth and exclusion of sunlight in many plantations, caused further aggravation.[1]

These remarks apply on Exmoor where, in the 1920s, the Commission acquired a large area in the Brendon Hills and south of Dunster. On Croydon Hill, particularly, the blanket effect of planting regiments of conifers was alien to the neighbourhood, though time has softened the outlines somewhat, but naturalists complain of the absence of birds and general lack of wildlife sounds and colours. The same criticism applies to the plantations on Kennisham Hill and in Chargot Wood, though relieved by the attractive Luxborough valley which runs between Croydon and Brendon Hills.

The Commission dominated forestry between the two world wars, and in the 1930s – as earlier described – when the demand for public access to the countryside was growing together with the idea for National Parks, the Commission took the lead and created its own National Forest Parks. Three were in operation by 1939, and more followed after the war, but not on Exmoor. In this period private forestry did not revive as expected. Landowners were deterred by adverse economic conditions and by what they considered inadequate grants for planting. Exmoor woods suffered in consequence, though natural regeneration made up some of the lost ground.

A New Dawn?

The Second World War was, ironically, a repeat performance of the First, in that – since the Forestry Commission plantations were as yet immature except for thinnings – recourse had to be made once again to existing mature (and semi-mature) stands of hardwood, and which in consequence were heavily reduced in acreage and volume once more. Exmoor did not escape. What the war did however was

1. Roger Miles: *Forestry in the English Landscape* (Faber).

to generate a great deal of thought and planning for the revival of forestry in peace time, both as to increasing the home production of timber, and the value of woodland for amenity and recreation. This led to the passage of three Forestry Acts immediately after the war – 1945, 1947 and 1951: which, between them projected the expansion of State forests, provided for the dedication of private woods, controlled felling in order to ensure a minimum reserve of growing timber, and paved the way for consultations with planning authorities on amenity and Tree Preservation Orders.

In Somerset, the county planning department took particular care to try to make the new legislation work: essentially by means of regular consultation between everyone concerned – planners, landowners, representatives of the Forestry Commission and, not least, the Nature Conservancy then at work demarcating Sites of Special Scientific Interest (SSSIs). All this seemed to go well, conflicts were few, compromises frequent, both before and immediately after the designation of Exmoor as a National Park in 1954. It, therefore, came as a shock when, late in 1957, the National Park Authority was first apprised of the negotiations between the Fortescue estate and the Forestry Commission to plant up some 1,200 acres of The Chains – the heart of the moorland and the watershed of the principal rivers – with conifers and build access roads. Thanks to public outcry and vigorous objections by the ENPA, the proposal was withdrawn, as described in Chapter 2; but it is worth repeating that, had the Forestry Commission wished to proceed with planting, nothing could have stopped it, since forestry was exempt from planning control.

The Chains row produced reverberations. One was the purchase of the area by Somerset County Council; another was the foundation of the Exmoor Society; yet another was an officially inspired survey to assess where and how afforestation might take place without detriment to the character of the Park. This proved timely, because the retreat of the Forestry Commission was countered by the advent of private forestry or 'financial' syndicates, supported by the Timber Growers' Organisation (an offshoot of the CLA), bent on taking advantage of tax concessions, to plant up other sites: for which incidentally the syndicates had no need to advise the ENPA as the Commission had done. One syndicate was already buying up land in Devon, and *The Times* reported plans to acquire 100,000 acres of 'bare land' in the south-west, plus 150,000 acres of existing woods – a total later inflated to 300,000 – with the purpose of supporting a chipboard factory at Okehampton. Where was the land to come from, and how much from the National Parks? The suggestion was 30,000 acres from Dartmoor and 20,000 acres from Exmoor; and there was nothing in the law to prevent it. The reaction was prompt. The CPRE and a Joint Action Group led by the formidable Lady Sayer of the Dartmoor Preservation Society, and John Coleman-Cooke, founder of the Exmoor Society, published a statement in January 1961, arguing the case against wholesale tree planting, and calling for the afforestation of open land to be covered by planning control.

The Minister said 'No', but once again public outcry was sufficiently strong to produce, in this case, a paper compromise, namely the Voluntary Scheme over Afforestation, which was accepted in principle by the contending parties and accorded more or less with the Exmoor Afforestation Survey, recently completed. The Scheme succeeded anyway in discouraging the planting of open moorland, and diverted private forestry to more suitable sites in the valleys. Progress, however, was hazardous, and soon the syndicates were trying a new tack, i.e. to re-stock existing woods (as opposed to open land) with conifers. This move was not covered by the Voluntary Scheme, and no one would negotiate. So, to its great credit, the ENPA (Somerset Committee) slammed Tree Preservation Orders on seven important woodlands, covering 700 acres – an action upheld by the Minister after public enquiry, and compelled the syndicates to talk across the table before sending in the bulldozers. At the same time a new investigation was ordered, entitled The Exmoor Woodland Survey, which was confined largely to a study of landscape values and the need, once again, to consult other interests (water, Nature conservation, recreation, et al.) in good time. The new Survey was completed in 1964, covering the entire Park and, by reason of its expertise had some effect, for it relied entirely on persuasion for results. But it also induced the ENPA to take another positive step: to lease or purchase (with grant-aid), or accept as a gift, areas of amenity woodland under actual or potential threat. By these means the Authority acquired c.1,000 acres (405 ha.) of forest property scattered between Dulverton and the north coast, as set out in the Table overleaf. This total is more than that owned by any other National Park Authority, while the 20,756 acres (8,400 ha.) of woods of all kinds on Exmoor is equivalent to c.12 per cent of the total area of the Park.

Woodlands belonging to the ENPA   *Hectares*

Dulverton
  Burridge Wood, Weir Cleave, Paddons Wood,
    Hawkridge Ridge   32.9
Haddon Hill
  Hadborough Plantation   18.2
Minehead
  Woodcombe Plantation, Woodcombe Brake, Whitecross
    Plantation, Moor Wood, Culvercliff Woods   61.0
Lynton
  Kibsworthy Wood   0.2
Porlock
  Hawkcombe Woods, Embelle Wood, Culbone Wood,
    Ashley Combe   279.8
Winsford
  Bye Common Woodland   0.7

        (1,000.5 acres)   404.1

Woodlands managed by the ENPA

Lynton
  Hollerday Hill   10.3
Minehead
  Greenaleigh Farm Woodlands   5.9
Nettlecombe
  Kingsdown Clump   1.4

        (43.4 acres)   17.6

Management

Inevitably ownership of woodland generates problems of management, but it was not until the reorganisation of the ENPA in 1974 as a single undivided Authority, with headquarters offices and staff based on Exmoor House, Dulverton, that it was possible to appoint a full-time forester: even then he had to depend on part-time assistance in the woods. His first task was to compile a register of all the woodland in the care of the ENPA and to assess its condition and needs, a job completed in 1975. Two years later, the forestry chapter in the National Park Plan added a review of all the principal woods on Exmoor, their location, status and owner-ship, and confirmed the policy of control by means of consultation as the best, indeed the only practicable safeguard in the absence of compulsory powers, other than TPOs. In that same year, 1977, Peter Garthwaite, an eminent forestry consultant, was called in to advise. In general he approved of the way in which woodland in the Park was being managed, but recommended the planting of a greater mix of hardwoods (beech, sweet chestnut, as well as oak, the dominant species), and commented on the huge backlog of thinning. That, of course, was part of the price of owning areas of woodland, where management had in the past been at a minimum if not totally absent, and where great numbers of trees were going back.

Burridge and Red Lion Woods, for example, consisting of 46 acres of partly coppiced oakwood north-west of Dulverton, listed as a SSSI, and an attractive sight at most seasons of the year, have little commercial value. However, since three of the objectives posed by Garthwaite were 'amenity and landscape value', 'habitat for wildlife', and 'public enjoyment' – to combine these with commerce is a formidable proposition. Such is the dilemma confronting the Authority in all its woods and operations, and which prompted the foundation of the Exmoor Woodland Conservation Fund, to which the public is invited to contribute and in 1990 stood at over £13,000. Some of the money has already been spent on conservation work at Hollerday Hill, Lynton and Moor Wood, Minehead. The hope is that the more planting the Fund finances, the quicker the Fund will grow; in other words, results breed resources.

The Four Aims

It is evident from this account how hard the going has been to try to fulfil the aims of the National Parks Act 1949 in regard to forestry. Similar difficulties applied, even more severely, to halting the reclamation of moorland for agriculture, and which had to wait for the Porchester Report 1977 before a solution came in sight. Yet in forestry progress never actually stopped. For example, the Forestry Commission (which had already introduced National Forestry Parks) paid increasing attention to the needs of recreation and amenity. In 1963 it appointed Miss (later Dame) Sylvia Crowe as its landscape consultant, and since then landscaping has become a regular commitment.

In July 1985 the Government announced a new policy for broadleaved woodlands. It recognised their value as part of the landscape heritage, also for recreation (walking, orienteering, etc), for Nature conservation, and the surprising fact that (from 3/4 million hectares of woods plus a further 90 million individual trees) hardwoods yielded 20 per cent of the country's wood production. It fell primarily to the Forestry Commission to implement the new policy, in collaboration with other statutory and voluntary organisations, and which in essence amounted to injecting advice and money into the business of improving and extending existing plantations, as well as planting new ones: all directed towards the four objectives already mentioned – enhancement of the landscape, recreation, Nature conservation, and wood production.

The ironical fact is that, contrary to expectation, the new policy does not lack sources of money or grant-aid arrangements; but has practically choked the market with a surplus of them. For example, the schemes 'on offer' range from:

Forestry Commission Woodland Grant Scheme to aid fresh planting and natural regeneration, additional of course to existing FC grant-aided schemes for forest owners.

Countryside Commission Scheme (administered by county councils) for small amenity woodlands under 0.25 ha.

MAFF Farm Woodland Scheme to encourage farmers to plant up agricultural land with trees (minimum 3 ha.), as a measure of 'diversification'; and its *Farm and Conservation Grant Scheme* for amenity planting and shelter belts on farms.

Nor is that the end of the list for there are schemes operated by the Crown Commission, the Woodland Trust, the ENPA, and several other bodies, private and public.

Where does an Exmoor, or any other, farmer start? The whole scenario needs clarification, and is simply a symptom of the piecemeal approach to the support of forestry and farming, in particular in upland areas such as Exmoor; and it adds force to the concept of 'whole farm management', envisaged by the adoption and extension of Environmentally Sensitive Areas (ESAs), see Chapter 3.

One statutory agency of prime importance to Exmoor is the Nature Conservancy Council, established by Act of Parliament in 1973 'for the purposes of Nature conservation and fostering the understanding thereof'. It replaced the Nature Conservancy, created by Royal Charter in 1949 as Britain's first official conservation agency, and is funded by the Department of the Environment. At the time of writing, the NCC has no National Nature Reserve on Exmoor, but it does have seven Sites of Special Scientific Interest (SSSIs) listed in Chapter 4, in four of which trees are an important element. These four are the *Barle Valley*, a long narrow strip running from near Dulverton to South Hill, Withypool; the *Dunkery* area (including Holnicote and Porlock Common); *Watersmeet*, running from Brendon to Lynmouth with southern arms along Hoaroak and Farley Waters; and *West Exmoor*, a $5\frac{1}{2}$ mile stretch of coast from Hollerday Hill, Lynton, to The Mare and Colt, below Holdstone Down, with a southern arm along the river Heddon and its main tributary. All these support important areas of ancient sessile oak woodland, with lichens and associated flora, qualifying them for protection as SSSIs. To ensure protection the NCC purchases or leases land, or enters into management agreements with landowners – who incur severe penalties if they break the rules – and it can fall back on compulsory purchase orders if all else fails. It means, in practice, that the NCC is a more effective body than for instance any of the National Park Authorities: in that the latter still have no ultimate weapon – Moorland Conservation Orders, proposed by Porchester, having been denied by Parliament. Moreover, in my view, the gathering force of conservation – as the prime purpose of land use in National Parks – will strengthen the hand of the NCC, if it decides to increase the number of SSSIs or even declare all the moorland areas of Exmoor a National Nature Reserve.

If the NCC is to be merged with the Countryside Commission in England – following the agreed merger in Wales (1991) and in Scotland (1992) – then conservation will indeed become the prime power within National Parks.

Of the 20,000 + acres of woodland on Exmoor, about half is in private ownership, and the balance split between the Forestry Commission (c.20 per cent), National Trust (c.20 per cent), and c.10 per cent between the ENPA and the Crown Commission. However, neither the owners of the land, nor the grant-giving agencies are the sole organisations concerned with forestry on Exmoor. For instance, the Exmoor Society includes the care of woodlands, trees and hedges as essential components of the landscape, which it is pledged to defend. Also the Exmoor Natural History Society is deeply involved in the whole spectrum of fauna and flora associated with the woods. It has established a Nature trail in Treborough Woods, maintains nest boxes at Treborough, Hawkcombe, Horner, and other woodland areas; and it lists – among much other valuable material – the broadleaves, conifer and allied species in its *magnum opus, The Flora and Fauna of Exmoor* (1988).

Following an investigation of woodland lichens in 1987-8, the Somerset Trust for Nature Conservation conducted a general survey of Exmoor woodlands in 1979-80, primarily to identify the ancient woods, i.e. those which have existed since before 1600, and to establish their value in terms of Nature conservation. This survey revealed that over 20 per cent of Exmoor woods can still be classified as 'ancient' (compared with c.5 per cent in the rest of the country), hence their unique importance. It is likely that all the woods recorded in Domesday derive from the primeval post-Ice Age, and can be identified by certain species of plants. Lichens in particular are important as clues to the age of trees, also to changes in light and humidity, and to the absence of air pollution. In general ancient woods provide controls for scientific research, habitats for floral communities (especially the vulnerable ones), and are 'reservoirs from which the wildlife of the wider countryside can be maintained'. These are clearly summarised in the recent review of the National Park Plan, and in an article contributed to the *Exmoor Review* 1983 by Rob Jarman, then Conservation Officer of the Trust and in charge of the survey.

A Look Both Ways

History reveals patterns. Until the 17th century man regarded wood as later he did coal: the latter, for long his sole source of primary energy, at least in industry. Likewise wood served a hundred purposes in its day, and man could not do without it. However, he did virtually nothing about the trees he was squandering, but relied on natural re-generation and coppicing. In the 18th century landowners planted trees in great profusion, for both commerce and amenity; but in the 19th, iron and steel began to replace timber for ship building and other forms of construction. Softwood was imported, and the hardwood stands became ornamental parks and game reserves. In the present century forestry revived, principally through the plantation of conifers, which are fast-growing and a viable commercial crop. That is still the case today; however, the scene has begun to change again. Farm land is in surplus and, as a nation, we are fast becoming aware that, by 'conquering' and plundering Nature, we shall certainly cut our own throats. Broadleaves are now to be nurtured and financially assisted, because they are good for wildlife and good to look at.

Exmoor fortunately still has relatively large areas of traditional species of broadleaved trees, e.g. oak and oak coppice, stands of beech and ash, and hedgerow trees. Properly managed – for they are not monuments of stone – they need thinning, felling and re-planting like their softwood counterparts, though on a far longer time scale, and the legacy of neglected woodland is immense. It is likely that the ancient woodlands cover some 7,413 acres/3,000 ha. and it is significant that the ENPA tree nursery at Allerford cultivates seed from locally acclimatised stock, thereby maintaining a genetic link with primeval woodland. And so it is the hardwoods that contribute so much to the natural beauty and many of the wildlife habitats that – together with the moors and in-bye farmland – compose our heritage of landscape on Exmoor.

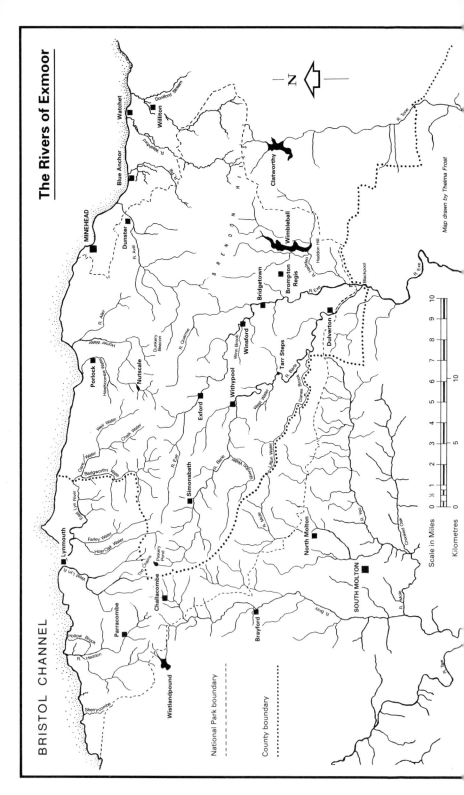

The Rivers of Exmoor

BRISTOL CHANNEL

Map drawn by Thelma Frost

Scale in Miles

Kilometres

National Park boundary

County boundary

CHAPTER SIX

Rivers and 'Waters'

Rivers and streams of every kind cover Exmoor like the veins in a human hand. They not only provide the habitats for trout and salmon and a host of micro-life but, in the past, supplied the power that turned the water wheels of flour and grist mills, sawmills, barn machinery, and small industrial plants, such as the crepe mill (now a laundry) in Dulverton. Wheels, some of great size, were installed at the various iron ore and copper mines on Exmoor – at Bampfylde, Bremley, Cornham Ford, and Wheal Eliza, operating pumps, whims, crushers, etc. The great Bampfylde Wheel, on the river Mole, was 50 feet in diameter by 5 feet wide. The earliest electricity generating stations depended on water, as at Lynmouth, installed in 1890, drawing on the East Lyn; and there were other early plants at Dulverton and Porlock; also in certain country houses and estates, e.g. Chargot near Luxborough, and Pixton near Dulverton.

Noel Allen, has related how he tramped 300 miles or so along and around the major rivers and reservoirs of the National Park.[1] The term 'water', he says, 'is a particularly happy Exmoor word given to a length of water which is not quite a river, but too big to pass as a stream'. And he calculates that, with some thirty named rivers and 'waters' marked on the Ordnance Survey map of Exmoor, averaging about ten miles each in length, the total of 300 must be further increased by hundreds more miles of unnamed brooks and tributaries. This chapter is based on his experiences and my own observations, and I have included further notes in the section devoted to Freshwater Fishing under *Field Sports*.

1. *The Waters of Exmoor*, (Exmoor Press).

For the purpose of what follows, it is helpful to divide the National Park into two main areas, east and west of the A.396 (Dulverton-Minehead road).

East of the A.396

Four rivers belong to this area: three flow north, one south. The first northern one, furthest east, is unnamed. It rises in Galloping Bottom, a short distance north-east of Raleighs Cross, flows through Pond Wood, fills the ponds at Combe Sydenham, thence to Monksilver and close to the road as far as Yarde. At that point it turns sharply north-east to the sea. The second is the **Washford** river, which springs from several sources. One group starts at different points below the ridge road between Raleighs Cross and Beulah Chapel, one of its brooks running beside the old Mineral Railway Incline, now overgrown and hard to penetrate. Another small stream rises in Leigh Woods above a 40-foot waterfall, and joins its fellows at Comberow at the foot of the Incline. A different source issues from Chargot Wood where it feeds several fish ponds, and then runs down via Kingsbridge and Druidscombe to Roadwater, where it meets the tributary from Comberow to become the Washford river proper. Below Roadwater it has a clear run, past the ruins of Cleeve Abbey, through Washford village and down to the the sea at Watchet. The third northern river is the **Pill**, which rises just inside the National Park south of Withycombe, runs through Rodhuish, and gathers a group of small streams before joining the sea at Blue Anchor.

The only south-flowing river of consequence is the **Haddeo**, which rises in the area of Cuckolds Combe in the Brendon Hills and flows into the eastern arm of **Wimbleball** reservoir (now christened a Lake), constructed 1974-77. The northern arm is fed by several unnamed streams that rise from springs north of Withiel Florey and enter the Lake above Bessom Bridge. Wimbleball is impressive. It is the largest and latest reservoir on Exmoor, built to supply water to Taunton, Bridgwater, Tiverton and Exeter, with a total capacity of $4\frac{3}{4}$ million gallons when full; and has already proved itself during the dry summers of 1989 and 1990. There are other striking features – the 161-foot high concrete dam across the head of the Haddeo river valley, the miles of footpaths and bridleways round the edge, camping and picnic sites, and provision for sailing and fishing. The fact that the Lake serves so many purposes additional to the impounding of water, is due to comprehensive planning from the start, and to imaginative designs for tree planting and landscaping, drawn originally by Dame Sylvia Crowe, which enhance the beautiful L-shape of the Lake and attract a variety of water and other birds. Below the Lake, the Haddeo continues on its course down a narrow wooded valley, past the hamlet of Hartford where it is joined by the little **Pulham** river coming down from Heath Poult Cross by way of Brompton Regis. Soon it reaches the small village of Bury and joins the Exe at Pixy Copse, east of Pixton Park. The path from Bury up to the dam is called Lady Harriet's Drive, after Lady Harriet Acland who, in the late 1700s, had it constructed as a carriage drive to give easy access from Pixton up to the outlying parts of the estate near Wiveliscombe.

West of the A.396

Dunkery Hill and the high ground running east-west across the north of the Park, almost as far as Parracombe, resembles a transverse backbone (with a few extra vertebrae), without which Exmoor would lose its physical identity. This backbone is the source of most of the moorland rivers – a watershed from which some flow north, some south.

North-flowing – described from east to west

The head waters of the **Avill** resemble the tentacles of an octopus, or several octopi, some stretching from the outer slopes of Dunkery, some from the tip of the Brendons, some from Croydon Hill. All these waters congregate near Timberscombe to form the main stream which flows round Dunster, passing under a packhorse bridge at Gallox and driving the restored watermill (with its two wheels) on the edge of the village, before running under the A.39 and the West Somerset Railway track close to Dunster station, and thence out to sea at Dunster Beach.

In its upper reaches, **Horner Water** bears several names. As **Chetsford Water** it rises in the high moorland near Alderman's Barrow and, as **Nutscale Water**, runs down to the **Nutscale** reservoir, which sits in a steep valley, a thousand feet up, about a mile east of Lucott Cross. It covers some 24 acres and was built between 1925 and 1941 to supply Minehead. It is the subject of a pamphlet, now rare, written in 1937 by Alfred Vowles, the popular

historian and photographer of Exmoor, in anticipation of its
ceremonial opening. However, the war intervened, and when the
work was finally completed in 1941, nothing could be published
about it for reasons of security. Below the reservoir, the stream
becomes **Horner Water** which flows in a circular route into Horner
Woods, and pulls in a couple of tributaries, one of them the **East
Water**, coming through Cloutsham. Once clear of the woods, it
makes a bee line for the sea via Horner hamlet, West Luccombe, and
Bossington, where it is joined by the Aller.

The **Aller** is described as a 'rivulet' some three miles long, rising
in a complex of sources in the area between the north-east edge of
Dunkery and the plantations north of Wootton Courtenay, supplemented further on by the trickle that comes down from Selworthy
Combe. Approaching Allerford , the Aller once provided power for
Piles Mill, which has been converted by the National Trust into a
Study Centre. In the village the stream is crossed by the attractive
packhorse bridge, passes behind the old school, now transformed
into an admirable Rural Life Museum, and then runs on to the
junction with Horner Water at Lynch. The outlet in Porlock Bay is
complicated by a barrier of pebbles built up by the tides, through
which the fresh water has to find its way.

Hawkcombe Water rises from springs at Hawkcombe Head in
the neighbourhood of Porlock Common and Whitstones at c.1,400
feet. It soon enters the steep wooded valley that bears its name –
much of it oak belonging to the National Park Authority – and
picks up a couple of tributaries, one from the north not far from its
source, the other from the south from the direction of Berry Castle,
an obscure Iron Age fort. The stream then flows into the outskirts
and through Porlock village. At one time its fall and speed were
sufficient to drive the wheels of two mills, in operation until the end
of the last century. Later they were refurbished and converted into
plants generating electricity that supplied power and light to the
village up to the last war. Below Porlock, the Water flows through
level meadows and marshland until it reaches the sea.

The two Lyn Rivers

West of Porlock Weir, several small streams find their way down
from the woods and high ground north of the A.39, and fall over
the cliff into the sea. However, the next significant group begins
with those that feed the **East Lyn**, not strictly a river in its own

right, but the name given to a combination of Waters, one flowing into another, and renowned individually for their fish and wild natural beauty.

Furthest east is **Weir Water** – hence in a sense the true source – which rises in a marshy area close to Lucott Cross. In its course northward it is swelled by three small streams – one has a name, **Colley Water** – until it bears round west to Robber's Bridge and Oareford, where it is joined by **Chalk Water**. Claude Wade (see the section on Freshwater Fishing) caught 123 trout above Weir Wood on one occasion, and compared Weir and Chalk by saying that the latter always had a brown peaty tinge and the former not. In spate, according to him, Chalk turned red, and Weir light brown or 'kharki' (sic).

North and east of Larkbarrow, one of the Knight farmsteads destroyed by gunnery practice in the last war, is a large marshy area known as Madacombe, which is the source of **Chalk Water**, visible and invisible at first in the form of trickles that gather force in a northward flow between Kittuck (Kite Oak), South Common and Black Hill to the west, and Mill Hill to the east. Halfway along, at a junction of small valleys and streams called Three Combes Foot, is a remarkable round 'stell' or sheep shelter, built of stone with beech trees growing on the perimeter. This dates from about the year 1846, when Larkbarrow was carved out of the moor. The stell has proved its worth ever since, particularly in the fearful storm-bound winter of 1962-3, when sheep sought refuge here and were found alive by shepherds brought by helicopter. The Water widens and deepens under the lee of Mill Hill as it approaches Oareford where, united with Weir Water, it becomes Oare Water for the next stretch.

A big pool, scoured out by the input of Chalk into Weir marks the start of **Oare Water**, which soon bends northward beside a lone beech and conifer wood on the right bank, and runs close to the narrow road all the way. There is high ground on both sides, Yenworthy Common to the north and Oare Common to the south, both rising to c.1,200 feet. Opposite Oare Church – we are now coming into R.D. Blackmore country- a lane crosses the stream at Oare Bridge and climbs steeply up to the A.39 coast road between Porlock and Lynmouth. Trees overhang the stream for most of the rest of its course between Oare and Malmsmead, which is the junction with **Badgworthy Water**.

'Badgery', as it is pronounced, is formed by several streams – by **Hoccombe Water** that runs down from Brendon Two Gates, picking up a side stream from west of Trout Hill; and by a spread of streams that issue from the Pinfords and Long Combe under the lee of Tom's Hill. From the union of all these, the Water flows north down a lovely valley, much of it wooded, drawing in two important tributaries from the west, both of which play a part in the composition of Blackmore's *Lorna Doone*. For example, the Water Slide derives from **Lank Combe** where the stream does indeed flow over a slab of rock or two; while the Doone village – claimed by enthusiasts as located at the head of Lank Combe – could only have been conjured out of the ruins of the medieval hermits' settlement at the junction with Hoccombe Combe (not **Hoccombe Water**). Be that as it may, the popularity of the novel and the beauty of the valley have been drawing visitors for the past 120 years, and since they come in the spring and summer during the fishing season, the effect on fishing can be imagined. Wade was complaining about it as far back as the 1870s. Coming down to Malmsmead (now a tourist honeypot), the river runs beside some grass fields, under a bridge and over a ford before joining up with Oare Water. From that point westward it is known as the **East Lyn**.

As far as Brendon Village, the **East Lyn** runs through an open grassland valley, bordered by steep slopes, pleasant but undramatic. Beyond Brendon, the river changes in character, widening, full of boulders, running between high, steep and wooded hangars. At Rockford the road turns inland, up the steep hill past Brendon Church, while the river rushes on below through a series of pools, famed for their fish, curling round and through Barton Wood, thick with hardwoods and conifers. At Watersmeet – as the name implies – the East Lyn is joined by two tributaries, **Farley Water** and **Hoaroak Water**, which have already combined further upstream at Hillsford Bridge.

Farley Water rises in the peat bog of Exe Plain at the eastern extremity of The Chains watershed, not far from Brendon Two Gates. The oozing water soon cuts a gully and gathers further trickles as it runs northward between Cheriton Ridge on the west and Pig Hill and Middle Hill on the east. On the way down springs at Holcombe Burrows add to the flow, which courses along a wooded valley leading to the small settlement of Bridge Ball, and ultimately to Hillsford Bridge and the junction with Hoaroak Water.

Hoaroak Water rises in a re-entrant of The Chains only half-a-mile west of Exe Head, a remarkably short distance on the watershed from which the Hoaroak flows north and the Exe east and south. Another headwater stream starts further west along the edge of The Chains and joins the main stream to flow down the valley floor of wild moorland grass and rush. Soon it reaches the Hoaroak Tree, planted in 1917, the third on this spot since the 17th century, and marking the parish and county boundary. It is a poor stunted specimen, not surprising perhaps at this elevation and exposed to all the storms that sweep up The Chains valley. The stream flows on between Furzehill Common and Cheriton Ridge, notable for the number of prehistoric sites (hut circles, standing stones, and tumuli) in such an isolated area. Inside Devon stands Roborough Castle, an Iron Age fort, high up on the left bank. Close by, the woods begin to clothe the stream as it drops by a series of spectacular waterfalls between Combe Park and Watersmeet.

From here to the sea the **East Lyn** runs between wooded cliffs of the most dramatic aspect. Myrtleberry Cleave and Lyn Cleave on the left bank, Wind Hill on the right, rising sheer in places to just under 1,000 feet. That the river turns into a torrent after heavy rain is no surprise: due to the narrowness of the gorge, the obstacles of rock in mid-stream, and the steep fall from the high moorland of some of the tributaries. In August 1952 there was simply not enough space to contain the wall of water tearing down from The Chains and Brendon Common, hence all the havoc at Lynmouth – and elsewhere – and shocking loss of life.

The **West Lyn** is composed of several streams, of which the main one (which bears the name) rises in two places on the north face of The Chains, one above Thornhill, the other at Benjamy. These two combine and fall fast towards the settlement of Furzehill, east of Ilkerton Ridge, and on to Barbrook. The second stream, **Thornworthy Water**, rises in the heights close to the Longstone, runs past the isolated farm of Shallowford, where it pulls in a brook from the east, and continues on through small fields, past Thornworthy, until it links up with a tributary from Woolhanger at the foot of Barham Hill. Together they flow along West Ilkerton Common where they are joined by yet another tributary that rises in Woolhanger Common, and so onward beside the A.39 to Barbrook, the junction with the main stream. Barbrook was the scene of devastation in 1952, which necessitated the widening of the river bed and the building of a new bridge in 1956. Lower down, the river contracts again in the wooded gorge that runs past Lynbridge and into Glen Lyn, with its spectacular rocks and waterfalls, before joining the East Lyn, a short distance from the sea.

West of the Lyns

There are two streams of note, west of Lynmouth within the National Park boundary. The first is **Hollow Brook**, short and precipitous. It rises above Martinhoe Church, runs down a ravine where it drops 70 feet over Hollow Brook Falls, and continues to the edge of the cliff where it leaps over the edge in a spectacular double cascade – impossible to view except from the sea.

The second is the **Heddon** river that rises south-east of Parracombe on the edge of Challacombe Common and passes through the village, which also suffered in the 1952 floods. Much damage was done to the bridge, the inn, and houses in the centre; and three people lost their lives in the parish. Below the village the river runs through grass fields until the high ground closes in, South Down on the east, Heale Down on the west. Steep woods then accompany road and river as far as Hunters Inn where the Heddon passes under a bridge, which carries the narrow road over the moorland to Combe Martin. Nearby is the junction with a tributary that starts far back in the area of Kentisbury Down and known (if it has a name at all) as **Trentishoe Water**. The two streams unite for the last mile towards the sea, first through high woodland and then out into the open under sheer slopes with patches of scree, before the outlet on the beach. Although there is no sign of a proper harbour other than a deserted lime kiln – evidence of ketches landing coal and limestone at high tide – Heddon's Mouth is rooted in the folk history of smuggling on Exmoor coast.

South-flowing – described from east to west

The **Exe**, from which the Moor takes its name, is the longest of all the Exmoor rivers, rising at Exe Head, a bleak spot 1,450 feet up at the eastern end of The Chains. Gathering strength as it goes from the saturated stretches of peat and rush, it runs south-east below Warren Farm, drawing in moorland waters from the direction of Elsworthy and Wellshead Allotment to the north, before turning down to Exford. It then circles round the Iron Age fort of Road Castle and threads along a narrow valley, flanked by steep bracken-covered slopes till it receives the **Larcombe Brook** at the bridge a mile or so before Winsford. This village boasts half-a-dozen

15 The East Lyn near Rockford

16 The valley of the Exe at Hele Bridge

17   Origins at Pinkery Pond

The River Barle

18   Above Wheal Eliza

19   *The Barle at Dulverton*

20   The Danesbrook near Slade Bridge – a rabbit's eye view

21   Nutscale Reservoir

bridges, but the **Winn Brook** – a small tributary that rises by Comers Gate and comes in from the west – is crossed by a splash or ford, hence the place name. At Coppleham Cross the Exe is joined by its main tributary, the river **Quarme**, a sizeable stream whose source is at Hoar Moor, east of Exford Common. Travelling east the Quarme pulls in several streamlets from Codsend Moors until it strikes Luckwell Bridge, where it passes under the B.3224 road between Exford and Wheddon Cross. Soon afterwards it takes a turn to the south, and accompanies the A.396, running due south in a wooded sheltered valley down to its junction with the Exe.

From here on the Exe becomes a broad river, some 30 feet wide, running in meadows alongside or within sight of the main road. After Bridgetown with its charming cricket ground, where the ball from a not-so-big hit has to be netted from the water, the southward run is flanked by steep hills on either side, clothed with dark conifers and older oaks. Road and river wind past single houses and small settlements, a deserted quarry and, at Barlynch, the relics of the ancient priory dissolved in 1538. The Exe then runs under Hele Bridge – which carries the side road to Dulverton – and, at Weir on the Pixton estate, opposite Pixy Copse, it is joined by the **Haddeo** river, already described. At this point the Exe runs out of the National Park, shortly before its link with the **Barle** above Blackpool, famous for its salmon, and subsequent entry into Devon and Exebridge.

The infant **Barle** flows through a tunnel out of Pinkery Pond, the seven-acre stretch of water dug out of The Chains peat at the behest of John Knight about 150 years ago: all for a purpose no one has been able to ascertain, although theories about it are numerous and recurring. It has been emptied twice in the past in the search for suicides, when the fish left stranded were gobbled up by herons. The Barle is joined by a side stream below Pinkery Farm, flows under the B.3358, Simonsbath-Challacombe road, at Goat Hill, continues south-east via Cornham Ford, close to a 19th century mine adit now sealed, and pulls in feeders such as **Bale Water** that rises south of Exe Head, and another one that runs down Limecombe before reaching Simonsbath in the very heart of the National Park. The next stretch is lonely, beautiful and full of history: the old shaft at Wheal Eliza, another mining venture and the scene of a child murder; and Cow Castle, an Iron Age fort, 200 feet high beside its smaller Calf, separated from Picked Stones plantation by **White Water** coming down from Cloven Rocks to the north. Further on, at Sherdon Hutch, the main stream is joined by **Sherdon Water** that rises up near Kinsford Gate and where the upper reaches bear the title of **Kinsford Water**. Then comes the medieval Landacre Bridge, with five pointed arches, repaired from time to time but never widened – sandwiched between Bradymoor on the left bank and the north-facing slopes of Withypool Common on the right, topped by Brightworthy Barrows at 1,400 feet. Down below, in a meadow opposite the bridge, the Free Suitors and others used to assemble for one of the two annual courts of the old Royal Forest of Exmoor. The place is busy with tourists in the summer. However, peace is re-gained on the way down to Withypool, graced by another handsome bridge built only about a century ago in place of an earlier bridge which had long disappeared and a packhorse crossing further upstream. Just below the village, the Barle is joined by **Pennycombe Water**, rising near Honeymead, running down a steep valley, past Chibbet (with its splash) and Halsgrove, picking up a feeder from Blackland, and ending its course at Garliscombe Mill, last at work in 1920-1. From there on it is delightful walking alongside the river in the deep wooded valley that winds down to Tarr Steps, honeypot-in-chief, but always impressive for its immense stone slabs, anchored on piers set in the river bed. Its age, prehistoric or medieval, is a matter of debate but, despite occasional damage by flood (always repaired), it looks good for another thousand years.

Shortly before the Steps, **West Water** flows down from Worth Hill to the north-west, while **Little River** runs in from Spire Cross up on Winsford Hill. Thick oak woods clothe the river banks for most of the rest of the way down to Dulverton. At a spot between the prehistoric castles of Brewers and Mounsey, thicketed and hard to find, is the junction with **Danesbrook**. This is an important river in its own right, a continuation of **Litton Water** with sources on Twitchen Ridge and Halscombe Allotment in the area above Upper Willingford Bridge. Lower down it is swelled by a stream from Molland Common, before joining the Barle as noted. Marsh Bridge, almost an outlier of Dulverton a mile further on, is a cast iron structure, and stands beside a miniature bridge spanning a brook. From here the Barle sweeps on to Dulverton, swings away from a weir and leat that once powered four mills in the town, and passes down the west boundary under the venerable five-arched bridge crossed by the road from Brushford. Beyond the Carnarvon Arms Hotel, it flows a short distance south-east to join the Exe above Blackpool.

At the south-western end of Exmoor, two rivers – the **Bray** and the **Mole** – rise a short distance inside the boundary of the National Park; but for most of their southward course flow beyond it until they join forces, first with each other, and then with the river Taw at King's Nympton, the latter flowing north-westward into the estuary at Barnstaple.

The **Bray** rises in a cleeve close to the Long Stone at the western extremity of The Chains, a lonely peaty place redolent of the prehistoric past. Gathering runnels from the area of Radworthy, it enters the northern tip of **Challacombe** reservoir built in 1936 to supply Ilfracombe. Lying at about 1,000 feet, 400 yards long and covering four acres, its capacity is limited, and the fishing is in private hands. Below the reservoir, the Bray flows through Challacombe village, close to the Black Venus Inn, and down to the bridge at Rooksfoot, where it is joined by a tributary from the slopes of Shoulsbury Castle, a prehistoric site where – in 1986 – the Meteorological Office proposed to erect an unsightly radar dome, happily rejected. Further on, at the edge of the Park boundary, the river runs past a deserted mill below the outlier of Barton Town and the parish church, perched 900 feet up and a mile from the centre of the village. The Bray then continues its course south, outside the Park, first to Brayford and then to Newtown Bridge below the village of Charles, where it receives a stream that rises in a complex of sources from the area of Bray Common and Whitefield Down.

The **Mole** rises just west of Sandyway Cross, travels along the edge of Long Wood, pulling in several streams from Span Head and the general area of Fyldon Common, before reaching Heasley Mill, the centre of vigorous mining activities in the last century. There are many reminders – spoil heaps, the ruins of a wheel house and, if you know where to look, the deepest shaft on Exmoor. Before mining, Heasley Mill boasted a woollen mill and a tannery; but all this has long given way to what is now a calm little backwater. Here the Mole passes under the stone bridge, runs along the Park boundary, and then turns down to the Moltons where it is soon joined by the river **Yeo**, rising in the Ansteys.

I wrote at the beginning of this chapter that the Exmoor rivers resembled veins in a human hand. What else distinguishes them? First, their purity, for their waters are rarely polluted by run-off of farm slurry or nitrates. They abound with game fish, provide habitats for wildlife in great abundance, and in many places are a joy for walkers. They can of course be wayward, subject to sudden spates and floods almost overnight that, in extreme instances as in August 1952, can cause great damage and even loss of life; but that is inherent in the character of wild Exmoor.

CHAPTER SEVEN

Commons and Ponies

COMMONS

I explained in Chapter 1 how the Commons Preservation Society, founded in 1865, led the fight to save the commons round London from exploitation by developers, and then entered the fray to protect rural commons and open spaces. The Society came too late to save some thirty commons on Exmoor, lost between 1841 and 1872; nonetheless it was thanks to unyielding and Herculean efforts that a residue of common land was rescued at all, and that access to *urban* commons was conceded under the Law of Property Act 1925. Strangely, the parallel right has never, with certain exceptions, been granted in respect of *rural* commons, though *de facto* access usually exists – certainly on Exmoor.

The next important move had to wait thirty years when, in 1955, a Royal Commission was appointed 'to recommend what changes, if any, are desirable in the law relating to common land'. The report, issued in 1958, revealed that commons and manorial wastes (equivalent areas but without rights of common) in England and Wales had shrunk to 1.5 million acres. The Commission made three recommendations: that all common land should be identified and registered; that it should be open to the public as of right; and that it should be properly managed.

Action on the first recommendation began with the passage of the Commons Registration Act 1965, whereby all relevant information as to the location and extent of the commons, ownership and rights was to be recorded and kept on file by borough and county councils – all this to be done within three years, with a further two years for objections. The time-scale was not long enough. Some areas failed to be registered, others were wrongly registered: so that far too much time had to be spent on preliminaries before the Commons Commissioners were able to consider the applications of substance. This, together with various omissions and obscurities in the Act, led to unnecessary losses of common land throughout the country.

All common land is owned by someone – individuals or corporate bodies – but it carries certain rights which, apart from the owner's interests, can be exercised by others. These rights include pasturage (grazing), pannage (pig foraging), estovers (wood), turbary (turf), piscary (fish), and soil (sand, gravel etc). On Exmoor all but one of these rights are virtually extinct. Grazing however survives and is much in use. Moreover since 11,800 acres/4,777 ha. of common land lie within the boundaries of the National Park, they are of vital importance, both to the farmers who hold grazing rights, and to the public who enjoy them for walking, riding, studying Nature, or simply looking at the view. The main areas (with acreage/hectarage) are:

Somerset: Alcombe Hill (188.2/76.2); Doverhay Down (54.5/22.1); Dunkery Hill-Cutcombe (791.7/291.4); Dunkery Erish (11.8/4.8); Dunkery Hill-Wootton Courtenay (75.5/30.6); Winsford Hill, Draydon Knap (1,337.7/541.6); Withypool (1,891.5/765.8)

Devon: Brendon (2,138.2/865.7); Cheriton Ridge, Malmsmead Hill (1,241.6/502.7); Furzehill (102.5/41.5); Heale Moor (15.3/6.2); Holdstone Down (486.8/197.1); Ilkerton Ridge (725.6/293.8): North Cleave (40.5/16.4); Trentishoe Down, East Cleave (587.3/237.8): Valley of Rocks (96.8/39.2); Venford (42.2/17.1): West Anstey (733/296.8).

Exmoor came through the registration stage remarkably well. Common land was lost only in a handful of cases: for instance at Ashway Side and Varle Hill, east of Tarr Steps, where the common was de-registered due to 'unity of seizin', which means that the ownership of the land and the holding of the common rights were vested in the same person; also at Bye Common, north-west of Winsford, where the owner split possession with the only commoner, and de-registered it. The ENPA then purchased 46 acres of the property where, in the early 1980s, it conducted an experiment in the control of bracken over 8 acres of steep land.

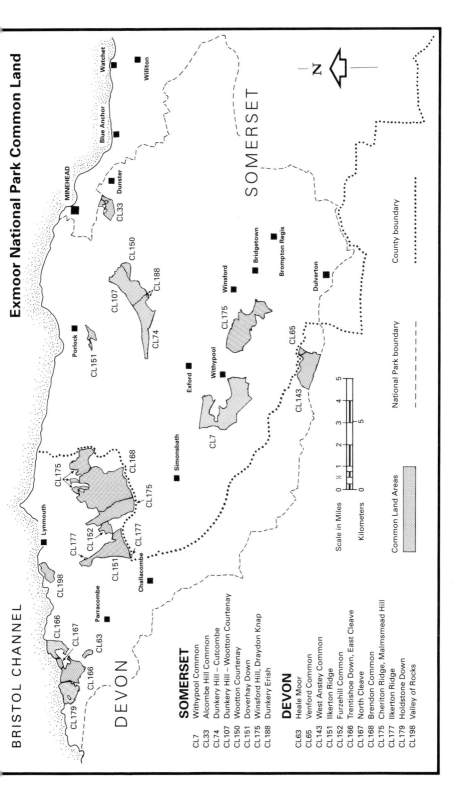

Exmoor National Park Common Land

BRISTOL CHANNEL

DEVON

SOMERSET

SOMERSET

SOMERSET

CL7   Withypool Common
CL33   Alcombe Hill Common
CL74   Dunkery Hill – Cutcombe
CL107 Dunkery Hill – Wootton Courtenay
CL150 Wootton Courtenay
CL151 Doverhay Down
CL175 Winsford Hill, Draydon Knap
CL188 Dunkery Erish

DEVON

CL63   Heale Moor
CL65   Venford Common
CL143 West Anstey Common
CL151 Ilkerton Ridge
CL152 Furzehill Common
CL166 Trentishoe Down, East Cleave
CL167 North Cleave
CL168 Brendon Common
CL175 Cheriton Ridge, Malmsmead Hill
CL177 Ilkerton Ridge
CL179 Holdstone Down
CL198 Valley of Rocks

Scale in Miles

0   ½ 1   2   3   4   5

Kilometers

0   5

Common Land Areas

National Park boundary

County boundary

N

West Anstey Common

The most critical case on Exmoor concerned West Anstey Common which was provisionally registered in August 1967 on the application of West Anstey Parish Meeting. The Common covered 733 acres/296.8 ha. and included – confusingly – five sections (or sub-commons) known as Anstey Rhiney Moor, Guphill Common, Anstey Money Common, Woodland Common, and part of Twitchen Common.

The first objection was entered in 1981 by Ernest John Nicholls and George Elston Nicholls in respect of the section known as Woodland Common (105 acres) in the south-east corner of the main common. The Nicholls claimed that the land was their private property without common rights. Although there were several claimants of rights, none pressed their claims, and so the Commissioner, L. F. Morris Smith, accepted the Nicholls's objection, which meant that Woodland Common was deleted from the Register in January 1982. Subsequently the Nicholls signed a Management Agreement with the ENPA and fenced the land, which was described as 'mixed heath' consisting of ling, bracken, gorse and rough grasses. The fencing cost £5,540, towards which a 50 per cent grant of £2,777 was received. The Management Agreement attracted an average annual payment by the ENPA in excess of £3,000 over the three years it lasted, 1983-6.

The next move was prompted by the fact that, at the 1981 hearing, the Commissioner had confirmed the registration of the rest of West Anstey Common, to which no objection had been received. On 26 May 1983 Hugh Michael James Harrison, owner of the sections known as Anstey Rhiney Moor and Guphill Common, applied to the High Court for a re-hearing on the grounds that, since an objection to one part of the Common had been sustained, the status of the whole area was put in question, and that the Commissioner had erred in law in failing to enquire into the validity of registration of the rest of the Common. The High Court, however, upheld the Commissioner, and in October 1983 the appeal was dismissed.

Sadly, however, for the pockets of everyone concerned, the matter was not allowed to rest there. In December 1984 Hugh Harrison took the case to the Court of Appeal; and so the whole business had to be re-stated and re-argued in great detail from the beginning. It transpired that several commoners had entered claims for rights over the Harrison section of the Common, and as no objection to these claims had been made within the prescribed period, these rights were duly registered. The Court held nonetheless that the de-registration of Woodland Common was not an isolated event, but had indeed put in question the status of the whole of West Anstey Common, and that the Commissioner should after all have enquired into the validity of the rights over the Harrison section before confirming registration. It was true that Harrison had appealed long out of time, but the Commissioner should have exercised discretion in his favour on this point. This second appeal was consequently allowed, which necessitated a re-hearing before the Commissioner.

The re-hearing was held in 1985 before Commissioner, A.A. Baden Fuller. It took ten days: 25-27 June in Exeter, 8-11 October in Dulverton, and 16-18 October in London. In view of the time spent in court on these and the previous occasions, the hiring of barristers and solicitors, the cost of travel and other items, it is hardly surprising that the total bill for the exercise exceeded £58,000 – all to reach a result that can very briefly be described. The report of the re-hearing, which filled 155 pages of A4 typescript, sets out in elaborate, repetitive and immensely complex detail the intricacies of the lawyers' pleadings, the Commissioner's comments, and the evidence of the numerous witnesses, one of whom (and there were others like him) admitted he had left West Anstey at the age of 12, many years before. As a piece of literature it reads like a chapter from *The Pickwick Papers*, with plenty of unconscious humour on the part of rabbit trappers and others who had worked on the Common, but were far from clear about facts and dates.

The Commissioner made it clear that the Court of Appeal had empowered him to come to a decision about the whole of West Anstey Common, including Woodland Common, even though the latter had been de-registered in 1982. The first question therefore was: Is West Anstey one common or five commons? He had no doubt about the answer – it was one common, 'an ordinary parish common . . . over which there were grazing rights appurtenant to a number of farms adjoining or near to it, all in the parish'. It followed that Woodland Common had to be re-registered and the fencing removed, and this was duly done in 1987.

Was it worth over £58,000 in legal and other costs, not to mention the money spent on subsidised fencing and on the Management Agreement with the ENPA? Those who paid may not have thought so, but the rest of us will be glad that the principle of *one common* was re-established and the objectionable fencing removed. Of interest is the fact that, in order to qualify as an interested party in the argument, the ENPA acquired (from one of the commoners) the right to graze a few ponies. Although doubts were expressed at the time of the legality of this move, counsel was consulted and the doubts set at rest. It is to the credit of the ENPA that it took this initiative, for West Anstey Common lies within the National Park boundary and must therefore be its concern.

The Register today (1990) records West Anstey Common as having six owners and eight commoners, with rights to graze a total of 1,233 sheep, 183 cattle and 36 ponies. If this rule were to be strictly obeyed, the animals would starve and the Common become a desert. The Commissioner at the re-hearing did his best to modify some of the exaggerated claims, but conceded he had no power in practice to regulate stocking, and no doubt the numbers in reality are far lower than those in the Register; but it does point a moral – the need for management.

Management

Although all the common land on Exmoor is covered by the ENPA's Conservation Map (successor to Porchester Maps 1 and 2), and is, therefore, 90 per cent safe from ploughing and other sorts of agricultural disturbance, the state of the sward on many of the commons is bad, in some instances shocking. Gorse and bracken, neither palatable to stock, are spreading fast and displacing the heathers and grasses on which the animals feed. Swaling, i.e. burning off shrubby growth in the spring to allow the young shoots to come through, frequently gets out of hand and wipes out acres at a time. Overstocking does serious damage, especially to the heathers which are the glory of wild Exmoor. Winter feeding with silage or hay carted out to sheep and cattle on a common breaks all the rules of good husbandry. Silage sours the ground, hay seeds will often 'take' and drive out heather, trampling will destroy any good sward in the winter. A deplorable case is that of Winsford Hill which is continuously overstocked and 'poached' all the year round.

It all comes back to management which means, among other things, agreed limitation of the number and types of animals allowed free range over a common; controlled swaling; and prohibition of grazing during the winter months by all stock – with two exceptions.

One is the Exmoor ponies, which are few in number and an endangered species, that depend on rough grazing all the year round without carted food to ensure hardiness – see later in this chapter. The other, of course, is the wild red deer, which roam where they will, feed off farmers' roots when really hungry, and for whom common land is part of their habitat. At present there are two Commoners' Associations on Exmoor – one for Withypool, the other for Brendon Common – but, as yet, neither is effective in terms of management; nor can they cope with public access where and when it becomes a problem – for instance at Landacre on public holidays and summer weekends; but none of these things are, any longer, matters of purely local concern.

In 1983 the Countryside Commission set up the Common Land Forum, a body representative of all the main interests – farming, landowning, conservation, recreation, and local government – whose object was to clarify problems left by registration, and to draft plans for new legislation designed to implement the two recommendations of the Royal Commission in 1958, but not yet proceeded with: namely management and public access. After $2\frac{1}{2}$ years of tough negotiation a consensus was reached, and the Forum published its report, *Management Schemes for Commons*. This was a remarkable achievement in the light of legal complexities and of all the competing claims and interests in an overcrowded countryside. The Government promised repeatedly to introduce legislation based on the Forum's findings, but failed in fact to find time for a Bill. Moreover at a relatively late stage in the proceedings, objections were raised by owners of grouse moors, who formed themselves into the Moorland Association with about 150 members, involving some 650,000 acres, about half being common land.

Grouse – even more than pheasant and partridge shooting – is big game in terms of money; it attracts wealthy sportsmen from overseas, and earns an estate an important slice of income, all in a short season between 12 August and 7 December. Sir Anthony Milbank, Chairman of the Moorland Association, was reported in *The Independent* as saying: 'There's nothing in the shooting world that is more exciting than shooting at fast-moving grouse in large packs. Later in the season when the birds become wilder and they are driven on the wind there is no more challenging quarry'. In a normal season he reckoned on a bag of 2,000 birds from his 4,000 acres in North Yorkshire.

On 7 July 1990, just before the end of the Parliamentary session, David Trippier, Minister of State for the Environment, made it plain in a written statement, that there would be no legislation before the next general election, and that in any event the idea of *de jure* access (i.e. as of right) would be rejected. Instead he proposed local negotiations between the interested parties and if those failed, then the Secretary of State for the Environment would have the final say. He added – without actually referring to grouse – that arrangements for access would have to take account of cases where common land was important for conservation and other uses. He was referring to disturbance by the public of other ground-nesting birds (e.g. curlews), and indeed of all species of fauna and flora that depend on commons for their habitat – a fair point.

Neither side in the controversy was satisfied with this statement. Kate Ashbrook, Secretary of the Open Spaces Society, said: 'We are not trying to stop people shooting grouse. We object to them being so greedy that they want to restrict access to their commons throughout the year'. Sir Anthony Milbank was no less pessimistic: 'I can see more years stretching ahead of unnecessary warring between the parties'.

Is there a case for an Exmoor Commons Act on the lines of the Dartmoor Commons Act 1985, which might sidestep the need for national legislation but exert the same force solely for Exmoor? Ian Mercer, then Dartmoor National Park Officer, told me that there has been a Dartmoor Commoners' Association – a federation of local associations – since 1954. 'It had been formed to give evidence to the Royal Commission, and it was that body which set off the whole process of obtaining the Dartmoor Commons Act'. Owing to the scattered nature of commons on Exmoor, and the inadequacy of the two Associations that do exist, the prospect – in my opinion – of an Act for Exmoor is not good. Effective management associations, consisting of owners, commoners, representatives of local government and of conservation interests, would be needed for each block (or associated blocks) of common land: and which would have the will and the power to agree stocking levels (and enforce them), control swaling, and fulfil other duties consistent with livestock husbandry and conservation. Such an Act – difficult to draft and administer – would be better than nothing. Far the best solution, however, is national legislation as originally promised for the implementation of the Common Land Forum proposals. Management by voluntary means, i.e. without the force of law, is unlikely to be effective.

THE EXMOOR PONY – an endangered species?

The connection between Exmoor commons and Exmoor ponies is vital. Running free and grazing common land in the hills are essential elements for the hardiness and other characteristics of the breed.

The pure-bred Exmoor pony is of ancient lineage. Some say it is the only true survivor of Britain's original 'wild horse', and that 'today's Exmoor ponies are the only remaining breed to show the jaw development found in fossilized bones dating back six hundred thousand years to the tundra-like conditions of the Ice Age'. This is hard to prove, though it is certainly a matter of serious research: as is the fact that, when our island was still joined to the Continent, there was more than one variety of wild horse at large in Europe, and that groups of such horses may have roamed over Britain until the sea broke down the land bridges and created the English Channel, thus preventing further free passage from the south.

At first, no doubt, ponies and horses were hunted for meat as were other wild animals; but gradually, as the practicable possibilities emerged, man found they could be domesticated for riding and driving, for hauling carts, sledges and ploughs. This must have been happening at latest by the Bronze Age, c.1500 BC or earlier, an epoch to which the Exmoor-type pony can safely trace its origins. A thousand years later, when the Iron Age was replacing the Bronze, the climate in Britain and northern Europe began to deteriorate, becoming wetter and colder – a change that converted the vegetation of the hills from palatable pasture to rough sward and bog grasses, heather, gorse, bracken, and bilberry; and it was then that the Exmoors, already useful servants to man, demonstrated their unique ability to stand up to unfavourable conditions, living out winter and summer on the high moorland and sustaining themselves on the wild herbage without additional feeding or artificial shelter. They have done so ever since.

Their remarkable stamina derives principally from certain physical attributes. For example, the winter coat consists of two layers – an inner one composed of fine hairs which retain body warmth, and an outer one of coarser texture that is weatherproof. Neither rain nor snow can penetrate, but are shed both by the coat and by the vigorous action of tail, mane, forelock, and beard. Colour is characteristic too. Originally it served to conceal the pony in its moorland habitat against predators; since then it has provided those distinctive features that mark the Exmoor among other pony breeds – the brown colouration of the coat and long thick tail, mealy muzzle, and ring round the eye, known as the 'toad' eye. As to size, the Exmoor ranges from c.46-50 inches ($11\frac{1}{2}$-12/hands) in height; it is stocky and strong, having a deep chest and large girth, indicative of a capacious digestive system capable of absorbing rough fibrous food to which it has to resort in winter. Teeth of course play a vital part, and are so shaped that the pony can bite cleanly without tearing or damaging the plant, and can chew and swallow the toughest herbage until well into its old age.

Whether the Celtic tribes that fought the Roman invaders before and after the beginning of the Christian era used Exmoors for battle is not known for certain; but it is an attractive theory, for their build and vigour would have served them in good stead as chariot horses, though they were probably too small and light for cavalry charges. Fighting is unlikely however to have been their principal purpose. Most Exmoors would have ranged over their native territory, isolated from the main tribal movements of the Dark Ages, and in a much larger area of North Devon and West Somerset than when it was formally delineated as a Royal Forest or hunting ground at the Norman Conquest. From then on the Exmoor region became a kind of reserve, a treeless waste, populated by the wild red deer and predators, such as wolves; but also by flocks of sheep, and herds of Exmoor mares and foals guarded by their stallions, the property of settlers who mustered and marked them at intervals throughout the year.

We know from the Domesday Survey of 1085 that ponies – or 'widge beasts' as they were called – figured in the records of the manors; and that later, whenever the Forest was perambulated or inspected, those privileged householders – the Free Suitors of Hawkridge and Withypool and the Suitors at Large – conducted regular drifts or round-ups of stock, including ponies, in return for their grazing and other rights within the Forest. Moreover, once the boundaries had been stabilised (enclosing an area of c.20,000 acres based on Simonsbath), and the administration assigned by lease to a Warden in the early 16th century, then virtually no change of significance occurred for the following 300 years. Thus the Exmoors continued to breed and survive, without interference, in hardy isolation, many of them belonging to the Warden of the day: which, in the late 18th and early 19th centuries, meant the Acland family.

However, not even Exmoor could escape the impact of world events. As stated earlier, a plan to grow timber for naval ship-building led to the enclosure of the Forest by Act of Parliament in 1815, and its subsequent division into allotments – 10,000 + acres going to the Crown, 3,000 acres to Sir Thomas Acland, the last Warden, and the remainder in smaller lots to the other owners and rights-holders. Then the timber plan was abandoned, and almost the entire Forest sold to John Knight from Worcestershire, who set about draining and ploughing the moorland for cultivation. The full story is told elsewhere, but suffice it to say here that, while John Knight and his son, Frederic, invested vast sums of money and huge exertions into converting their Exmoor lands into – ultimately viable farms and shepherdings, they also incurred some outright failures. Iron ore mining was one, cross-breeding the Exmoors was another. In the latter case John Knight imported a Dongola Barb stallion to mate with the mares and produce a 'refined pony' of the Exmoor type. He had some success in that the geldings and some of the fillies sold well; but he entirely failed to breed an animal capable of out-wintering on the moorland which, presumably, had been a prime object of the exercise, and it was not continued.

Fortunately Sir Thomas Acland had decided, when the Forest was enclosed, to drive a selection of the best stock down to Winsford Hill, and so founded the renowned Anchor Herd of pure-bred Exmoors, still the largest herd today. When the Winsford estate was sold in 1926, some of the grazing rights were retained so that the Anchor ponies – based on Old Ashway Farm – continued to run on the Hill. The situation was not altered when the late Sir Richard Acland handed over the Exmoor estate to the National Trust at the end of the Second World War; nor, soon afterwards, when the Anchor Herd passed to Frank Green of Dulverton, and subsequently to the present owner, Mrs Ronnie Wallace, of Ashwick Farm.

The Aclands not only saved the Exmoor Pony as described, but kept the earliest Stud Book, a document of unique value which sadly has not survived. They were not, however, the only breeders of note. A number of ponies were bought in by local farmers, among them the Miltons of Withypool. Writing in the *Exmoor Review 1968*, Fred Milton of Weatherslade Farm described how his great-great-grandfather, Nicholas, became tenant of Landacre in 1807 and kept a number of Exmoors on Withypool Common. 'His sons also learned to look after them especially young Nicholas II, who spent much of his time riding his pony, shepherding and looking after the stock of ponies'. Though illiterate, Nicholas was hard-working and shrewd, 'and the rigid way in which he checked up on his neighbours' animals on the Common certainly didn't win him any popularity'. Fred's father, Charles John, took a keen interest in Exmoor ponies, 'and in 1890 played the responsible part of collecting, marking and selling for his father, uncles and brothers. During the 1880s the sales for Exmoors were good, but early in the 1890s the prices at Bampton dropped considerably, although those at Bridgwater kept up'. Attempts to rail the ponies from Dulverton to Bridgwater proved too expensive, while driving them there – a two-day journey with an overnight stop at Crowcombe – tired and lamed them. However, Bampton Fair, held on the last Thursday in October, came increasingly to the notice of dealers from the north, and so prices improved in the early 1900s and stayed steady, at least until the depression of the 1930s. Fred himself learned to ride at an early age and rode regularly to school. During the summer, after school hours, he used to ride to the Common shepherding and taking with him the collie sheepdog. As his father also bought grass keep up to ten miles away, Fred spent eight hours in the saddle on many occasions; but that was a tribute too to the stamina of his mount, a real tough Exmoor pony, at its best always when ridden for work. The Milton Herd, running on Withypool Common, plays a leading part today.

The Exmoor Pony Society

Before the end of the last century, moves were being made to regulate and promote the interests of the various pony breeds in Britain. The National Pony Society was founded in 1893 and in 1898 the Sir Thomas Acland of the day was appointed 'Convenor of Representatives' of the Exmoor breed. A year later, 'the Exmoor Division of the National Pony Society consisting of five members was founded, and began registrations in its own section of the Stud Book with five stallions and 25 mares. In 1921 Earl Fortescue, whose family had purchased the reversion of the Knights' Simonsbath estate in 1879, became the first President of an independent Exmoor Pony Society, and was joined by Sir Francis Acland as Vice President, R.V. Le Bas of Winsford as the Society's first Secretary, J. Follett Pugsley of Tiverton, Captain R. Hern of Porlock, and Col. V.C.A. Munckton of Hatch Beauchamp, who administered the

Society's affairs for twenty years after the Second World War. He was duly succeeded by Jeanne Head of Rodhuish, then Ken Walker, and he – in turn – by David Mansell of Dulverton, the present Secretary, who works with a General Purposes Committee, meeting regularly at Exford.'

Thanks to Col. Munckton, the Society first published its separate Stud Book in 1963, with a record of 715 pure-bred animals registered since 1921. A sequence of events marks the breeder's year – a stallion parade in May; followed by some two dozen agricultural or horse shows during the summer open to Exmoors, either in classes reserved for the breed or in mixed classes of Mountain and Moorland ponies; most important, obviously, is the Society's own show held at Exford in the second week of August in conjunction with the Devon and Somerset Staghounds. Finally, comes the autumn gathering of all the stock that has been running out on the moor, for inspection for registration – the vital requisite for maintaining the purity of the breed. The pure-bred suckers, as the foals are called, are individually examined and 'if accepted as good specimens, they are given an individual number and then branded with that number on the near flank, together with the Society's star and their herd number on the near shoulder. That is how you can be sure that the pony shown to you is a true Exmoor'.

All sales of pure-breds are now conducted privately or through the Society, the traditional market for Exmoors at Bampton Fair in October having now come to an end; but un-registered or cross-bred stock can be bought at horse sales. However, the admirable activities of the Society do not hide the fact that, despite undoubted interest in the breed both on Exmoor and in other parts of the country and abroad, the number of moorland herds is low. At present (1990) there are very few stallion bloodlines, and only five herds kept by individual breeders on Exmoor commons, plus two founded by the Exmoor National Park Authority – one running on Haddon Hill, the other on Larkbarrow. One other moorland herd is kept in comparable conditions on the fells in Cumbria. While most Exmoors are bred for riding, there is a certain resistance to their use as children's ponies because, it is said, they are too strong and stubborn for the purpose. This is hotly denied by David Mansell and others, who insist that the Exmoor makes 'a smashing family pony; they're so tough they can be ridden by adults as well as older children'. Moreover, riding is not the only use. Increasing attention is being paid to driving as demonstrated by – among others – Peter

Dean in Cumbria and Melanie Wright at South Molton: which, after all, is no more than revival, since – not so long ago – Exmoors were used on farms for every purpose, in traps and putt carts, as well as for shepherding and hacking. Nonetheless one trembles to think what might happen if a virus attacked the breed, when it is estimated that there are only about 500 pure-bred Exmoors of all ages in existence, of whom less than half range the moorland.

The relationship between moorland stock and those kept in domesticated conditions is fundamental to the survival of the breed, and has been clearly explained by Dr Sue Baker:

> Those ponies that range over the commons of Exmoor or the fells of Cumbria are the reservoir of the genetic heritage from the once totally wild ponies. The wild-type for all those features adapted to the natural environment is conserved by the ponies which remain subject to the law of natural selection. The features we know so well of colouring, coat structure, and conformation, plus the hidden adaptations, such as the digestive capabilities, are what make the Exmoor so special. Every member of the Society therefore shares a commitment to conserving this remarkable animal, to shielding the ponies from unnatural change.
>
> Of equal importance are those members who own ponies under domesticated conditions. In modern life, if an object or an animal serves no purpose, then its very existence is threatened. If the Exmoor enthusiasts did not want to own, show, ride or drive Exmoors, there would be no demand for foals at all other than for meat. This would inevitably reduce the number of breeding herds living free to below a critical level and, no doubt, to their ultimate demise. The existence of the moorland herds is precarious enough, even with all the support of the members around the country. The domestic owners do indeed have a vital part to play. It is not just a case of economics or market demand, but the total commitment of our riders, drivers and show supporters that reaffirms the importance of maintaining the free-living herds. Survival is founded on interdependence.[1]

What of the future? In a paper entitled *Planning for 1992, The Way Forward*, the Society makes a number of important proposals in view of the control over horse and pony breeding to be exercised by the European Economic Community (EEC). One concerns the identification of Exmoors, only effective through hot-branding, and the use of specific brand-marks to conform to the details of

1. *Exmoor Review*, 1990.

registration in the Stud Book. Another envisages the substitution of a passport for the present certificate of registration, which should contain a wider range of information about physical features, pedigree, and ownership; and that one set of criteria as to identification should apply in all countries, operated through a single breed Society and single Stud Book, mandatory throughout the EEC. To this end, financial support at a very modest level is requested either from the EEC direct or from the British authorities.

It is certainly encouraging that the Exmoor Pony is looking ahead in this practical way for, without common sense allied to a visionary understanding of the role of the Pony, the species would indeed be endangered.

CHAPTER EIGHT

Field Sports

Hunting, Shooting, Freshwater Fishing

In a region such as Exmoor, which has substantial stretches of moorland, high pastures, and woodland, ribbed with hills and serrated with rivers and combes – in short a relatively remote region, rich in wildlife, with a long history of man in contact with Nature – it is inevitable that field sports should be sewn into the fabric of the entire scene. The fact, too, that Exmoor is a National Park, administered under special safeguards in one corner of our industrialised suburbanised island, has meant that the three principal sports described in this chapter – hunting, shooting, and fishing – have to be strictly organised in order to survive. Furthermore, all three are under hostile or disruptive pressure from two mutually exclusive categories of opponent: those who oppose them on moral grounds; and those who want to participate in larger numbers than the sports can manage or the territory support. In what follows, I write not as a participant or opponent, but as an observer without commitment.

HUNTING

It should not be forgotten that, only fifty years ago, the horse was the main motive power in farming and was used for many other purposes as well. This fact is reflected today, for instance, in the survival – precarious though it may be – of the Exmoor Pony; likewise of other equine breeds that once pulled the plough or carried the farmer to market. In sport, above all, the horse has never lost its popularity. It is the means *par excellence* whereby numerous people of all ages enjoy the open air and the countryside at first hand; and that is evident from the number and variety of events that would not take place without it.

In this connection the role of the horse in hunting has, since earliest recorded history, held prime place, and it still does. The local Exmoor newspaper, *The West Somerset Free Press*, publishes every week through the season reports of hunts and hunting appointments on Exmoor, relating to the Devon and Somerset Staghounds, five packs of foxhounds, and one of beagles. In 1990 these included the Exmoor Foxhounds, founded in 1869 by Nicholas Snow of Oare, now kennelled at Simonsbath, whose territory takes in the Royal Forest, and an area between the Bratton Fleming – Blackmore Gate road in the west and Wheddon Cross in the east; Dulverton East Foxhounds, with kennels at East Anstey, which broadly cover the south-east corner of the National Park, i.e. from the Bampton – South Molton road up to a line drawn between Winsford and Upton; Dulverton West Foxhounds, with kennels at Stoke Rivers, which hunt the country south and west of the line, Hawkridge to Ilfracombe; West Somerset Foxhounds, with kennels at Carhampton, which hunt along the coast east of Minehead and take in most of the Brendon Hills; Minehead Harriers (foxhounds nonetheless), kennelled at Wootton Courtenay, which cover a relatively small area bounded by Dunster, Porlock, and Wheddon Cross; finally, Crowcombe Beagles, with kennels at Oake, near Milverton, which patrol the Brendons and the Quantocks. All these packs – like the Staghounds – are self-supporting and owe their continued existence to the enthusiasm of their supporters, and upon income from subscriptions, 'caps' at meets, point-to-point races (entry fees for qualified horses, sponsorship, car park and other charges), dances, whist drives, and so on, throughout the year. Without voluntary activities of these kinds, the packs would disappear, but that they do survive is practical evidence of their popularity.

However, the chase of the fox and the hare is obviously not confined to, nor specially characteristic of, Exmoor where most people – when they refer to hunting and for whatever reason – think first of the Devon and Somerset Staghounds. Their history and that of their predecessors stretches far back into the past, and is bound up with the evolution of the Royal Forest from the Norman Conquest onwards, when hunting the deer was a prerogative of the king and jealously guarded. For our purposes however we need look back no further in time than the 18th century: since when there has been a plentiful stock of sporting and family histories, volumes of reminiscences and the like, from which it is possible to draw a connected account.

The Historical Background

We know that, in 1740, Edward Dyke of Pixton (near Dulverton) was described as Forester of Exmoor and Master of the North Devon Staghounds. Six years later he died and was succeeded as Master by Sir Thomas Dyke Acland, 7th Baronet, who bought the lease of the Royal Forest in 1767 from the third Earl of Orford, thereby becoming 'the first Warden to keep a pack of staghounds since Sir Hugh Pollard III' in the early 17th century. Sir Thomas's wife was Elizabeth, niece and heiress of Edward Dyke, and he added her name to his own. Known as 'His Honour', Thomas also inherited, through his wife, both Pixton and Holnicote; and so, as a full-blooded sporting squire, he spent every winter and spring hunting over some fifty square miles of Exmoor, maintaining kennels at Holnicote, Jury and Highercombe (the last two near Dulverton). He also entertained with 'princely splendour' all and sundry, keeping enormous stocks of linen and plate at both Holnicote and Pixton.

In 1775 he passed the Mastership of the Staghounds to Major (later Colonel) Bassett of Watermouth, who remained MSH intermittently until his death in 1802. Meanwhile Sir Thomas 'His Honour' had himself died in 1785 and, due to the early deaths of his eldest son and his grandson, the baronetcy passed to his second son, another Thomas, who was as devoted to hunting and hospitality as his father, though less adept at controlling expenditure. However, with his death in 1794, the Acland ownership of Pixton came to an end, although the family did not lose the Wardenship of the Royal Forest until the latter was 'disafforested' by Act of Parliament in 1815.

As regards the nature of hunting in those days, the most notable source of information is the diary kept by the Rev. John Boyse, incumbent of Hawkridge-cum-Withypool, one of the most devoted staghunters of the period – or any period – so much so that one wonders how he fitted in his not very arduous pastoral duties.

According to tradition the parson would start the day's hunt clad in sober black; but when the hounds were laid on, he exchanged his black coat for a white flannel jacket – until the end of the day when he changed back again to black in order to avoid giving offence to certain parishioners. Boyse's diary ran from 1776 to 1816, and although the entries were brief and telegraphic (a blessing, as lengthy descriptions of 'runs' are inclined to pall), it contained some memorable passages:

> *1789, October 18th.* Drew the Shillets. The hounds killed several sheep. Sir Thomas ordered the huntsman to hang himself and the whole pack.

> *1802, October 21st.* Found a stag in Longwood. Ran him to Hawkridge Ridge. Down to Dulverton Town. Came to water at Hele Bridge . . . A most excellent chase as ever was rode.

He then added, by way of an aside:

> On this day the ever memorable and glorious battle was fought off Trafalgar in which the great Lord Nelson fell.

After Colonel Bassett's death, the pack passed through various hands until Early Fortescue came to the rescue, 1812-1818, at Castle Hill, Filleigh, where he entertained royally and paid all the expenses of the Hunt out of his own pocket: that is until the costs of a general election 'made further tenure of the mastership impossible'; in other words, when too much money had to be sunk in bribes.

After this, the hounds were kept going as a subscription pack, which meant that a few landowners contributed a handsome fifty guineas each, though not all promises were honoured and the deficit had to be met by some other means, for there was then no regular system of annual subscription or capping at meets. Moreover deer poaching was rife, and even encouraged by a number of farmers who, as noted by Boyse, were infuriated by the damage done to crops, fences and sheep by the deer, hounds and riders. Strangely enough the deer population was not thought to be large, around only 200 in the year 1820, although within which boundaries was not stated. That may have accounted for the difficulty in finding deer, and that a day's hunting was often unusually long and strenuous. One Master warned against running a young stag as it 'kills hounds and horses, without killing the deer you pursue'.

In the early 1820s support for hunting deteriorated to such an extent that, in 1825, the hounds had to be sold off to a 'German baron', and for the next two years no hunting took place on Exmoor at all. That it somehow survived over the next thirty years was due principally to the efforts of Dr Charles Palk Collyns, surgeon apothecary of Dulverton, ably assisted until 1833 by Sir Arthur Chichester of Youlston, near Barnstaple. Collyns was the author of the classic, *Notes on the Chase of the Wild Red Deer in the Counties of Devon and Somerset*, published by Longman Green in 1862. He bewailed contemporary trends:

> Time was when the deer roamed wild over the whole of the north, and great part of the south of Devon, and over a large part of the west of Somerset, but they have been driven by high farming and denser population from their ancient fastnesses, and have now taken their stand within a narrowed circle, and are to be found chiefly on Exmoor, and the wild and wooded regions about and around that once trackless waste. Even there the ploughshare creaks and mattock rings; new fences daily encroach upon the space still left to the monarch of the forest; and perhaps the present generation may witness the death of the last of the wild red deer in Devon and Somerset.

And that was written well over a century ago!

Collyns's career was, in its way, a social commentary of the times. As mentioned, he was a leading G.P. and citizen of Dulverton. Bleeding, cupping, and purging were still customary treatments for most ailments and, in support of his prowess as a doctor, Collyns was said to display a basin of blood outside his surgery in High Street every Sunday morning. He rode everywhere – to his patients out on the moor however distant – and combined medical practice with hunting and immense exertions towards keeping the staghounds in being. Recollecting that no deer had been hunted since 1833, he wrote:

> It was at this time – in the year 1837, when the prospect seemed blank and dreary – that I made an effort to revive the sport; and I claim for myself the credit for having, by untiring labour and persevering industry, succeeded in creating a stimulus to which the existence of a pack of staghounds at the present moment is, I humbly venture to say, mainly due.

Collyns collected subscriptions as best he could and acted as treasurer. He also succeeded in assembling a pack, thenceforward known as the 'Devon and Somerset Staghounds', which is still the name they bear today. However, troubles were far from over. By 1841 it had become clear that money was still short, and that Collyns was personally owed £531. Fortunately he was bailed out by the Hon. Newton Fellowes (later Lord Portsmouth) who agreed to keep the pack at his own expense at Eggesford, except when they were actually engaged in hunting, so that subscriptions could go towards reducing the debt which, by 1847, had fallen to £75 – a sum incidentally never 'liquidated'. Things continued on a hand-to-mouth basis until 1855, when a fresh saviour appeared in the person of Mordaunt Fenwick (he added Bisset to his surname later), who happened to be renting Pixton from Lord Carnarvon for the sake of the shooting.

Such was local pressure, however, that Fenwick Bisset, though a novice, was persuaded to try his hand as Master for one year: in the event the term was extended to 27 years, 1855-1881, during which time he not only overcame initial discouragements and later crises (the hounds were decimated by rabies in 1878-9), but laid firm foundations for the conduct and continuation of the sport, and personally paid for the building of kennels at Exford in 1875-6, at a cost of £7,000. Bisset was however fortunate in his friends. At the outset he managed to assemble 18 couple of hounds, presented to him by three well-wishers, including Froude Bellew, squire of Anstey, who in 1861 leased him his house, stables and kennels at Rhyll for several years. He was also able to rely on strong supporters in key areas during the first critical decade – Frederic Knight at Simonsbath, Nicholas Snow at Oare, Henry Dene at Barnstaple, Sir Thomas Acland at Holnicote, and several others around Dulverton including Dr Collyns, Lord Carnarvon, Stucley Lucas at Baronsdown, and John Arthur Locke at Northmoor. He was also well served by Jack Babbage, an experienced huntsman, by Arthur Heal as whip, and by Jim Blackmore as harbourer.

Although poaching continued, it was more than offset by a heavy increase in the deer population, with which even the growing popularity of the 'D & S' was barely able to cope. The opening meet at Cloutsham was becoming – in Bisset's own words, 'a rabble and a fair'; while the visit of the Prince of Wales on 22 August 1879, an unique and memorable event, attracted a vast crowd. H.J. Marshall gives a vivid account in his book, *Exmoor, Sporting and Otherwise* (Eyre & Spottiswoode). The meet took place at Hawkcombe Head on a fine morning after a night of rain. The Prince arrived in an open carriage with his host, Mr Luttrell, Prince Louis of Battenberg, Lord Charles Beresford, and Parson Jack

Russell, all mounting their horses at Culbone Stables. Arthur Heal, who had succeeded Jack Babbage as huntsman in 1871, arrived with the pack at 10.30 am, and soon rode off with the harbourer and tufters (three couple of well-tried hounds) to rouse a stag. But the job proved impossible owing to the huge concourse of followers – over a thousand (sic) riding and many more on foot, it was said. So the hunt moved off to Badgworthy Woods where Nicholas Snow had harboured a warrantable stag, and soon the pack was laid on. Then followed a long circular run, past Brendon Two Gates, over Exe Plain, down into Hoaroak Valley, up to Cheriton Ridge, back over Brendon Common, and down to Badgworthy Water where the stag was brought to bay, lassoed by Arthur Heal and given the *coup de grâce* by the Prince himself, who drove Arthur's knife straight into the beast's heart, Scottish fashion.

Arthur, famed for his skill and knowledge of both deer and moor, retired in 1889. Six years earlier he and his bachelor son, Fred, who farmed at North Ley, Exford, had piloted Richard Jefferies, the naturalist writer, over Exmoor and briefed him about the deer and the hunt. Jefferies's book, *Red Deer,* published by Longman in 1884, is a fine example of the author's ability to communicate essential facts in an attractive style about the life cycle and habits of the deer, and the methods and pattern of hunting. In writing about Jefferies and Exmoor in a book of my own, *Exmoor Writers* (Exmoor Press), I was able to include an interesting postscript given me by Fred Clarke of Dene Court, Bishops Lydeard. This concerned his brother, Arthur, the world-famous science fiction author, who had come across a worn copy of *Red Deer* and found it to be sheltering several letters from Jefferies addressed to Fred Heal. Jefferies had presented Fred with a copy of his book and corresponded with him on points of fact about the deer, which underlined the debt he owed to the Heal family for their expert assistance. Jefferies was a liberal dispenser of his own works: so much so that Longman, his publisher, complained once that he had already given away sixteen copies of one title, so why couldn't his friends buy some?

Fresh Blood and More Money

Farming was depressed in the generation before 1914, thanks to Free Trade and the flow of cheap corn, chilled beef and lamb that poured into the country from North and South America and

Australasia, undercutting home produced food. This put a sudden stop to high farming in Britain and, on Exmoor, to wholesale reclamation of moorland on the scale undertaken by John and Frederic Knight at Simonsbath, and on a smaller scale by many others with less resources. At the same time it attracted well-heeled families from the towns to buy country properties, organise house parties, and devote themselves to hunting, shooting and fishing. Such at Dulverton were Sir Frederic Wills, the tobacco magnate, who bought Northmoor; Heber Mardon, the Bristol printer, who built Ashwick, and Frank Green, the Wakefield industrialist, who bought Ashwick in the 1920s, when farming was still depressed and land relatively cheap. The 'new' families soon settled in alongside the long-landed ones and established themselves in the higher echelons of local society. Any losses in farming were borne with equanimity, being far out-weighed by the prestige of landownership and the sporting and social pleasures it afforded them.

Their arrival brought economic benefits too – to tradesmen in the local towns and villages, and to craftsmen of several sorts, farriers, smiths, saddlers and harness makers, wheelwrights, purveyors of guns, cartridges, and fishing tackle, etc. In Dulverton some fifty people were regularly engaged in tailoring and dress-making, depending largely on orders received every year for new outfits for grooms and hunt servants, and sensible clothing for the daughters of the gentry and their maids. After the completion of the railway line between Taunton and Barnstaple in 1873, the influx of seasonal visitors grew apace, most of them coming for sport. This generated plenty of business for the hotels, e.g. the Anchor at Exebridge, the Lion and the Lamb at Dulverton, the Crown and the White Horse at Exford, the Royal Oak at Withypool and Winsford, and the Carnarvon Arms at Brushford, which was built expressly for the purpose in 1873-4.

This injection of wealth, and undoubted prosperity generated by the pursuit of field sports, meant that the finances of the Devon and Somerset Staghounds presented few further difficulties of any substance. Not only had Fenwick Bisset placed the hunt on a firm foundation as described, but instead of having to rely on the affluence of the Master and a handful of friends, money was now forthcoming from numerous supporters who all enjoyed the hunting and were therefore keen for it to continue. For similar reasons, there were fewer problems in finding Masters. In 1881 the Mastership returned to the Fortescue family after some sixty years,

Viscount Ebrington holding the post until 1887. He was succeeded by a series of six Masters up to the outbreak of the First World War. Among them was C.H. Basset of Watermouth 1887-1893, who introduced spring stag hunting, mid-March to end of April; also R.A. Sanders (later Lord Bayford) 1895-1907, who married Lucy Halliday of Glenthorne. In his time the deer increased so greatly that they were doing serious damage over a wide area. It prompted, for example, the Earl of Lovelace at Ashley Combe to erect, at great expense, a high wire fence round all his cultivated land and woods right down to the sea, the first deer fence in the district. Lovelace also planted more than 800 acres of the neighbouring Culbone and Yearnor hills with conifers, which in due course provided the deer with a fine new refuge – never his original intention!

To cope with the deer population during the 1890s, hunting took place on three or four days a week, and kills were estimated at around 100 a year – which produced an outcry against slaughter! By way of relieving pressure on the 'D & S', Sir John Heathcoat-Amory of Knightshayes started the Tiverton Staghounds in 1896, hunting the country south of the Taunton-Barnstaple railway line; while two short-lived packs, based on Barnstaple, were active between 1901 and 1911. By that time the deer were thought to number about 1,500, and the number of kills by all the packs rose to c.250 a year: after which the problem abated. On the other side of the moor, but not until 1920, E. J. Stanley of Quantock Lodge founded the Quantock Staghounds to hunt the deer that had proliferated in that area ever since Fenwick Bisset had introduced the original stock in the 1860s. They too were doing great damage and had to be controlled. The last of the 'D & S' Masters before 1914 was Morland Greig, who was killed at Gallipoli in 1915.

The flavour of this period can, perhaps, best be appreciated by reference to another classic about Exmoor, Fred Goss's *Memories of a Stag Harbourer* (Witherby): an articulate and attractively written life story, which illuminates the harbourer's work with a variety of anecdote and, above all, imparts a clear impression of the sense of affinity with Nature felt by all Fred's friends on and off the hunting field, irrespective of class – though everyone 'knew his station'. Fred was born at Brompton Regis in 1873, was educated at the village school, and then went to live with his grandfather, old Jim Wensley, at Hartford in the Haddeo valley. Jim was a carpenter on the Pixton estate and a true countryman, who taught Fred all he

knew about the locality and the ways of Nature. As a result the
young man made himself indispensable to Andrew Miles, keeper at
Pixton and official harbourer to the 'D & S', eventually succeeding
him in both jobs at the age of 21. Ten years later he was appointed
head keeper at Pixton and moved from his cottage at Frogwell
Lodge to one at Weir. In effect, Fred converted harbouring into a
profession without neglecting his duties as a keeper.

The job of harbouring, he explains, is threefold. First of all, to
watch where a suitable or 'warrantable' stag or hind (the sex
depending on the month within the hunting season) has made its
lair. Secondly, to report observations to the Master at the morning
meet. Thirdly, to assist the huntsman and a few chosen hounds,
known as 'tufters', to rouse the animal, so that the pack can be laid
on for the day's hunting. The skill of the harbourer resides in a
whole range of abilities: his knowledge of the territory; the likely
places, e.g. patches of woodland, where the deer will lie up;
phenomena such as a mud bath where it will roll or 'soil'; a
depression in the bracken where it will crouch down or go 'quat'
and hide; such habits as when an old stag will drive out a young one
to draw off the hounds while it stays hidden; the significance of a
'slot' (imprint of the hoof) which may reveal sex, size, and age of
the animal and the direction it has taken; likewise 'fewmets' or
droppings which may indicate what it has been feeding on and
where. All this and more constitutes the core of a fascinating book.
Fred Goss retired in 1921, was given a handsome testimonial and
appointed sub-agent to the Pixton estate. He was succeeded by Ned
Lang, headkeeper of the Miltons estate; meanwhile the sequence of
'D & S' huntsmen had also been sustained by a series of notable
characters since Arthur Heal's retirement in 1889 – first Anthony
Huxtable, then Sidney Tucker, and then Ernest Bawden appointed
in 1917.

Consolidation and Change

The period between the two world wars was similar to that
before 1914 in that farming was still depressed (despite a short burst
of subsidised corn growing during the war), so that the moorland
was generally untouched by the plough. Hunting revived quickly,
and the 'D & S' flourished under the Mastership of Colonel Wiggin
1918-1935. Wiggin was a benefactor in several respects, starting the

puppy show at Exford and, with two other landowners, donating
Dunkery Hill to the National Trust in 1935, the year of his
retirement. He was also involved in a move taken by the Hunt
Committee to safeguard its hold upon a key area of territory. In
1926 the Committee bought from Sir Edward Mountain, owner of
the Oare and Brendon estates, Oare Deer Park and Manor Allotment and, on the Devon side of the river, the whole Badgworthy
Enclosure including the wood and the site of the hermits' houses,
also the manorial rights over Brendon Common as far west as
Hoaroak Water. All this property was vested in the Badgworthy
Land Company, which later received, by way of gift, two tenanted
farms – Hinam from Miss B.K. Abbot (Master of the 'D & S'
during the war), and Walland, including Blagdon Wood, from C.
Smith-Bingham. The Company also acquired Burrow Wood, near
Winsford, so that the total land-owning, including manorial and
sporting rights, now amounts to nearly 7,000 acres, all within the
Park boundary: and includes the kennels at Exford with about 27
acres of land.

In addition the Company owns the hunting rights over many
thousands of acres of Exmoor and North Devon: such rights, as
distinct from sporting rights, only entitle the Hunt to take wild
deer, foxes and hares, and not game. The rights run with the land
and the Company licenses the Masters of the various packs of
hounds to exercise them. The practical effect of hunting rights is
that no owner or occupier of land over which they run, can bring an
action for trespass against the Hunt. This agreement has worked
well for some thirty years. In 1976 all the shares in the Company
owned by the directors were transferred to the Badgworthy Trust, a
registered charity with the object of promoting, for the benefit of
the public, the protection of lands and buildings of beauty, historic
interest, or scientific and ecological value within the Park. Since
1976 the Trust has taken steps actively to conserve its moorland and
woodland properties, in the belief that this is fully compatible
with the encouragement of hunting, especially stag hunting, by
providing suitable habitats for the deer as well as foxes.

The Second World War brought radical changes to Exmoor in
that, under Government direction and aid, large stretches of
moorland and rough grazing were ploughed for cropping or
re-seeding, fences erected, and much wild land used for military
training. Casualties and damage due to enemy action or the activities
of troops were on a relatively small scale, and only a handful of

reminders are left today. It is not thought that the population of the deer was seriously affected. Poaching by troops and other invaders out to supplement the meat ration may have accounted for a few head; otherwise, as in the First World War, the 'D & S' was barely able to keep the numbers in check, even with the aid of regular deer drives organised by the War Agricultural Committees.

For and Against

Hunting revived after the war but, in contrast to the period after 1918, certain changes had come to stay. First of all, the wartime policy of underwriting farming for the maximum production of food was enshrined in the Agriculture Act 1947, which meant that subsidised ploughing and fencing continued in peace as in war. Inevitably this imposed restraints upon riding across arable and leys, while wire always adds hazards to hunting, especially to hounds.

Another more serious problem for the 'D & S' was the growth of the anti-hunting lobby, and the moves made in Parliament during the first post-war Labour Government to promote Private Members' Bills to prohibit field sports of all kinds. These moves failed, but they induced an enquiry into the whole question of 'Cruelty to Wild Animals' and the appointment by Parliament of a Committee, chaired by John Scott Henderson KC, which produced a Report under that title, published by HMSO in 1951. So far as it went, this was a thorough piece of work, the Committee taking evidence from a wide spectrum of individuals and organisations ranging, on the one hand, from the British Field Sports Society (BFSS) and several hunting and other associations, including the 'D & S', to animal welfare organisations such as the Royal Society for the Prevention of Cruelty to Animals (RSPCA), the National Society for the Abolition of Cruel Sports (NSACS), and the League Against Cruel Sports (LACS).

The Committee stated three reasons for the existence of hunting – provision of food, sport, and the control of animal population; and that these three had arisen in the course of history in that order. As regards red deer on Exmoor, the first two – food and sport – had run together at least since Norman times, but that sport had taken over by the 18th century, while the need to control numbers of deer had become evident by the late 19th. By the end of that century, deer hunting – as we have seen – was strongly established as an organised sport, having a clearly defined season for hunting stags and hinds, and a code of practice (to use a modern term) expressed in harbouring, tufting, and – at the kill – by the use of a 12-bore shot gun with a special cartridge, or a humane killer of the pistol type.

The opposition advanced two main objections – ethical (or moral) and social: namely, that hunting was cruel, several cases being quoted in which it was alleged that deer had been mauled or mutilated; secondly that it was socially deplorable, implying that those engaged in the sport belonged to the 'idle rich'. On the other hand, while conceding that the deer population had to be controlled – to reduce damage to crops, hedges and trees, to prevent the deer outgrowing the natural feeding capacity of the ground, and to eliminate the old and ill – it was claimed that shooting by skilled marksmen using a rifle was both practicable and efficient, and did not involve cruelty.

In its discussion of all the arguments, the Committee refused to be drawn on the question of ethics – was hunting cruel or wasn't it? Nonetheless it did consider the *degree* of cruelty involved, which amounted to a tacit admission of the existence of cruelty, for any reference to 'degree' implied cruelty at the outset and, in the context of Nature, 'red in tooth and claw', undeniable. However, in all that followed, the Committee concentrated on clarifying the issues wherever possible and on reaching a balanced assessment of the claims of each side. In so doing it found, for example, that the specific evidence of cruelty (mauling, mutilation, terrorising of the quarry, etc) was not proven, but the product of hearsay, misconception of animal behaviour, and ignorance of hunting practice, often exaggerated by Press reports, for which the subject made good copy. They also found that the alternative of shooting was just as open to inflict cruelty by wounding, as well as being dangerous in a relatively small area, such as Exmoor; that hunting was no longer the preserve of the rich, but popular among people of moderate means; that, while the kill was the logical end to the chase, death was not the prime purpose, but enjoyment of a day following the hounds was; that culling by means of hunting was safe and effective; finally, that hunting in general provided a healthy and traditional form of recreation, generating a variety of events, such as point-to-points, shows, and other items associated with the horse, which were both a valuable source of income, as well as of entertainment to a large number of people in the countryside, and in

22 *West Anstey Common*

23 *Winsford Hill from the Wambarrows*

24   Exmoor ponies in their natural habitat

25   Two year old Exmoor pony colt

27   Returning after a day's hunting

Devon and Somerset Staghounds

28   The Puppy Show at the Kennels, Exford

29 *Stocking the Lyn*

30 Concrete raceways showing settlement areas at Exe Valley Fishery

31 Mansel Jaquet tieing flies at Exford Show

32 *Propitiating the good spirits at the Carhampton Wassail*

33 *The Minehead Hobby Horse in winter quarters, John Leech holding the tail*

34 *The Hunting of the Earl of Rone, Combe Martin: Grenadiers, the Earl revived (centre left) and the Hobby Horse*

35 *Dunster Show*

36 *Judging horseflesh at Exford Show*

Exmoor in particular. The findings of the Committee, which recommended that hunting of the red deer should be allowed to continue, have repeatedly been reinforced by writers as diverse as S.H. Burton in his standard work, *Exmoor* (Hodder & Stoughton), Lord Porchester in his official report, *A Study of Exmoor* (HMSO), and E.R. Lloyd in *The Wild Red Deer of Exmoor* (Exmoor Press), the latter writing from the inside, with a lifetime knowledge of the deer, the moor, and hunting.

The Committee's Report however did nothing to discourage the anti-hunting lobby, and meets on Exmoor were invaded on several occasions by objectors, many of them brought by bus from places as far afield as Bristol. The 'demos' reached their apogee during the 1960s, when a well-known local farmer and character, Bob Nancekivell, was Joint Master of the 'D & S'. No violence occurred, but the man who attracted most odium was a prominent representative of the LACS, E.A. Hemingway, who organised a public meeting in Dulverton Town Hall that nearly ended with his being thrown into the river Barle by a group of young farmers.

A far more effective weapon was the progressive acquisition by the LACS of sporting rights on certain farms within the hunting territory, and of various properties at strategic locations, dubbed 'sanctuaries'. One is at Baronsdown, near Dulverton; another at Pitleigh, near Cutcombe – over 30 sites being so acquired, totalling some 1,200 acres in all. In 1985 the LACS brought a case for trespass against the 'D & S ', a test case heard before Mr Justice Park, which resulted in the Hunt being fined £180 for seven instances of proven trespass, a trifling sum as compared with the enormous bill for costs of £70,000 awarded against the defendant, though this sum was duly reduced by £19,000 by the Taxing Master. Contributions from hunt supporters all over the country flowed in to the 'D & S' – a significant indication of support for the principle at stake – but the most important outcome was the ruling, couched as follows:

> Where a Master of Staghounds takes out a pack and deliberately sets it in pursuit of a stag knowing there is a real risk that in pursuit hounds may enter or cross prohibited land, the Master will be liable for trespass if he intends to cause hounds to enter such land, or if by his failure to exercise proper control, he causes them to do so.

This ruling made it clear, if there had been any doubt before, that hunting as a sport was lawful, and that any incursion over prohibited land during a day's hunt was not automatically a subject for trespass, but only if there was evidence of intent or negligence. It is understood that maps showing the whereabouts of LACS 'sanctuaries' have since been issued to all members and supporters of the Hunt, with clear instructions about the meaning of trespass, and that high deer fencing has been erected round Pitleigh by a group of these same supporters.

Another source of trouble concerns the behaviour of Hunt followers – leaving gates open, disturbing ewes in lamb, and so on, matters which have always dogged the Hunt, with which, however, the Master and Secretary can usually cope. But they are often powerless to deal with traffic jams on popular hunting days, or with a new nuisance, not necessarily caused by Hunt followers, but often imputed to them. This relates to damage done to the moorland and pasture in open country by people in 4-wheel drive vehicles, on motor cycles and even mountain bikes, intent solely on their own advantage. It is difficult to catch these offenders and the remedy lies with the landowners who permit access. However, one case taken to court and given an examplery fine might prove the best cure. It would certainly attract the support of conservation bodies.

Traffic jams and damage to the moorland – real or alleged – are, however, among the least of the accusations levelled against hunting. The hostility of the LACS on moral grounds is unlikely to diminish. What had once been an irritant has now become a serious threat, a recent symptom being the motion passed at the AGM of the National Trust (albeit on a very low poll) to ban hunting over the 20,000 acres of Trust land on Exmoor, though not ratified by the Council. More serious still is the prospect of a Private Members' or Government Bill in a future Parliament led by Labour, though no political party likes losing rural votes 'for a pastime' in every sense of that phrase.

There seems also to be a shift in the background of opinion on Exmoor itself. Hitherto hunting has been supported by the majority of hill and other farmers, who put up with the damage done by deer to crops and hedges for the sake of the sport. Not all farmers, it is claimed, are of this mind. Their attitude is conditioned by the great increase in deer numbers over the past decade, due in part to the prohibition of the use of guns (except under licence) by the Wildlife and Countryside Act 1981 for killing surplus animals. One observer, whose passion is watching and photographing deer, has taken a careful count and now estimates the total population at around

3,000, twice the accustomed estimate. If that is true, it would account for the undoubted increase in legal shooting of deer by certain landowners, or game dealers licensed to do the shooting, and who profit from the demand for antlers as trophies and sale of venison. Poaching also is prevalent; even so the deer continue to increase at an estimated 25 per cent a year.

Controlling the deer population on Exmoor is a key issue and the reason for two opposing views: on the one hand, that culling by hunting is ineffective; and, on the other, that shooting is potential genocide. Another complaint concerns the over-kill of mature stags, whether hunted or shot. Noel Allen, the naturalist and author, who recognises that hunting is a traditional sport, irrespective of class, and entrenched in the pleasures and social customs of Exmoor, has said:

> The problem today and perhaps casting a shadow over the future is the indiscriminate shooting of deer for venison. Invariably the biggest and best deer are shot with little concern for the maintenance of a balanced population. The same is true of most culling undertaken when deer are damaging crops and trees. The ratio of male to female calves at birth is on a 1:1 basis which is Nature's way of indicating the proper balance. There are however far more hinds on Exmoor than male deer and the ratio is more like 4:1.
>
> On the other hand an indiscriminate preservation of the red deer would be disastrous, for this would mean an annual population increase of some 25 per cent and rapid over-stocking. This in turn would lead to shortage of food, weaker deer succumbing to disease and more poaching with its attendant cruelty. At present uncontrolled shooting results in an imbalance of the herds as regards both sex and age. In brief, more prime stags need to survive to maintain a strong, healthy, and vigorous population. With this, and with much of their habitat in 'safe hands', the future of the red deer of Exmoor can be assured. Here they can live a full and satisfying life, and give us the delight of watching them contented and free.[1]

The reality, in my opinion, is that the conflict over hunting, deer in particular, will never be resolved by argument, for the subject is too emotive to be settled by reason alone. If a conclusion is ultimately reached, it will be thanks to pressure. Either the anti-hunting lobby (which is by no means the same thing as the conservation one) will, *faute de mieux*, accept hunting as a component in the

1. Noel Allen: *Exmoor's Wild Red Deer* (Exmoor Press).

campaign to protect the countryside; or hunting will be prohibited by political and predominantly urban interests. If that happens, then it is likely that the wild red deer of Exmoor will indeed be shot and trapped to extinction.

SHOOTING

In Chapter 10 of the Exmoor classic, *Memories of a Stag Harbourer*, the author, Fred Goss, states that he was appointed head keeper to the Pixton estate in 1904, but combined this work with that of stag harbourer which he had begun ten years earlier. He wrote:

> To my other occupations that of pheasant rearing was now added. The labour necessary for this can be gathered from the fact that the shoots there were often big shoots that included a day of 960 head and many others when the numbers were round about 400 and 500 head . . . Altogether I reared birds for about fifteen years to the total of somewhere about 35,000 – the largest number for any one year being 6,000.

His calendar was made up as follows:

April. Harbouring for spring stag hunting.
May-July. Pheasant rearing.
July (latter part) to 20th October. Harbouring for stag hunting;
October – 1st February. Organising shooting days; harbouring hinds and rendering general assistance to the Hunt as required.
February-March. Largely occupied in catching up stock pheasants for eggs for the coming season.

Goss then refers to 'all the minor jobs inseparable from harbouring and keepering': which would have included shooting predators and hanging some of them on gibbets 'pour encourager les autres', e.g. stoats, weasels, rats, foxes, badgers, and birds of prey such as kestrels, sparrow hawks, and buzzards, all of which he specifies. He would quite likely also have seen to coppicing and the planting of certain shrubs as cover for the birds. In *Forestry in the English Landscape* (Faber), Roger Miles has described the situation in the last century, particularly as it would have applied to Exmoor:

> With the perfection of the central-fire cartridge by Daw in 1861 and the subsequent improvement of breech-loading sporting guns, the success of fashionable shooting parties was usually measured by the

numbers of birds slain. The rearing of sufficient birds and their proper presentation to the guns therefore required the services of skilled gamekeepers, and in many estate woodlands their requirements took priority over those of the forester. Gamekeeping, like the preservation of deer in royal forests centuries earlier, helped to conserve the woods but contributed little to their proper management. Although good forestry practice is not incompatible with game preservation and many of the conifer species can provide excellent harbourage for birds, this was not generally appreciated in the nineteenth century. Coppices provided good cover for game and, in some degree, their retention could be justified for sporting reasons. It became common practice to plant shrubs where no coppice existed under standard trees; snowberry, *Leycesteria*, rhododendron, and laurel being popular for this purpose.

The expansive days of large shooting parties and big bags, so characteristic of country house life in the late Victorian and Edwardian eras, were sustained to a surprising degree right up to 1939. As a weekend guest in that *milieu* you were expected to wear tweed plus-fours or 'shooting knickers' (sic), whatever they were, out in the field; but you also had to pack your suitcase with one good suit and a dinner jacket for the evening, which might be spent dancing or playing cards. Naturally you brought your 12-bore gun (possibly a pair), a supply of cartridges (decanted into a bag on the shoot), and sufficient cash with which to tip the gamekeeper, your personal loader (if that was the scale of the enterprise), and possibly others as well, not forgetting the formidable butler or major domo of the household. The visit, even excluding transport, was not cheap.

My maternal grandfather, who got through a great deal of money as a young man and never did much work, except when in the Army during the Boer War, became in effect a professional guest. Equipped with a pair of Purdey guns, and a satchel full of expensive handmade shoes, he spent the winter going round from one country house to another, shooting, gambling, and 'noticing' the women.

*   *   *   *   *   *   *   *   *   *   *

The last world war and its aftermath said goodbye to most of that. Of course, well-heeled landowners continued to invite their friends to shooting parties, but on large estates stark economics accelerated the move away from private hospitality towards commercial enterprise.

Nowadays it is the syndicate of guns that pays the bill for game shooting, and this has become apparent on the dozen or so sizeable shoots in and around the confines of Exmoor National Park.

Briefly the pattern looks like this. At one end of the scale a landowner with, say, a thousand acres more or less, leases the shooting rights to a tenant, who is not likely to be a farmer but an independent *entrepreneur*. He or his representative will manage the operation from first to last: which means, for a start, that, unlike Fred Goss, he will not be spending February and March catching stock pheasants for eggs! Instead he will purchase day-old chicks or poults at six weeks from a specialist rearer, who keeps a stock of brood birds, hatches the eggs in incubators, and sells the young birds on. If he buys day-olds, the manager keeps them initially in small confined pens, with a brooder or heater, before transferring them to larger units, always with adequate space but strictly guarded and closed at night. At poult stage the birds will be penned in the shooting area, and continue to be hand fed and watered. By the age of ten weeks or so, or when they are fully feathered, the birds will be free to fly out of the pens and roost in the trees, and so get acclimatised to the 'wild'. However supplementary feeding will go on (by hand or automatic feeder) until the birds are fully able to forage for themselves. Care has to be exercised lest they become domesticated and forget that they have been raised for the 'kill'! They must all be 'wild' by about a month before the shooting season begins.

Since most of the shoots on Exmoor are wooded, and since trees and undercover are their natural habitat, pheasants are the principal game and are shot between 1 October and 31 January. Originally introduced from south-west Asia, there is something very oriental in the splendid appearance of the cock bird, with its bright red cheek patches, greenish-black head, white ring round the neck, and variegated brown and yellow plumage flecked with black. Its call is unmistakable – loud, explosive, and indignant, followed by heavy wing beats and a slow take-off. By contrast the hen is very unassuming in her nondescript brown. Both have long tails, and feed on seeds, berries, and grain.

Recently, on Exmoor, it has become the custom to shoot partridges and ducks first, as from 1st September. There are two kinds of partridge, the common grey and red-legged or 'Frenchman', distinctive for its red bill and legs, rust red tail, and dark upright bars on its flanks. Both kinds collect in coveys, sit tight until flushed, and then rise all at once. In descent, they will skim over the ground and run a fair distance before settling. Shooting partridges and duck has not only stimulated the production of young birds of these two species, but encouraged the provision of feeding grounds outside the woods; for example, partridges are partial to fields of roots and stubbles, and along broad headlands untouched by sprays. Flight ponds, long familiar on Exmoor, are now being dug for commercial reasons, partly for stocking with trout, partly as habitats for ducks and other water birds; but these ponds have to be carefully guarded against pollution by pesticides, nitrates, and farm wastes.

The story of black and red grouse on Exmoor is a sad one. According to John Coleman-Cooke, farmers remembered their for-bears talking of large packs of both species at large on the heights of the moor, though by about 1900 they were beginning to decline.[1] The downward process continued until, in 1962, it was estimated that the resident population of black grouse amounted to only 27 males and 17 hens; red grouse were not mentioned at all. Coleman-Cooke, as a naturalist and Exmoor enthusiast, pleaded for the revival of this beautiful game: the cock bird, in full plumage, big and blue-black with scarlet wattle and lyre-shaped tail; the hen in her soft brown dress, flecked with gold, white and black. At a 'lek' or mating place, which some said they had seen in secret parts of Exmoor, the cocks pranced aggressively about, and gave vent to a cooing and bubbling call. Why the decline? Not due to over-shooting, it was thought, but more likely to the loss of food and habitat – heather, sedge, bracken, and above all whortleberries – as a result of reclamation of moorland.

Seventeen years later, Sir Dennis Stucley bewailed the total loss of all game birds on Exmoor in the fearful winter of 1962-3 – pheasants, partridges, and grouse – destroyed by hungry predators even if they had survived the cold. He recalled that two attempts had been made to re-stock the black game. One small group of chicks, reared in Perthshire, had been sent by train from Edinburgh to Taunton in 1968. The birds had arrived in good order, but shortly afterwards developed blackhead and died. Another attempt was made in June 1969. A bantam and eleven chicks were sent from Perthshire as before, and Mr. Loosemore, Sir Dennis's gamekeeper at North Molton, took charge of them. A second brood intended for the Dunkery area was lost owing to a railway strike, the chicks being left to die in a rail siding. At North Molton:

1. *Exmoor Review*, 1963.

We took every precaution to guard against blackhead and indeed any other disease. A site was used at the top of North Molton park on an old grass court, 650 feet above sea level and facing North Molton Hill which rises to 1,550 feet. Strips of heather and whortleberries were planted across the tennis court, so that some of these moorland plants were included whenever the pen was moved. An oak tree gave partial shade from the afternoon sun – exceptionally important in that warm summer. The tennis court had never been contaminated by other poultry.

The chicks were fed on turkey pellets, plenty of fresh lettuce and a handful of ants' eggs twice a day, containing plenty of ants and eggs . . . All eleven chicks grew at a great pace and were virtually fully grown by 20 August . . . After about five weeks Scots pine branches and birch were suspended in their pen, the birds set about the buds and shoots at once, it was interesting to note how keenly they appreciated this natural food.[1]

Sir Dennis went on to describe how the birds were carefully released near the moor – by removing the roof of the pen and letting them find their own way out – and how several birds were spotted during the autumn out on the moorland. What happened later, in fact what became of them and their possible descendants, he does not relate – he was writing in 1979 – but sadly there are no black game on Exmoor now.

*   *   *   *   *   *   *   *   *   *

Sporting interests claim that rearing game birds confers benefits on the environment. For instance, the planting of shrubs in woodland, and the care of hedges, provide food for butterflies and bees, and encourage the growth of orchids and other wild flowers. Also the control by game keepers of predators – attracted by the concentration of young game birds in limited areas of woodland – is a beneficent practice if not pushed too far. Fred Goss's gibbets, for example, are a thing of the past, as is the old obsession with extermination. That of course is to the good, but such improvements are often cancelled out in the public eye when, in the late summer, roads around places like Dulverton and Winsford are littered with young pheasants barely able to fly, and notices have to be erected along the roadsides warning the public not to drive over

1. *Exmoor Review*, 1980.

them. There is another cause for concern. So great on occasions is the number of birds shot, especially at the end of the season, that it far exceeds the ability to dispose of them in the market; so they have to be buried. No comment is necessary! However, the British Field Sports Society and shooting organisations are well aware of the bad image so created, and are endeavouring to introduce a code of shooting practice, also a 'white list' of registered shoots that conform to the practice, and even a scheme for marketing pheasants – not only to deal with a spate of dead birds but, for business reasons, to promote the sale of pheasant flesh for its dietary qualities, high in protein, low in fat.

Large shooting syndicates are not easy to join, so great is the demand, other than for the odd day's shooting. If you do succeed in joining for a season, you have to have plenty of cash, as operating expenses are high at every stage of the sport. The shooting manager has, as we know, to stock the estate with sufficient birds to last the season, which will depend – among other factors – on the type of land and cover, and the quality of the shoot. It is not easy to estimate. To quote an example: in order to provide for three days' shooting a week for three months, or forty shooting days, and allow for, say, 200 shootable birds per day, the manager would have to raise – allowing for losses – 10-11,000 birds. He employs the keeper who is responsible for every stage of growth, and for the maintenance of the habitat. He employs the team of beaters, whose job is to move in extended line – slowly so that not all the birds are flushed at once – tapping trees and beating brush and cover towards the guns, who are stationed at key points or 'stands' round the edge of woods or clearings; he also employs the pickers-up who, as the name implies, pick up the dead and wounded birds, for which retrieving dogs will be needed.

All this adds up to a heavy outlay, exclusive of overheads and before profit is calculated; consequently the gun has to foot a correspondingly heavy bill. In a syndicate of ten guns, on a '200-bird day', the charge for each gun could be £20 per bird: thus 20 × 20 = £4,000 divided by 10, or £400 per gun per day and the privilege of keeping only one brace of birds! But that is not all. The gun is expected, as has always been the custom, to tip the keeper, and pay his own loader if he has one (usually a local man). In all, a gun would have to spend £50 – £100 on these unavoidable extras, exclusive of the cost of cartridges (at £3.50 for 25), and of the original purchase of his 12-bore shotgun, or pair of them. Such a gun – like a car or a house – can command a wide range of price according to quality: in this case from c.£250 to c.£15,000.

It is obvious that shooting on this scale is a rich man's hobby, while the capital required by the owner of the shooting rights, even with a potential turnover of c.£200,000 per season, will be very large. It means, increasingly, that outside interests are moving in to Exmoor shoots, so that members of syndicates are reputed to be coming from all over Europe and even from North and South America. That such people patronise local hotels, restaurants, sports and other shops, and provide some seasonal employment, confers benefits upon the economy to a limited degree; but it also means that native sportsmen are being progressively excluded.

It is however true that, here and there, owners are still to be found who operate on a relatively modest scale: rearing their own birds, walking them up instead of driving them, and so providing sport at correspondingly lower cost. Or again, friends and neighbours will get together simply to share expenses in cash and kind for an occasional day's sport, relying even on game bred naturally in the wild. Walking round the farm of an evening, as I used to do, stalking pigeons (very 'fly' they were) and rabbits before the days of myxomatosis, seems very far off in time. Now that rabbits are becoming resistant and popping up again, those days may possibly return – provided the EEC does not issue some directive to the contrary!

FRESHWATER FISHING

Literature about fishing on Exmoor – apart from information about licences, permits, where to fish, and the habits of the fish themselves – is not large: certainly much less than that about hunting. But because it says so much about the fascination of the sport on Exmoor it is worth referring to in some detail. One of the earliest and most readable accounts is to be found in the first volume of memoirs by the Rev. W.H. Thornton, entitled *Reminiscences of an Old West Country Clergyman* (Andrew Iredale). Thornton was the first incumbent of the living at Simonsbath in the newly created parish of Exmoor, 1856-60. He knew the neighbourhood pretty well already, having spent two years with a private tutor at Selworthy before being ordained and appointed curate to the Vicar of Lynton. At Selworthy in 1848 he 'took to fishing as keen as if I had been a heron or kingfisher'.

We were never in those days particular as to poaching, but, whether or no, I filled my pouch like an otter, and I often now think of my own early and great performances with the rod, and in saddle on the moors. I like to visit the very topmost waters, fish with a short line, fine gut, and a single fly, often a red one with a white tip to the body. I would throw myself down quite flat, and wriggle up the brookside like a snake, throwing my fly into the small pits and narrow stickles most successfully.

In those days I generally carried a basket which held fourteen pounds weight of trout, and, after learning to fish, I did not consider that I had done well if I did not succeed in filling it . . . dearly did I love the woody, tangled brook which runs down from Holnicote, through Bossington, to the sea, near Hurlestone Point.

Sometimes with a worm, sometimes with a bluebottle, sometimes with infinite pains with artificial flies, I would fish that tiny brook, and its trout, if not numerous, were large and fat. When it rained hard, and thunder was to be heard, several of us would make a clot with worms and worsted, and go down at night with a bag and a lantern to catch eels, and an occasional trout in the brook.

From some cause or other the clear streams in the north of Devon are much more tenanted by eels than are the rivers in the south; and great was the scramble of pupil and farm boys as at midnight, and in streaming rain, the eels would disengage themselves from the worsted, and glide about in the long grass of the meadow, endeavouring to escape and get back to their homes. At other times I would go down to the ditches in Porlock marsh to catch eels with an eel spear, ever so many at a time. Really I scarcely know how I found time to get at all these rivers, but in 1848-9 it was my custom to fish the Timberscombe brook, Chalkwater, Exe, Barle, Lyn, Horner and Hawcome (sic) brooks, and last, but not least, the little stream of Holnicote. No one ever said me nay.

The next writer, chronologically, was H.C. Cutcliffe, a surgeon whose *The Art of Trout Fishing in Rapid Streams* was published in South Molton in 1863. Unfortunately his style is so prolix and convoluted that it involves a great deal of sustained effort in order to extract the sense of what he is trying to say. He also has a talent for stating the obvious, though his comments are usually valid.

Cutcliffe fished the Bray and the upper reaches of the Mole, and records his experiences in ten chapters, broadly assigned to observations on the movements and feeding habits of the trout, especially its rapacity; the variety of bait – flies (natural and artificial), maggots, worms, and minnows (natural and artificial); methods of making flies, the materials and colours to be used; preference for the hackle and objection to the winged fly on rapid streams, 'because the wings are so soon washed down upon the shank of the hook, and therefore lose the appearance which they have when dry'; advice on tackle and use of rubber boots for wading (a new idea apparently); and a small item to which, typical of the writer, he devotes two pages on the need to carry two small hooks or crooks 'for the purpose of cutting off any little bough or twig, rush bush, or thorn, in which my flies may accidentally become entangled'. Eventually he grasps the nettle:

> Keep behind his tail, fish up stream, and keep your head as close to the level of the water as you can. Keep as short a line at all times as possible – creep and crawl – get down to the water's edge, or into the stream itself – use every artifice you can for concealment – throw, up stream, but do not, if you can help it, let out line to reach a fish. Throw boldly and with exact precision . . .

Next in order comes Claude F. Wade, London barrister, whose *Exmoor Streams. Notes and Jottings with Practical Hints for Anglers* was published by Chatto in 1903. It is easy to read. Wade began fishing in 1861, mostly on the East and West Lyn and their tributaries, but also in the upper waters of the Barle (from Landacre to Pinkery Pond), and occasionally at Heddon's Mouth. On his head he wore 'a black bowler hat or a very old and dingy white one . . . and not a cap, because you ought to be able to wind at least two collars round your headgear'. This was not his only eccentricity. Staying at Lynton or Lynmouth, he would hire a trap to take him to his destinations, but that was before the development of the twin villages into tourist resorts and the construction of the cliff railway; likewise before the publication in 1869 of Blackmore's Lorna Doone, which began its bestselling career in the 1870s – all of which he deplored. On a visit to Badgworthy Water, he related how he came to the 'so-called "Lorna's Bower"'.

> This is a very prosaic looking cottage farm that used once to be called "Cloud". Lorna isn't there, and I don't think ever was, but a nice old lady now is, who will yarn to you for hours together, give you plenty of ginger beer or tea of the best quality, and ask you to write your name in the visitors' book.

Salmon, trout and sea trout abounded in the Lyn, but poaching or 'snatching' was rife, and the waters subject to raids by '"hotel fishermen", I mean fishermen who made their livelihood by providing *table d'hotes* with Exmoor trout.'

> One poor old tailor I remember for years and years, from my boyhood upwards; he could walk, or rather "slip along", very fast, generally dressed in old shiny black clothes, with a keen pointed nose. You could never be out before him – he was always in front of you with his seedy looking rod and basket and his bag of worms – and very often you met him in the lanes hurrying home with a load of fish for the "Castle" cook.

Wade was careful to make friends with the riparian owners, especially the important ones – Nicholas Snow at Oare, Frederic Knight at Simonsbath, and Sir Thomas Acland's agent at Holnicote. He offers pages of advice on the technique of fishing and the various species, and lovingly describes every pool and cranny of the East Lyn, his favourite stream; but of course his ardour must have exacerbated the very publicity he so deplored! He was not snobbish about worms:

> As to worm fishing for trout in general, don't you believe that it is an inferior kind of sport and hardly to be named amongst fly fishermen. This is all utter nonsense and is only put forward by those who fancy themselves at fly fishing and know more or less about it, but who are utterly ignorant in the art of worm fishing, which they pretend to despise, simply because they don't understand it.

A generation later, Claude Luttrell remarked in his *Sporting Recollections of a Younger Son*, published by Duckworth in 1925, that he was nine years old and present at the famous staghunt in which the Prince of Wales took part in 1879. Thereafter he grew up into an enthusiastic all-round sportsman, who hunted, fished and shot. He was friendly with Nicholas Snow and regularly fished the Lyn rivers and their tributaries, having the free run of Snow's property. The trout, he notes, were small but delicious, though not exciting to catch. However, 'the real pleasure came from the surroundings':

> It is a real joy to fish streams like Weir and Chalk with heather on either side, and every variety of water, from deep dark pools to quick-running stickles, as you fish your way up the winding combes: a lovely wild country where you may fish all day and never see a

tripper. I am afraid one cannot say the same of Badgworthy Water, as an endless stream of trippers follow the path by the side of the river on their way to from the Doone Valley.

He also caught salmon that came up from the sea at Lynmouth, even though it got poached 'when the water is clear enough to see them', and observed that 'Mr Snow was a first-rate fisherman, but he couldn't beat the record of Parson Froude (of Knowstone), who caught 315 trout in one day'.

In recent years most writing about fishing on Exmoor has appeared either in the *Exmoor Review* or in one of the two books, *The Fish of Exmoor* and *The Waters of Exmoor*, published by the Exmoor Press. Among the contributors are James Connell, who began fishing as a schoolboy in 1919, when he and his brother hooked trout with worms 'in the beautiful little brook that runs down Worthy Combe'. Afterwards, in holidays, he fished in a more orthodox manner in most of the Exmoor streams, notably Sherdon Water and Danesbrook which he described as:

> . . . alike in many ways, fast flowing, clear as crystal, when not in spate, and full of lovely rocky pools and stickles, but the Danesbrook is much more wooded in its lower reaches, whereas the Sherdon is very open apart from large beech hedges on the left bank . . . One of the joys of fishing these lovely streams is that you often see the deer in their natural state, so quiet and peaceful are the surroundings.

Other knowledgeable and experienced fishermen, whose work has appeared in the *Review* or the Exmoor Press books, and who infuse it with a passion, not only for the sport but also for the ambience of a day by an Exmoor stream, include Kenneth Mansfield, Brigadier A. E. Snow, Stanley Woodrow, Audrey Bonham-Carter, Maria Poles and Mansel Jaquet. The principal author of *The Fish of Exmoor* is H.B. Maund, who bought the Exe Valley Fishery in 1953, a business now operated by his son, Hugh.

Trout

The wild brown trout is the native fish in Exmoor rivers. It does not migrate, and it is small. The life cycle starts in September when the parent fish move upstream to beds of gravel in the shallows, where the hen digs a small trench or 'redd' in which she lays her eggs or ova. The cock fish then fertilises the eggs with semen or 'milt', and then covers in the redd. In thirty days after spawning, the eggs become 'eyed ova' and eighty days later they become alevins; after a further three weeks they turn into 'fry' or 'fingerlings'. The alevin feeds on single-celled organisms present in the water – comparable to plankton in the sea – from which it can readily be understood how vital it is that a fishing stream should be clean and unpolluted. This is one reason why, for instance, the river Barle or the tributaries of the East Lyn have such a high reputation, as they flow fast over rocky beds and clear quickly after spate. Farm slurry, nitrate or other pollutants are lethal for river life. After about a year the young trout becomes an adult fish and lives all its life in the river in which it is spawned, usually staying within a specific stretch of water. Its life expectancy can be as long as ten years, and it will be ready to spawn after a year or so.

Until recently the brown trout rarely averaged more than 5 oz. in weight (3-4 to the lb). Its lack of size is due to the shortage of food, influenced by the acidity of the moorland water which – at the source – trickles out of the peat and tends to discourage the proliferation of larvae, gnats, and other species of insect brought into the stream by wind and water, and which constitute the trout's diet. Some of the insects thrive on the weed along the banks, and consequently are deprived when the plants are torn away by storm and spate. However, though small, the brown trout is a vigorous game fish, and provides plenty of sport for anglers.

In 1968-70 an epidemic of Ulcerated Dermal Necrosis (UDN) – a skin infection – attacked both salmon and trout and heavily reduced the fish stock, especially of trout. This, in turn, diminished the competition for food among the survivors, so that – in the past decade or so – the brown trout have tended to increase in size and weight, so that specimens of $\frac{1}{2}$ lb or so are occasionally caught. Although some limited stocking is carried out by riparian owners, most brown trout maintain their numbers by natural breeding in the manner described. Their survival depends on their ability to see and catch food on the surface or under the water; also to avoid the attentions of predators, such as birds and cannibal fish, and of course man. The season for brown trout fishing runs from mid-March to 30 September, and in small numbers it is present in reservoirs and lakes as well as in rivers. Lake 'brownies', thanks to greater variety and quantity of food, can reach several pounds in weight.

Rainbow trout were originally imported into the UK from the west coast of North America. There are two varieties: *irideus*, spring

spawning; and *shasta*, autumn spawning. It does not normally breed
in British rivers – though escapees are found in some Exmoor rivers
– but is raised in large numbers in hatcheries for stocking reservoirs
and lakes. The rainbow grows more quickly than the brown, and
can attain 2 lbs within two years. Its life, however, is shorter, usually
5-6 years, and it tends to congregate in shoals.

Sea trout or peal is a variety of brown trout that has taken to sea
feeding, and behaves much like salmon in that it is migratory and
returns to fresh water to spawn. It usually comes from the sea in
July, and normally is only to be found in such Exmoor rivers as the
Bray and West Lyn.

Salmon

Salmon do not feed in fresh water, but enter the river of their
origin from the sea as maiden fish at various stages of the season.
Thus the spring run is followed by a smaller summer run, and a
much larger (usually) movement in the autumn. At these times the
fish force their way upstream to spawn, much as trout do; that is,
the female or hen salmon digs a redd in the gravel bed, lays her eggs
which are then fertilised by the cock. Sometimes they do not
succeed in reaching the headwaters, but can be seen depositing eggs
in pools up and down the river; or if they do find a suitable spot in
the shallows, they may be so large (10 lbs or more) that their backs
may actually stick out of the water and render them easy prey to
marauders. Unlike trout, the act of spawning is so traumatic that the
first may be the last time that a pair will undertake it. After it is
completed – when their sole objective is a safe return to the sea – the
parent fish will be so exhausted that the majority will die or be killed
by predators. Their appearance also undergoes a change. They lose
colour and condition, in which state they are termed 'kelts' and are
safe at least from anglers, who are forbidden to fish for them then.

For the newly hatched ova, the life cycle continues in their
becoming, first, alevins, and then fry or 'parr', when they look much
like small trout, but with a forked tail instead of a straight one, and
a shorter mouth. They feed on microlife and, at the age of 2-3 as
'smolts', take on a silvery sheen and make their way down to the
sea, by which time they will measure 9-10 inches. The next part of
their life is a mystery – indeed the whole cycle is a wonder – but it
is thought that they disappear into the depths of the North Atlantic
or Arctic in the neighbourhood of Greenland, where they eat

voraciously and build up muscle and tissue for their return to the same river where they were spawned. This they do after a year away (when they are known as 'grilse'), or later when they have grown into mature salmon (weighing 15-30 lbs), before re-enacting the cycle of reproduction.

In 1968-70 the epidemic of UDN decimated the spring run of salmon, possibly because the temperature of the water favoured the spread of the disease, as compared with the autumn; nonetheless the reduction in numbers of the trout – afflicted by the same infection – allowed the salmon to proliferate in the Exmoor rivers, among which the Barle, Exe and East Lyn are accounted as having the best runs. UDN is happily on the wane, but its cause and cure are not known.

Angling

The enormous increase in the popularity of freshwater fishing over the past twenty years has been reflected in the corresponding rise in demand for fishing in Exmoor rivers, where trout and salmon maintain their population by natural breeding, and are only now recovering from depletion caused by UDN. On the other hand almost all the stock for still water fishing, i.e. in reservoirs, lakes and ponds, is provided by hatcheries, mostly rainbow trout. With certain exceptions, such brown trout as inhabit still waters come from feeder streams and not hatcheries.

Only three reservoirs are located within the boundaries of the National Park. Wimbleball in the Brendons (see Chapter 6) is the largest, covering 374 acres, and is managed by South West Water p.l.c. It was opened for fishing in 1980, since when many thousands of trout have been caught, and re-stocking runs at about 25,000 head a year. The season runs from early April to end of September, permits are supplied on the spot, tackle can be hired, and fishing conducted from bank or boat. The other two reservoirs (also mentioned) – Nutscale and Challacombe – are private preserves.

Two more reservoirs lie just outside the Park boundary. Clatworthy (Wessex Water p.l.c) is fed by the river Tone, which rises on Brendon Hill. It covers 130 acres, offers boat and bank fishing, and is open from mid-March to mid-October. Wistlandpound, situated a short distance south of Blackmore Gate, is a 41-acre lake with similar facilities. Of historical interest is the fact that it covers part of the old railway track between Lynton and Barnstaple.

Regulations are not complicated. An intending angler must first obtain a rod licence – one for brown trout, or a combined one for brown and sea trout and salmon. Rainbow and brown trout fishing in still waters is usually controlled by the sale of day tickets on the site. If new to the area the river angler is well advised to apply to the local agent for a permit for a day's fishing from the riparian owner. If, however, he knows his way about, he will contact the owner direct – who may be a private individual or a hotel or a fishing association. In any event, be he river or lake fisherman, the angler needs the appropriate rod licence. Charges by today's standards are not unreasonable, nor is the cost of fishing tackle (rod, reel and fishing line plus landing net), or of that important item of clothing, a pair of waders. To probe the depth of stream, a wading staff is also recommended.

In a river a trout's staple food during the season is waterbred insect life, available either as larvae rising to the surface (nymph), or as a fly floating on the surface after hatching (dun), or again as an adult fly returning to the water to lay eggs (spinner). The artificial fly must therefore imitate one of these stages, and whenever possible at favourable moments of light and weather. Thus a dry artificial fly must resemble the dun or surface spinner, and a wet artificial fly the nymph or spent and sinking spinner. Trout also prey on small fish – their own fry or minnows or sticklebacks – in which case the angler will offer an imitation of one of these.

Since this is not the appropriate place for a lengthy discussion of the habits of freshwater fish on Exmoor, or of the art of casting and catching fish, I append a short note and list of artificial flies recommended by my friend, Mansel Jaquet, a fisherman of great skill and experience, whose advice I have followed and quoted in these paragraphs. He is also well known for tieing flies, widely used in Exmoor waters.

Fishermen's Flies

Flies are either *dry* and imitate the natural insects on the water prior to taking off or when they have returned to the water to lay their eggs; or *wet*, when still in the water before reaching the surface to hatch, or submerged, when – after egg laying – they sink and drown. To look at, in the fly box, dry or wet flies look very similar. The difference is in the materials used, especially the hackles – the 'scarf' end at the eye. Wet fly hackles are hen feathers, soft and ready 'sinkers'. Dry fly hackles are cock feathers, bright and stiff, which float. Wet fly hooks are usually of heavier wire than those used for dry flies. Trout feed on flies both dry and wet, but the visible sign of a 'take' is different – the wet take being little more than a hump in the water, while the dry is much more obvious as the trout's snout is only just below the surface. If a fly is taken deep, the only sign will be a slight straightening of the line.

Wet Flies

March Brown has a large brown body and brown hairy wings in the natural form. It is very prolific in the early part of the season. A similar but not so prolific pattern occurs in May and June. The imitation fished wet is a good representation of the nymph. A first class early season fly.

Gold Ribbed Hare's Ear is a very useful general pattern doing much the same job as the March Brown, but also covering the nymphs of many of the Olives and Sedges. The Olives are *ephemeridae;* they have four *setae*, two upright wings, an olive coloured body and delicate olive coloured legs. They are delightfully dainty in flight, and rest on the surface of the water with wings up. A wide variety of Olives appear during the season.

Half Stone is a general representation of the hatching nymph of the early Olives. A favourite West Country fly.

Blue Quill, *Blue Dun*, and *Greenwell's Glory* are representations of the various stages of the many Olives in their life before hatching.

Infallible. From the beginning of May it is a very good general imitation of the *Iron Blue*, a small, very dark, and much appreciated member of the Olive family. When this hatch is in progress, trout will frequently feed on it to the exclusion of all other Olives, however large.

Pheasant Tail is far and away the best imitation of the spinner of all the Olives, and an excellent representation of the darker Sedges. A first class evening fly.

Black Midge represents, as the name implies, the tiny midges which fall into the water from bushes. It is better on enclosed and bushed waters than on open stretches.

Coachman has a high reputation as an evening fly. It is supposed to represent a moth.

Dry Flies

Blue Quill, Speckled Brown Quill and *Beacon Beige* are suitable for all the early Olives, the latter being used for the large Olive of spring. After mid-April turn to:

Tups Indispensable and *Ginger Quill.* The *Tup* imitates the Blue Winged Olive and, in its lighter coloured dressing, the Pale Watery Dun, a prolific West Country fly. The *Ginger Quill* is excellent for the Pale Watery and useful to imitate other small mid-season Olives.

Gold Ribbed Hare's Ear represents the hatching forms of Olives and Sedges. It is specially useful when there is a touch of colour in the water.

Pheasant Tail is suitable for all evening fishing throughout the season.

Greenwell's Glory is appropriate as an Olive variant.

Coachman is best for evening use, when nothing but moths are being taken.

Fish Breeding

The popularity of still water fishing has perforce stimulated the production of fish in hatcheries, some of which are to be found in or near the National Park. One of the longest established – indeed it is reputed to be the oldest still in active operation – is the Exe Valley Fishery at Exebridge, near Dulverton. It was started in 1885 by an enterprising farmer, who excavated six ponds and used his mill stream for irrigation. Unfortunately the enterprise failed, though the ponds remained. In 1900 a skilled trout farmer, T.F. Tracey, took over. He had learned his trade at the Braunton Trout

Fishery, then a small and busy concern, but long since defunct due to water abstraction in the area. Tracey re-opened the original ponds and dug out a number of new ones. He started a hatchery and drew his water from a source near Brushford, piping it into the fishery. Very soon he had a flourishing business and, thanks to his inventive flair, produced an oxygenated can with which he was able to supply distant markets with his fish. During the 1914-18 war he took Dulverton Rural District Council to court, owing to pollution from the town sewage plant; and eventually won the case after having had to take it to the House of Lords – a vital judgment that affected the whole future of freshwater fishing and fish farming.

In 1927 the Fishery passed into other hands, and is now owned and managed by Hugh Maund, whose father – as noted earlier – had bought it in 1953. Since that date the business and plant have greatly expanded to meet the heavy demand for rainbow stock from still water fisheries all over the country. At Exebridge the water is still drawn by leat from the the river Barle, and passes through a series of ponds (40 now), in which rainbow trout are raised from eggs to adult fish. In the process they are guarded against predators – such as herons and inland cormorants – by means of nets suspended over the ponds.

Strict attention is paid to the perils of pollution, both as to the intake of the water and its outflow, when the used water is allowed to settle either in settlement tanks or in settlement areas. This ensures that the water returned to the water course is almost as pure as when it was abstracted. Although there is no evidence that trout farm discharge ever harmed water courses, all responsible trout farmers ensure that the water returned is as clean as technology will allow.

CHAPTER NINE

Revels: Sacred and Profane

It may be surprising to reflect when buying a cake at Mrs Smith's
stall at the church fete, held every year in the Glebe Field, or sitting
in line listening to the Cadet Band, that you are participating in a
tradition that has continued – albeit with breaks – on that same spot
or in the churchyard yonder, for at least five hundred years, possibly
longer. Indeed, if you think back for enough, you could imagine
yourself the contemporary counterpart of some Ancient Briton or
his woman attending a rude, perhaps grisly, mid-summer festival,
dancing round a local Stonehenge and sacrificing something or
somebody!

However, let us be content with the less fanciful fact that,
throughout history, the land has been not only the foundation of
our survival but, *ipso facto*, our reason for rejoicing at having
survived at all. All over the English countryside, all sorts of rural
celebrations with a link to the past take place between January and
December. Hazel Eardley-Wilmot remarks that:

> In the eighteenth and well into the nineteenth century most parishes
> held – as before the Reformation – an annual 'Revel' to celebrate the
> feast day of their patron saint. In their heyday the Revels began with
> a church service and might last a week, and wrestling was the chief
> amusement. Perhaps the Church was trying to moderate the sport by
> annexing it.[1]

This passage vividly illustrates the point that, even today, there
are a number of shows and festivals – the title 'Revel' is still in use

1. Hazel Eardley-Wilmot: *Yesterday's Exmoor* (Exmoor Books).

at Hawkridge – which derive from the distant pagan past, but long since absorbed by Christianity; on the other hand there are plenty of others that have no religious connotation at all. Latterly, as a result of changes in farm practice and the prolonged neglect of folk custom, but also because of the increasing urbanisation of country life, a new pattern has emerged. Gone, for example, is the significance of haysel or haymaking. Silage starts in May and goes on so long as the grass grows, and hay – if made at all – takes its chance. In a good year the combine will clear winter sown wheat in June or July; and in a bad one it will pick up lodged barley in September or even October. The machine never stops. No more capering round the last sheaf in the field, no weaving of a corn neck or dolly. The old rituals have vanished because farming has transformed its technique, and we have lost touch with the mysteries of husbandry. Yet we are as keenly aware of the weather and seasons as ever. They are obsessive subjects of conversation. How do we reconcile the two sides of the paradox – that while we recognise the forces of Nature, we no longer bother to observe their spiritual significance? It is illogical, but we manage to get by illogically in two ways.

First, those old customs that are still more or less intact owe their survival to a mixture of habit, historical interest, and simple popularity. And if some of them do derive from the pagan past, e.g. fertility rites, then there is sufficient religion in them, in the broadest sense, to deserve remembrance if not actual observance. They are 'sacred'. It is no disrespect to equate them with Christianity, because adoption and adaptation has been the policy of the Church since early times; and so it is no coincidence that the pagan rites of spring and renewal of life run along with the celebration of Christ's resurrection at Easter. Moreover it is often the Church, and the Church only, that records the sequence of farm festivals on saints' and other holy days, which we either take for granted or have just forgotten. Rogation, for example, when we ask for a blessing on the crops at a critical stage of growth; or Lammas in early August, which used to mark the first fruits of the harvest. Reminders are salutary, even if at the time they seem no longer to have practical significance.

Secondly, there are all the country pursuits and events that we enjoy for their own sake and for the sheer pleasure they give us – rambling, bird-watching, riding, fishing, shooting, hunting, etc. and the whole sequence of summer shows and meetings – especially those that involve the horse. They have no ritual significance, but are important too for practical reasons, as they appeal – not only to country people, but to thousands who want to get out of town and away from office and factory, to enjoy exercise and fresh air or seek solitude if they can find it. That moreover is one of the principal objects of National Parks. As there is no religion in 'revels' of this kind, they are – in the technical sense – 'profane' or 'not holy', and I refer to some of them later in this chapter.

SACRED

With one exception – harvest – I am not concerned with customs popular elsewhere in the country or, for that matter, universally observed: such as the making and eating of pancakes on Shrove Tuesday (consuming the leftovers before the start of Lent), or hot cross buns on Good Friday, or bonfires and fireworks on Guy Fawkes Day. Here I have chosen half-a-dozen customs, sacred in origin, which, simply by survival on Exmoor celebrate a very long local tradition.

Plough Sunday

The forerunner of this day, Plough Monday, was intended to signal the return to work after Christmas festivities. What happened was that a crowd of youths hauled a decorated plough round the village, soliciting gifts in money or kind, making a great noise; reluctant donors had their gardens ploughed by way of recompense. Obviously little serious work was done; and so when the custom dwindled away about 75 years ago, it was soon either abandoned altogether or replaced by a more civilised observance on the first Sunday after Epiphany. This survives in one place on the edge of Exmoor, and I am obliged to Terry Squire, churchwarden at Bratton Fleming parish church, for the following account.

> During the early part of the service, members of the Blackmoor Gate Young Farmers Club enter the church carrying the old Huxtable horse plough. The Young Farmers, wearing white overalls, place the plough on the chancel step. The vicar is then invited to come down from the sanctuary and give a blessing, which he does and concludes by laying his hand on the plough with the words, 'God speed the plough', echoed by the congregation. Appropriate hymns are sung and the lessons are usually read by Young Farmers. The plough is

normally stored in a chamber at the foot of the tower and re-appears later in the year, when it forms a centre piece, suitably decorated, at the Harvest Thanksgiving Services during the first week in October.

As someone once said: 'I like the service. If Harvest Festival is "thank you", the Blessing of the Plough is "please".'

Wassail

January is a bleak month. Christmas is over and New Year come and gone. All greetings cards and decorations must be taken down on Twelfth Night, 5 January, at least since the calendar was corrected in 1752. According to the folk diary however, the next day, 6 January, was Old Christmas Day; and Old Twelfth Night, 17 January, was celebrated before the war in orchards all over Exmoor by the custom of wassailing. In Old English 'Wes Hal' was a toast meaning 'Be Hale', much the same as now. The custom almost died out after 1945, but is now enjoying a certain revival. So far as I know it has been observed without a break on the due date at the Butchers' Arms at Carhampton. In the evening the company gathers in the bar and, at about 8.00 pm, is led off by the 'chief gun', accompanied by a band of local musicians into the orchard behind the house, where a bonfire has been lit. I was present in 1990 and it was the landlord, Peter Robinson, who then invited Jim Binding to sing the Wassail Song which runs traditionally as follows:

> Old Apple Tree we wassail thee
> And hoping thou wilt bear
> For the Lord doth know
> Where we shall be
> Till apples come another year
> To bloom well, to bear well
> So merry let us be
> Let every man take off his hat
> And shout out to the old Apple Tree

We all joined in the chorus:

> Old Apple Tree we wassail thee
> And hoping thou wilt bear
> Hats full, caps full, dree bushel bags full
> And a little heap under the stairs
> Hip Hip Hurrah

At this point the two shotguns were fired to scare away the evil spirits, and toast dipped in hot cider placed – by Mrs Robinson – in the branches of the tree for the benefit of the robins, the good spirits. The company was then regaled with hot cider, and more songs sung round the bonfire, before returning to the bar for the rest of the evening. This is a lively contemporary event. Friends from all over the country come every year, some bring musical instruments, some just to sing, and some just to listen and reminisce.

We now move on to the month of May, when two Exmoor customs of long ancestry are celebrated with such vigour and pageantry that they deserve to be described at some length.

The Minehead Hobby Horse

No horsing on Sunday!

Otherwise the Minehead Hobby Horse – its shape, play and antics are vigorously intact. What is this strange beast, what does it do, where does it come from?

Today, essentially, there is only one horse – the Sailors' Horse – though there have been others in the past and fresh ones may yet be foaled; but of them, later.

The Sailors' Horse is indeed an odd animal: about 8 feet long, like a boat upside down, traditionally constructed over a substantial frame of Sedgemoor withy sticks – like those once used for lobster pots – all lashed together with tarred cord. The frame is covered with hessian or sacking – possibly sailcloth in the past, for the smell of the sea is always there – painted all over with multi-coloured roundels and topped with strings of ribbon that hang down over it. Amidships in the frame stands the carrier who bears the whole contraption (weighing well over a hundredweight) on his shoulders; and he also wears a dome-shaped be-ribboned 'head' and a fearsome painted mask, encircled with sheep's wool, that hides his face. Nor is that all. Attached to the 'head' is a mast or tall plume of feathers and rags, that sticks up like part of a Regency head-dress and nods naughtily as the carrier cavorts. Most important is the long rope tail, tipped with a fistful of real cow's tail and bound with ribbon, that runs round the carrier's neck and over his shoulders and then on up to the bow – a practical feature that helps balance the 'boat'.

While allowance must be made for occasional changes in personnel and precise sequence of events from year to year, this is the team and this is what they do:

Horse Carrier. John Leech, Roland Thresher, Neil Miller. Owing to the Horse's weight, these three replace each other every half-hour or so.

Drummers. John Land, Bob Miller.

Melodeon Players. Alan Baker, Peter Creech, Ken Dibble.

There are no Gullivers nowadays. They were men who used to act as a kind of body guard and extract money from bystanders, even entering people's houses; but rough play in the last century (resulting in a death) put an end to them anyway as companions to the Sailors' Horse, though they have appeared with other Horses now and then.

The Horse makes its first appearance on the last day of April (or a day earlier if it is a Sunday), and then proceeds as follows:

May Eve. This is known as 'Warning' or 'Show Night'. The team assembles at about 6.00 pm at the Old Ship Aground inn on the Quay, prances round the town, and shows that it is alive and well to the citizens of Minehead.

May Day. This is a holiday. Assembly is early – 5.00 am – at the inn, where the present landlord, 'Mac', and his family have in recent years heartened the team with rum and coffee; then off they go up to Whitecross by way of Higher Town arriving at 6.00 am, not a moment later, as tradition demands. There the Vicar has been known to say prayers, followed by three cheers for the Horse, a little dance around, and back to the Quay for breakfast.

During the morning the team goes over to Dunster and makes for the Castle. As to what happened not so many years ago, I am indebted to Colonel Walter Luttrell, whose family lived in the Castle from the 14th century until quite recently, for the following account:

> My earliest memories of the Hobby Horse's annual May Day visit go back to when I used to be both terrified and fascinated by his prancing – I was then about 5. The Horse and accompanying drum and accordion, plus a couple of supporters, always arrived at about 10 o'clock and, after the Horse had recovered his breath after climbing

the Steep and the steps up to the Forecourt, we were treated to a 5-10 minute energetic display – ending with great obeisances to my father and mother, or 'paying homage to the Squire', as Alfie Webber (then in charge of the Horse) used to say. Then – off with the exceedingly heavy frame which was propped unceremoniously on its bows against the wall, while the carrier and his supporters downed several mugs of our home-brewed cider. A donation from the family and any house guests who might have been staying at the Castle (the collection invariably went to the Lifeboat) – then down the hill to perform in the village.

Nowadays the team is made no less welcome by the National Trust in the person of the Administrator, who provides refreshment and contributes cash – all before the team tours the village, dances by the Yarn Market and visits the pubs, before making for home. Later that day, after tea, the Horse issues again and tours Minehead, up the Avenue and round the streets, prancing and dancing to the Hobby Horse tunes, bowing to the bystanders and inviting them to contribute a coin through the slit, one on each side of the frame. Sometimes the sequence of events is reversed – Minehead in the morning and Dunster in the evening, but the performance is the same.

May 2nd. Since this is a working day and wages have to be earned, nothing happens until the evening when, in recent years, the team has been accustomed to visit Alcombe and call at the Britannia Inn.

May 3rd. Another working day, so the team assembles on the Quay at about 5.30 pm., prances along the front, calls perhaps at the Hobby Horse inn (formerly the Metropole Hotel), up the Avenue, past Wellington Square, and on up Bampton Street to Cher, where the 'booting' or 'bootee' ceremony takes place. By this time several hundred children and grown-ups have followed the Horse because they know what is coming next. Two of the relief carriers pick out a willing victim, who is held face down between them and receives ten taps from the Horse's bow, accompanied by a shout at each stroke, 'A-one, A-two', etc up to ten. Then the victim holds the hand of the carrier inside the slit and dances with the Horse, avoiding a lash with its tail! The ceremony is then repeated down in the town in Wellington Square until – after suitable lubrication – the Horse returns to the Quay and is stabled for another year. For most of the four days therefore it has had the freedom of the streets; and, after all is over, the takings (less the expenses of maintaining the Horse and the musical instruments) are given, as a rule, to the Royal National Lifeboat Institution.

There are, of course, variations to the proceedings and some interesting explanations. For instance 'booting' may have been connected with 'beating the bounds', which is the interpretation suggested in James Savage's *History of the Hundred of Carhampton* (1830); but there may be earlier references than that, and it is always implied, if not actually stated, that the custom was very old. One explanation is that the Hobby Horse formed part of the annual May Day games, which celebrated the return of spring, starting with a visit up to Bratton Ball to see the sun rise — hence a pagan fertility rite. Another explanation claims connection with the sea, commemorating the arrival of a phantom ship without captain or crew. Colonel Luttrell writes:

> As far as I know, it dates back "for ever". I have always thought that the visit to the Castle may have arisen from my forbears' ownership of Minehead harbour, as the Horse was entirely manned by fishermen and boatmen. Otherwise I have always been brought up on the rather nice idea that it originated from the successful scaring-off of a threatened landing by a Danish raiding party — the local inhabitants prancing about on the foreshore with branches of trees fore and aft to give the impression of mounted cavalry.

Herbert Kille, local historian and journalist, long associated with *The West Somerset Free Press* (and mentor of Jack Hurley who later served as editor and inaugurated the *Notes by the Way* column in that newspaper), wrote a lengthy essay on the Hobby Horse in which he referred to some recollections of old people, probably dating back to the middle of the last century:

> Old Minehead residents, long since passed away, have told of how in their youthful days, many of the inhabitants accompanied the Horse to Whitecross on May morning and, to the music of fiddle, and clarinet and drum, danced a "sort of Maypole dance" but without the Maypole. The prettiest girl among them was chosen to be Queen of the May, and it was part of the ceremonial for the Queen to be placed on the Horse and carried round.

He added:

It seems that, at about the time the Gullivers were abolished, the Hobby Horse lost its snappers. Previously it was armed with a formidable pair of snappers made of wood, covered with a hare's skin and ears, and fixed to the front of the body and operated with a cord by the man inside, which enabled him to catch hold of people and detain them until "largesse" had been paid.

. As to the music:

The music and instruments that accompany the Hobby Horse have changed a great deal over the years. In the early 19th century – as noted – they comprised fiddle, clarinet and drum; but by the end of the century only the drum survived. When the Horse was "split" about the year 1905 into the Sailors' Horse and the Town Horse, the music was supplied by melodeons or accordions and drums, and that is the situation today. The tune or tunes in the last century are now lost, and subsequent developments obscure. The tune that has been used for many years now is simply called *The Hobby Horse Tune*, with improvisations depending on the skill of the musicians.[1]

In fact the musicians today play a variety of renderings and versions taught them by one of the retired melodeon players, George James, who started playing in 1929 at the age of 13 on an instrument bought for him by his father on a day trip to Cardiff, costing 7s.6d. George taught himself to play the basic tune, very slowly at first. Dick Martin, then in charge of the Horse, needed an extra hand and gave George a day to practise and speed it up – which he did – and in due course improved sufficiently to join the regulars at the age of 15. 'Hard work', he said; and they *walked* all the way to Dunster and back, as they do now, and played for a full hour at the Castle. They also visited other 'big houses'.

The Hobby Horse tune is really a medley made up of *Soldier's Joy*, *Sailor come Home, Old Joe, the Boat is tipping over, Little Redwing*, and *Give me Five Minutes More*; but other popular tunes have also been played, for example, *Cock o' the North*, notably at the 'booting' ceremony; and there can be little doubt that contemporary melodies have at one time or another found their way into the repertoire. An interesting survival is a drum of great age, in the possession of John Leech – too old and precious to use, but a prized relic.

Alfie Webber and his brothers managed to keep the Horse

1. Robert Patten: *Exmoor Custom and Song* (Exmoor Press).

alive during the war, and on one occasion at least Alfie turned up at Whitecross alone to prevent any break with tradition. For a short time after the war the team was reduced to three – Horse (Alfie), melodeon (George) and drum (Ken Gubb). Then the custom returned to favour and was recognised afresh for its pageantry and historical interest. Today it is enjoying a vigorous re-surgence and has been watched by thousands on television.

Other Horses

Other Horses have come and gone in and around Minehead: for example, at Dunster (where the Horse was known as the 'Black Devil'), also at Woodcombe, Higher Town, and Bampton Street, each bearing the name of the place where the Horse was kept and promoted. There were several Children's Horses too. However, the best known and longest lived 'alternative' animal was the Town or Show Horse, first recorded in c.1905, when it was accompanied by a bevy of 'Maids'. This Horse was active until the last war and was afterwards revived by Jim Date, who stored it in a shed in Court Green and, with the assistance of Laurie Pidgeon, kept it going until the early 1960s when Laurie took over. Laurie was a busy man – running his own taxi service – but devoted a great deal of his spare time to putting life into the Town Horse. He re-made the withy frame, painted the hessian sacking, and re-introduced the Gullivers – for whom he made the costumes – as friendly attendants and street collectors. Sad to say he died in February 1990 in his 78th year, still happy to talk about his Horse – a few months earlier he had been asked to make one for the Watchet Festival, but by then he was too ill to do the job. Laurie was an artist too, and he kindly left me a painting of the Town Horse and its two musicians.

The two Horses – Sailors' and Town – were rivals, as indeed were all the Horses, and sometimes they clashed, though they would meet without fuss at Whitecross and Cher Steep. But the fact that more than one Horse has made its appearance and flourished for a time is, in my view, a symptom of strength, a tribute to the vitality of this immemorial custom. The Sailors' Horse remains, however, the original character who has never been displaced.

I hope that when the new Minehead Museum comes into its own at Townsend House, the Trustees will consider devoting one room, or part of one, to the Minehead Hobby Horse, its accoutrements and its apparel, displaying it not as something dead and gone, but as living history.

The Hunting of the Earl of Rone at Combe Martin

Unlike the celebrations associated with the Minehead Hobby Horse, continuous – so far as is known – since time immemorial, those relating to the Hunting of the Earl of Rone at Combe Martin were last enacted in the old style in 1837: hence a gap of 140 years or so until their recent reconstruction and revival. It is thought that the custom died when it did for a combination of reasons. First, it had got out of hand; the participants were nearly all reeling drunk by the time they reached the third of the nine village pubs in their itinerary, and were indulging in dangerous horseplay. In fact, one man fell down the steps of a cottage and broke his neck. Secondly, a newly arrived Baptist minister – by name of Winsor – was influential in having the proceedings stopped, because they scandalised him; and this was consonant with the changing mood of the times, which we now dub 'Victorian'. Thirdly, the Established Church was coming out of its long sleep, while Nonconformity – in all its aspects – was in full flow; both underpinned by the rapidly increasing wealth of the middle classes, and influenced by the Puritanism of church and chapel goers. However, the old ceremony was not lost for ever, in that, many years later, it was placed on record from a description given by three old men, who claimed to have witnessed it as children.

Up to 1837 the ceremony was observed on Ascension Day. In the preceding week a party of villagers, including the Fool and several men dressed as Grenadiers, perambulated the parish, collecting donations in aid of their search for the fugitive Earl of Rone. In the afternoon of the Day, they went up to Lady's Wood above the village where a mock fight took place and the Earl was captured. He was then made to ride a donkey, facing towards the tail, and taken back to the village where the whole party was joined by the other stock characters, including a Hobby Horse. At intervals the Grenadiers fired a volley, whereupon the Earl fell off the donkey amid public rejoicing but to the distress of the Fool and the Horse. Healed and revived, the Earl remounted on every occasion, and the procession continued its career down the village.

History and legend do not agree about the Earl and his adventures. In history there was indeed an Earl of Tyrone, Hugh O'Neill

(1540-1616), who fits into the period in which Elizabethan and Jacobean England was oppressing the Irish. In fact O'Neill declared his loyalty to James I, though he and the Earl of Tyrconnel, Rory O'Donnell, were both under suspicion, and duly incurred the hostility of Sir Arthur Chichester, the King's Deputy in Ireland and a member of the well-known North Devon family. On summons to London, presumably to answer charges, the two Earls decided to flee; and so in September 1607 – in company with their families and retainers – they embarked for Spain, but were driven off course by bad weather, eventually landing at the mouth of the Seine in Normandy, where they were kindly received by the King of France, Henry IV. Soon afterwards they travelled on to Spain, where they repaid hospitality by engaging in the Spanish wars in Flanders. O'Neill eventually died in Rome at the age of 76, as a pensioner of the King of Spain and the Pope.

Legend equates Rone with Tyrone and has it that the Earl was shipwrecked in the Bristol Channel, scrambling ashore at a cove, called Rapparee, between Combe Martin and Ilfracombe. The fugitive, the account continues, then made his way along the coast, surviving on water and ship's biscuits. However, 'on information received' or just plain rumour – that there was an outlaw hiding in the woods near Marinscombe (as the village was then called) – a party of soldiers was sent out from Barnstaple and apprehended the Earl in Lady's Wood. Subsequently he was dispatched to Exeter and executed for treason. This, of course, was not true, though the 'Earl' might possibly have been a fugitive from justice, perhaps a smuggler? And so, when the news of the flight of the two Earls percolated through to North Devon, popular opinion may have jumped to the conclusion that this was Tyrone.

The revival of the ceremony started in the 1960s, when W.J. (Buck) Taylor of the North Devon Movement asked the rhetorical question, 'What do you know about the Hunting of the Earl of Rone?' Thereafter, thanks to the researches of the North Devon Folk Troupe – which led to the re-discovery of the text about the 1837 Hunting – Buck Taylor's question was answered: to such good effect that, in 1970, the Troupe was able to perform a reconstruction of the event at the Barnstaple and Ilfracombe Carnivals, and present an 'animated account' on stage at the Queen's Hall, Barnstaple. Four years later, in 1974, when the Combe Martin Carnival was revived, the Hunting episode was added to the procession. This prompted a series of moves – discussions about the nature and future of the Hunting, and the happy circumstance that, in 1975, the new proprietors of the Top George Inn in Combe Martin showed a keen interest in the subject, and provided accommodation for the Horse. In that year, too, the old Hunting was replayed in its own right, before joining the Carnival procession; and so it was decided three years later to separate the two events – so many people were committed to both – and assign the Hunting to the Spring Holiday weekend at the end of May. In 1978, therefore, the ceremony was re-enacted in full at the appropriate date for the first time since 1837. By then an Earl of Rone Council had been set up to direct the ceremony and sustain tradition by, for instance, keeping a register of participants who must be residents of Combe Martin or who otherwise justify inclusion, subject to the Council's invitation.

However, the Hunting today is not totally static in form. On the one hand it sticks to tradition, so far as it is known, and care is exercised as to the choice of persons best suited to play the different characters. For instance, a strong man is needed to carry the Horse, which, like the one at Minehead, is a heavy burden, so that the carriers work in relays; another similarity is its decoration with coloured roundels and ribbons; but its shape differs, at Combe Martin more like a drum than a boat, and the carrier wears a conical hat (and mask), not a square one as at Minehead. Incidentally, the Horse still retains its grotesque proboscis – a pair of 'nappers' or 'snappers' for seizing reluctant donors during the walkabout. On the other hand, fresh elements have found their way or been allowed in – a junior performance by school pupils on one of the days, bell ringing during and dancing in the procession; and music, mostly folk tunes with variations, one called 'The Poor Old Horse' being regarded as the village's own tune.

As to the Fool, the Grenadiers, the Musicians, and, of course, the Hobby Horse itself, they are all stock characters in folk lore, who figure in seasonal festivals and other rural rejoicings. Very likely they are fertility rituals in origin, many of them adopted and tamed by the Christian Church, and transmuted into saints' days and other occasions in the church calendar. There is a large literature on the subject. The local element may concern the Horse's link with the sea – whatever its apparent shape, it is basically a boat – evident in the three Horses along the south-west coast, at Padstow, Combe Martin, and Minehead.

The vitality of the Hunting of the Earl of Rone in its reconstructed form today is undoubted, for it has become a collective village festival – not a weak revival – involving a crowd of participants and onlookers. The sequence of events over the Spring Holiday weekend speaks for itself.

Friday evening. Procession from bottom to top of village.

Saturday day. Junior procession from school around the village

Saturday evening. Barn dance in Town Hall. Music and dances provided by the Earl of Rone band. Presentation of badges.

Sunday afternoon. Procession from the parish limit near Berrynarbor all over the village.

Monday day. Village Revel.

Monday evening. Hunting the Earl. Full procession from London Inn to the beach. Final death of Earl and committal to the sea.

Harvest has Come

The 'sacred' Revel chosen for this part of the chapter is not, of course, confined to Exmoor, though there are local variations in most moorland parishes. It concerns the various events that distinguish the harvest of corn, vegetables and fruit, a sequence that runs from August to October, and includes Michaelmas on 29 September, which is also Quarter Day when rents always used to be paid (many are now) and farms – to be leased or sold – change hands, preceded by sales of live and dead stock. Seasonally, the end of September is the real end of the farming year, and the beginning of the next. Robert Patten refers to Harvest Home as the supper that followed the clearing of the last corn field, taking place in a barn on the farm. It was a Revel in every sense, and several of the old sort as depicted in Thomas Hardy's *Far from the Madding the Crowd* lasted at least into the present century. However, as the custom began to decline, it was progressively replaced by the Victorian Harvest Festival which, surprisingly, was formally issued as a complete church service by royal command as early as 1847. The 'command' took time to percolate widely into the countryside, but it was in the West Country that the new form of the festival was pioneered ⁄ another, rather late, example of Christian adaptation! –⁄

Two of the pioneers were the Rev. R.S. Hawker of Morwenstow in Cornwall, and the Rev. George Denison of East Brent in Somerset. They did so probably – and I quote Patten again – to 'maintain and make more acceptable an ancient and lusty custom, to inject life into a rural culture that was already beginning to decay, and to gain the support of the Nonconformist farmers who had strong ideas about temperance'.

Hawker had started in 1843 by reviving the ancient service of Lammas (first week of August), but held it at a later date in order to embrace the other products of the season; and so it became possible to decorate the church with all the autumn offerings – corn, fruit, flowers, vegetables, etc., in a manner familiar now. Harvest Festival always attracts a large congregation. Even occasional or absolute non-attenders experience a feeling deep down that thanks are due at this time of year to Nature, if not to God, and join in the hymns. On Exmoor, as elsewhere in the countryside, the Festival has long revived its social trappings – a party for children and tea for senior citizens, a supper with entertainment, perhaps a disco with dancing. It is in effect a return to a form of the old-fashioned Revel, though shorter and less crude.

*   *   *   *   *   *   *   *   *   *

We began with Plough Sunday, and so it seems right to close with the plough, the classic symbol of husbandry. Ploughing matches used regularly to take place in mid-October or early November, organised by the local agricultural association. One such was the Williton and Dunster Association, found in 1838, and in latter years the match was held at the Home Farm, Dunster, at the invitation of the President, Colonel Walter Luttrell. After a vigorous career of 135 years, the Association was wound up in 1973, due to lack of entries. Is that an omen?

PROFANE

In dividing rural celebrations into 'sacred' and 'profane', it is not possible to stick to logic all the way. While it could be argued that, historically, almost every sort of event – garden show, point-to-point, carnival, arts festival, etc – may be traceable through all the twists and turns of time to some religious origin, that would be stretching the definition to breaking-point. In any case many contemporary events are of relatively recent date, if not absolutely new, and by their nature, secular. The celebration in 1988 of Watchet's thousandth anniversary of the Danish raid of 988 was not only an innovation but unique. The Minehead and Exmoor Festival was launched as recently as 1962. The Lynton and Lynmouth Festival of the Arts and Countryside took place for the first time in 1990. The Dulverton Carnival, which has flourished, died and been revived more than once, is not of great age. The ordinary village garden show was started – probably in the last century – by the squire, either to encourage his labourers to cultivate the patches of land attached to their tied cottages, or for the particular benefit of allotment holders lately deprived of their common rights; or it may have been an act of self-help by working people, somewhat on the lines of the independent burial and sickness clubs that grew up before the days of National Insurance.

On Exmoor today, garden shows and similar attractions apart, the most popular and characteristic events are those that involve the horse, either as the principal performer or as playing some part in the programme. At Hawkridge in the heart of the moor, the Revel in its present form – now in its 45th year (1990) – is held on August Bank Holiday at Zeal Farm, the family home of John and Mary Pugsley. It is essentially a horse show, for the particular enjoyment of young people: starting with show jumping in the middle of the morning, followed by showing classes and a gymkhana. There is also a dog show, and a series of 'foot' events, capped by a tough $2\frac{1}{2}$ mile cross country race round the farm, starting in the Gymkhana Field, on to Slade Bridge, Anstey Common, Zeal Ford, and back up to the start. Prizes and rosettes are liberally distributed, and there are plenty of added attractions, such as stalls selling ices and white elephants, skittles and other side-shows. Although always held on the Monday following the patronal festival of the parish church, the Revel is basically entirely secular and home made, a true local event, but attended by hundreds of people from far beyond the parish boundary. It yields an annual profit of anything from £800 to £2,000, devoted primarily to the upkeep of the village institutions such as the church and village hall; but without the horse the Revel almost certainly would not take place at all.

Six miles to the east, as the crow flies, is another ancient settlement, Brompton Regis (Kingsbrompton), 800 feet up in a hilly pocket between Brendon Hill to the north and Haddon Hill to the south. The annual show, held in mid-August in the cricket field, is still vigorously supported after some forty years. In character it is similar to the Revel at Hawkridge, but larger and more varied as befits a larger place – with a sheep show, clay pigeon shooting, skittles at the George Inn, and a parade of the West Somerset Foxhounds: all additional to basic components, e.g. the mounted events, foot races (even a ferret race!), dog show, competitions and displays of produce and handicrafts, sections for children, and all the trade stands and sideshows.

Clearly the theme of the horse permeates spring and summer events at all levels all over Exmoor. It would be tedious to draw up a full list, but here is a selection from the 1990 calendar to indicate the range and variety. Point-to-points take place in late April and May, and I spent a glorious sunny afternoon on 26 May at the Dulverton East Foxhounds races high up on Mounsey Hill. On 3 June the West Somerset Polo Club organised an historic revival, playing its first competitive match for forty-five years, on this occasion in a field behind the Carnarvon Arms Hotel, Brushford. The club was founded – some say in 1889, others in 1904 at Allerford, moving to Dunster Lawns in 1910. From that date up to the first world war, and between the two wars, it enjoyed great popularity and was patronised by crack players from all over the world, notably by teams from India. The present (1990) chairman is Kevin Lamacraft of the Knowle Riding Centre, Timberscombe. On 25 July the West Somerset Foxhounds and the Minehead Harriers combined to present their annual Country Fair on Dunster Lawns, a mixed horse and hound show, blessed by good weather and a large attendance.

August was notable for three important events. On the 8th, the 98th Exford Horse Show – founded by Earl Fortescue in 1887 – took place at Court Hill, $1\frac{1}{2}$ miles outside the village. Jointly organised with the Devon and Somerset Staghounds, it is the main annual event for the Exmoor Pony Society: on this occasion with sixteen classes for both in-hand and driven ponies, stallions, mares, geldings, and young stock. Judging began at 8.30 am, and continued all day with classes for hunters and children's ponies, and breeds of sheep. The Staghounds were duly paraded in the afternoon, and the pink coats of the huntsman and the two whippers-in added a blaze of colour to another sunny day. On the 15th a one-day Horse Trial – dressage, showing, and cross country riding – was held on Maurice and Diana Scott's farm on Brendon Hill under the auspices of the British Horse Society. This is the national governing body for 'riding as a sport and recreation'. It is likewise the

authority for the Golden Horseshoe Ride, held earlier in the year in
June – its 100-mile course centred on Exford and taking in two 50-
mile circuits of varied country, extending to Dulverton, Wimbleball
and Dunkery. The BHS is also the parent body of the numerous
Pony Clubs (for children) and Riding Clubs (for adults and teenagers) in Britain, both with plenty of members in West Somerset.

The third event was the Dunster Show which took place on 17
August. It now fulfils a dual purpose, as the prime Exmoor Show
and as one of the best known in the whole of the south-west,
attracting numerous outside entries and over 150 trade stands
offering everything from farm machinery, cattle feed, timber and
clothing to such unusual subjects as prayer books and the protection
of cats. It is of historical interest to read about the first Dunster
Show, held on 2 September 1897, reported in the *The West Somerset
Free Press* as 'an offshoot of the old and popular Dunster Great
Market and Cattle Show'.

> For some years past, a strong opinion has existed among several
> members of the committee that there were great risks in bringing
> animals from a comfortable stall or pen, and exhibiting them in the
> first week in December upon a cold and oftimes wet and windy field
> with nothing more than a hedge for shelter.

Accordingly it was decided:

> . . . that a show of horses and breeding stock should be held early in
> September, and that the December show should be one for fat stock
> only. Mr Luttrell was approached, and he very generously gave the
> society permission to hold the summer show in the beautiful and
> picturesque lawns below the castle.

The 1897 catalogue listed a total of 21 classes – six for cattle, three
for sheep, eight for horses, one for driving, and two for jumping.
First prices were worth £4 or £5, and about 150 supporters
contributed from five shillings to £10 each. In contrast the 1990
catalogue included long lists of vice-presidents, patrons, members,
judges, stewards, officials, and commercial sponsors, with 131
classes of all kinds (some 60 devoted to ponies and horses), first
prizes £20 to £25, surprisingly low compared with 1897. Perhaps
the most telling comparison that struck me on the day was the
disproportionate amount of ground that had to be assigned to car
parking. Although the traffic inside, and to and from the Show was
well controlled, the sheer volume of cars, trailers, horse and trade

trucks, was a pointer to the extreme pressure now being exerted upon all such Shows and which threaten their very existence.

CHAPTER TEN

Access and Tourism

ACCESS

There are three main channels of access into Exmoor: walking or riding over open country, i.e. unfenced grass and heather moorland; across private land by rights-of-way (footpaths and bridleways); and travelling along the usual public highways.

As to open country, there are or should be few difficulties if you happen to be walking or riding over National Park property, where the right of public access is built into tenancy or management agreements; and the same applies to much of the land belonging to the National Trust, Forestry Commission and Crown Estate. Over common land there is *de facto* access only, but long accepted on Exmoor. Elsewhere you have no more right to walk or ride over private land inside the Park than you would outside; and if an owner objects to your presence on grounds of trespass, you are obliged to leave. If, however, he threatens you with legal action, he has to prove damage to obtain redress – normally a problematic business – in fact normally a nonsense, but it is not pleasant to engage in an altercation if you are innocent of evil intent. In practice if you, say, as a walker, behave in a civilised way, keep control of your dog where sheep are grazing, remove litter, and avoid starting a fire, trouble will not arise. Mutual good manners solve most problems, thanks often to the work of the National Park Rangers who, in effect, act as liaison officers between landowners, farmers, and the public. That quarrels still occur is due often to the mistaken belief that all land in a National Park is nationalised – or belongs to Prince Charles, as one lady said on television! – hence the right to

roam, particularly over moorland which, of course, is not cultivated
and does not 'look farmed' – so what's the harm in walking over it?
If you add that to the gut feeling that a British man or woman has
an innate right to enjoy the open countryside, then that goes far to
explain the impulse of the campaign organised by the Ramblers'
Association and expressed on 30 September 1990 as Forbidden
Britain Day. It is difficult not to sympathise, but sympathy alone
will not solve a genuine clash of rights and interests which flow,
ultimately, from the fact that Britain (England and Wales especially)
has a population too large for its landspace. Demand is simply
outrunning supply and, if not controlled, supply will be devastated
or destroyed.

As to rights-of-way, there is a network of footpaths and bridleways all over Exmoor, recorded on the Definitive Map, awarding
legal use to the public and maintained by the Park staff. They
include 258 miles/415km of footpaths (walkers only), 404 miles/
650km of bridleways (walkers and riders), and 40 miles/64km of
'roads used as public paths' (RUPPs), mostly old droves and green
lanes that vehicles rarely or no longer use – still a grey area in terms
of classification. Not long ago a representative of the Trail Riders
Fellowship, formed to protect the interests of 'recreational motor-
cyclists' consulted the National Park Committee. He pointed out
that his members made use of RUPPs and were legally entitled to do
so, and he wanted to ensure their preservation. As the Fellowship is
regarded as a respectable well-organised body, aiming to provide
young people with opportunities to enjoy riding their machines in
an orderly fashion, would they be welcome on Exmoor? I did not
hear the official reply when the question was put, but in my view it
has to be 'No', for there can be no possible accommodation in an
area whose prime purposes are to protect the landscape and its wild
life, and enable the public to enjoy solitude and natural beauty.
Nonetheless, the uncomfortable fact is that a motorcyclist can ride
his machine over any right-of-way (even footpaths) if the landowner
agrees. This makes for problems for the ENPA, and is one more
symptom of pressure upon the resources of the Park, and to which
I shall refer again later. There is a fourth category of right-of-way
on Exmoor, i.e. 25 miles/40km of 'permissive' paths which owners
allow the public to use. As these are without statutory status, they
are vulnerable, though no case has yet occurred of permission being
withdrawn, and the ENPA is always on the look-out for alternative
are/ routes. Finally, as already mentioned, there all all those paths

negotiated by the ENPA under management agreements – an important addition to the network, for example at Glenthorne, where exploratory footpaths have been almost doubled in length.

The fact that rights-of-way are maintained by the ENPA staff is a great asset: not only keeping the paths clear of seasonal growth, but coping with drainage, obstructions and repairing over a hundred footbridges, and keeping abreast of waymarking and signposting – all to a standard far higher than is usually found outside the Park boundaries. Incidentally, signposting (and waymarking) is a subject that has attracted criticism, mainly that it has been overdone to the extent that – short of a sudden hill mist that can lead you round in circles – you can generally find your way across the moor without recourse to a compass or even a map, simply by following the marks and the posts; and that this diminishes the mystery and wildness. There is some truth in this; but from my own experience as a young man walking in Europe, notably in Germany where waymarking was normal practice long before the Second World War, I found a dab of colour on a stone both helpful and unobtrusive. Moreover the more walkers that come to Exmoor, the more such signs are needed, if only to prevent intrusive wandering in our small National Park, of which two-thirds are productive farmland, and in which established rights-of-way are the agreed means of passage to the public. At the same time the walker or rider is protected by the Rights of Way Act 1990, which obliges an owner or tenant to restore the surface of any path, disturbed by ploughing or other field work, and lays down clear rules about the temporary diversion of a path and keeping its line clear of crops.

Rights-of-way, vital as they are for the quiet enjoyment of the countryside, are not so sacred that they can never be altered or adjusted *pace* the Ramblers' Association. Because a particular path, originally, say, a shortcut for labourers, has for years passed through a farmyard – that should not preclude it being re-routed by mutual agreement and at minimum cost, if it has now become a nuisance. Dogmatic rigidity generates conflicts, best avoided if no principle is at stake. Rights-of-way are a continuing commitment, subject to the needs and uses of the times, particularly in a National Park which is obliged by law to define and maintain them. For these reasons the ENPA plans to adopt the new terminology recommended by the Countryside Commission, viz. National Trails, Regional Routes, Local Walks and Rides, and Parish Paths, the last two catering for the majority of visitors and residents. The first two are long-distance paths. Exmoor has only one National Trail – the coast path that runs for some 35 miles between Minehead and Combe Martin, and is part of the South-West Peninsula Coast Path that terminates at Poole in Dorset, a total distance of over 500 miles. A magnificent route, the Exmoor section is fully described in an illustrated booklet published by the ENPA. There are two Regional Routes – the Tarka Trail, so-called after the adventures of Henry Williamson's otter, but which lies mostly outside the Park; and the Two Moors Way – projected some 25 years ago but not so well known as it deserves – which comes up from Dartmoor and enters Exmoor at Badlake Moor Cross, before running north for some 24 miles up to Lynmouth by way of Tarr Steps, Withypool, Exe Head, and Cheriton.[1]

The Exmoor Greenway

Looking back over its career as a National Park since designation in 1954, Exmoor has been well served as regards access on foot and on horseback, although the ENPA missed a golden opportunity in 1970 when it failed to follow up a report, published by the Exmoor Society on the possibility of converting part of the Taunton-Barnstaple railway line (axed by Dr Beeching in 1966) into a right-of-way. With the aid of a substantial grant from Butlin's of Minehead (thanks to the interest of Paul Winterforde-Young, personal advisor to Sir William Butlin), the Society commissioned a feasibility study from DART, the research unit at Dartington administered by Michael Dower, son of John Dower, and the author of *The Challenge of Leisure: The Fourth Wave* (Architectural Press). Hardly had the work begun when the Taunton-Minehead branch was closed down, and so it was agreed to include that line in the study too. By that time all the track west of East Anstey on the Taunton-Barnstaple had been sold off, but it was felt that the 22-mile stretch from Norton Fitzwarren offered many attractions, including a possible link with the Two Moors way. Furthermore British Rail had agreed not to offer any further sections of the line until the DART report had been completed and considered.

While his surveyor, Ross Gray, was at work, Michael Dower and other members of his staff consulted some forty organisations with

---

1. Its route is traced by Dennis Martin in *Exmoor Review 1990*, and in a Guide published by the Devon Ramblers' Association

potential interest in the project, and drew up a list of five types of recreational use – walking, riding, and cycling; picnicking and other 'passive' day activities; scenic driving by horse-drawn vehicle; field studies; and use of campsites, caravans and other accommodation. They concluded that all these uses were viable, especially for riding (estimating that 12,000 riders and 7,000 horses 'lived' within five miles of one or both of the lines) and for field studies, since the lines cut across varied geological strata and gave ready access to a wide variety of habitats. DART worked out alternative treatments for the lines and suggested three – a basic 'greenway'; a linear country park; and a variation on the latter, with a number of 'nodes', i.e. access to car parks, toilets, refreshment facilities, stables, etc, mostly sited at disused stations. DART also investigated the benefits that might accrue to the local economy and pointed out that it might well save local authorities having to make alternative provision elsewhere, in view of increasing pressure for recreation in or near the National Park. Finally tables were supplied, both for the Taunton-Barnstaple and the two lines together, setting out capital and annual running costs.

The Exmoor Greenway report was an exhaustive and professional study that provided the authorities with a piece of investigation that they should have undertaken themselves, had they had the initiative. It was submitted to the Countryside Commission and Devon and Somerset County Councils, distributed to numerous organisations, and widely publicised. In the end it was turned down as being 'financially unrealistic' (the figures of cost make laughable reading now). However, two crumbs of comfort emerged. One, a large one, was the revival of the Taunton-Minehead line as the West Somerset Railway, now popular and financially successful. The other, a small one, was the purchase by Somerset County Council of a short stretch of track from a point east of Langaller Bridge, Brushford, then westward for about $1\frac{1}{2}$ miles to Nightcott. This has now been recorded on the definitive rights-of-way map and is well used – but it is a sad little residue of the original bold plan.

The Incline

It is therefore greatly to be hoped that a future opportunity will be grasped and of similar significance. This concerns the possible conversion into a right-of-way of the old West Somerset Mineral Railway Incline or embankment which runs for about $\frac{3}{4}$ of a mile, and a gradient of 1 in 4, from Comberow up to the former winding house on top of Brendon Hill at O.S.024344. A striking example of Victorian engineering, it was a gigantic effort completed between 1858 and 1861. It carried a two-track cable line for hauling up empties and letting down trucks loaded with iron ore (mined between Raleighs Cross and Gupworthy) to the rail head at Comberow, and thence to Watchet harbour for shipment for smelting in South Wales. Mining ceased in 1883, but the railway continued in use until 1898. After a short and unsuccessful revival in 1907-10, the rails were lifted in 1919, and all the land and buildings sold in 1924. Dereliction followed, but all the mine adits and shafts were sealed and very few signs remain of the once-vigorous mining community.

The Incline is a monument in itself and remains remarkably intact. Part is grown over, but not impenetrably so. The two bridges (one halfway, the other at the bottom), the culverts, and the embankment itself, abandoned more than eighty years ago, are basically in good order. To convert it into a right-of-way would not only be feasible – what a challenge for a team of young volunteers! – but a delightful footpath in magnificent scenery and a useful link for walkers wither way, up or down. Whether it would be possible to extend the path from Comberow down to Watchet, combine the highway with stretches of the old railway bed (with diversions as necessary) remains to be seen; likewise along the ridge to Gupworthy. In any event the clearance of the Incline would come first, together with the restoration of the winding house, which still contains some of the original fittings (e.g. some of the large bolts anchoring the iron frames that supported the winding drums, and a timber baulk built into the wall to act as a shock absorber), and would serve well as an industrial museum and information or interpretation centre, with parking close by. The full history of the WSMR, the Incline, and the mining is told in the *West Somerset Mineral Railway and the story of the Brendon Hills Iron Mines* by Roger Sellick (David & Charles), also in *The Old Mineral Line*, an illustrated account with a shorter text by the same author (Exmoor Press). The Incline is also described, with colour and black-and-white photographs, by M.H. Jones in the *Exmoor Review 1987*. Recently the whole subject of restoration has been explored in a preliminary study, entitled *The Brendon Hill Enterprise*, by Dr. Glyn Court.

A serious problem for rights-of-way on Exmoor is erosion induced by over-use. Too many feet, too many hooves. Horses can make bridleways literally unusable, while riding schools are often guilty of wearing away the same few tracks with follow-my-leader strings of young riders. The most obvious example of erosion is on Dunkery, but it is not unique. Riverside paths and tracks over common land are suffering too, and the ENPA is engaged in a rights-of-way survey in order to assess what needs to be done. Happily the situation is not so horrific as on the Pennine Way; but we may yet see helicopters hovering over Dunkery, carrying blocks of stone to rebuild the cairn on the summit, and pave the track up from Dunkery Gate.

TOURISM

Access by car or other vehicle is far from satisfactory, even though Exmoor has not yet been invaded on the scale that afflicts Lakeland and the Peak District. The ENPA aims to 'absorb people without intrusion in the landscape' and draws comfort – mistakenly in my view – from statistics that seem to indicate that the 'number of visitors to Exmoor overall has changed little since the early 1970s', despite the construction of the M5 motorway and the North Devon Link Road, plus the proliferation of brown enamel notices on these and other highways directing motorists towards Exmoor.

Statistics of this kind are often suspect. I am inclined to believe that the number of 'staying' visitors, i.e. those accommodated in hotels, farm houses and guest houses, etc, has not significantly increased, in contrast to those who cater for themselves or go to camping and caravan sites, though accommodation even of this kind is limited. That means that day visitors account for most of the increase in summer traffic over the past decade, only too evident in the village streets and along the moorland roads. One reason is that Exmoor is small and accessible and easy to enjoy without having to stay overnight. Nearly everybody comes by car, coach or motor cycle, even if they intend to walk or ride a horse. The majority however are car-bound. They drive around the beauty spots, pull off the road along stretches of moorland, take out chairs and rugs, picnic, admire the view, go for short walks, and let the children romp in the heather.

That is as it should be, and it fulfils one of the objects of the National Park. To provide for car-bound enjoyment of this kind, the ENPA has constructed no fewer than 27 car parks and laybys 'ranging in size from the larger more formal ones as at Tarr Steps, to the many informal parking areas and laybys providing access to walks and viewpoints throughout Exmoor'. Comparable facilities are offered by other organisations, such as the Forestry Commission and National Trust, also by local authorities and private enterprise: so that, in total, the amount of parking space in and around the National Park is considerable.

Nonetheless, saturation is only a matter of time. The unpalatable fact is that the provision of parking, allied to the policy of attracting visitors to a handful of 'honeypots', e.g. Malmsmead, Tarr Steps, Lynmouth, Simonsbath, *et al.*, equipped with toilets and information boards, is at best a holding operation. Tourist traffic grows in direct proportion to the facilities available, but when saturation point is reached, the problem has to be solved – either by finding more room and more facilities, or by doing nothing. In the first case the time will come – and how far off is it? – when space for parking, without harm to the environment, will simply run out. At Dunster, for example, the large car park at the northern entrance to the village is nearly always full in the summer months, and a new one is being considered for the opposite (Timberscombe) end. That too will fill up. These two parks, another small one in Park Street, the very limited space in the middle of the High Street, the Castle park owned by the National Trust, and whatever other slots are available to the residents – all add up to a grotesquely large total in terms of space when related to the needs of shops and dwellings and the community at large. Dunster is over-run, and finding yet more space for cars will merely add to the congestion and frustration, and to the disruption of local life. Similar symptoms apply in varying degrees to Dulverton, Lynton/Lynmouth, Porlock and Combe Martin. If, however, nothing is done, saturation may automatically reduce the pressure, so that tourists will fight shy and cease to come in such large numbers, at any rate at the peak periods; but that admittedly is a counsel of despair.

Out on the moor, the problem so far is, of course, less intense. Even so, the day will come when the roads will become so heavy with holiday traffic that car owners may take the law into their own hands, disregard the 15-yard limit for pulling off the highway, drive around over open country and park wherever their cars will take them. Indeed this is already happening. Four-wheel-drive vehicles and motor cycles are capable of travelling cross country over most of Exmoor. Farmers use all-terrain vehicles or tractors to tend their sheep wherever they are; while a number of hunt followers, with permission of the landowners, cruise over open moorland in the same way. If such 'privileged' people carry on 'legitimately' in this manner, how can other members of the public, including trail riders, be expected to refrain from following their example? The pass has already been sold. That means that unless preventive and effective action is taken, large areas of the moorland will be scarred and the sward destroyed. Digging anti-vehicle ditches at selected points is effective but has its limitations, for obviously it is impossible to line every road with traps of this kind. The alternative is to impose exemplary fines whenever a 'pirate' can be caught and identified, but who will do the catching?

Cars are inseparable from tourism, and tourism generates business and money. The present economy of Exmoor largely depends on it, seasonal though it is: whether it be accommodation, or food and drink, or sales of other goods and services in shops, studios, and other outlets in the villages and small towns in or near the National Park. The declared principle of the ENPA is, not so much to initiate enterprise, as to guide it so as both to benefit local communities and prevent it from damaging the special character of the Park – in other words that it should be 'compatible with conservation', which must always take precedence. To this end the ENPA co-operates with the tourist agencies, notably the Exmoor Tourist Advisory Group (ETAG), which succeeded the Exmoor Tourism Development Action Programme launched in 1985.

In all these matters, however, the ENPA is walking a tight rope. The development of Information Centres at Dulverton, Dunster, Lynmouth, Combe Martin and County Gate, designed as the name implies to answer enquiries and impart information about the Park, but which also conduct brisk and profitable business in the sale of merchandise and a variety of publications (including its own excellent series on rights-of-way) about Exmoor, veers very closely to promotion as opposed to interpretation. The point is emphasised by the issue of the *Exmoor Visitor*, the free National Park news-paper, that enjoys an estimated readership of half-a-million, and contains a mixture of articles, a programme of guided walks, and pages of advertisements about accommodation, places to visit, and a mass of other commercial information. The inference is obvious. The more publicity, the greater the problems in containing the invasion that has already all but overwhelmed some of the other National Parks, where overcrowding and erosion have become twin nightmares. Appetite grows with eating. It is a classic dilemma.

Tourism in whatever form earns money, and that is important for the local economy, but there are snags. One is that it is seasonal and does not therefore provide the permanent employment, alternative to farming and forestry, which is so badly needed on Exmoor. Secondly, it attracts *entrepreneurs* – some of them professional thieves who rifle cars at the beauty spots! – who come in from the outside, cash in on the summer trade, and return from whence they came. Thirdly, as explained in a paper written for the Exmoor Society by Anne and Malcolm MacEwen in April 1986, the language of marketing (employed by the tourism programme) is demeaning to Exmoor and its visitors, who are treated as objects for exploitation:

> The natural and cultural resources of Exmoor are represented as 'products', the values of which are calculated in terms of their potential for generating income and which have to be 'marketed' in order to realise their financial potential . . . But when it comes to identifying the distinctive characteristics that have potential for tourism development, it selects 'the Lorna Doone connection', regional foods, crafts, and countryside activities, by which it means hunting, shooting and fishing. Walking, which is what a much larger proportion of those visiting Exmoor love doing, is not mentioned.
>
> The programme fails to point out that the real 'distinctive character' of Exmoor is that its semi-wild open country offers local people and visitors an opportunity to disengage from the pressures that impel their daily lives and to experience the restorative features of moorland and woods, cliffs and sea and all the many features of the natural and man-shaped world to be found in the National Park. Exmoor, in short, offers outstanding opportunities for informal recreation . . . that is, drives, outings, picnics, long walks, rambles or hikes of more than 2 miles . . . Yet the programme mentions Exmoor's national park status only in terms of providing 'a good market image'.

It is calculated that, already, tourism employs more people and generates more income than farming and forestry, the primary sources of work on Exmoor. That would seem to justify its expansion on economic grounds alone, so long as it stays within bounds and does not turn into Frankenstein's monster. The ENPA believes it can cope with the problem through education in the broadest sense: by enlarging the scope of the Information Centres, by continuing to organise guided walks and talks, by expanding the work of the Ranger service, by encouraging the visits of school groups, and by co-operating with the other interested organisations. That is the present position. The question is – can it be sustained and will it succeed?

The best answer, at the moment, is supplied in a speech to the International Council on Monuments and Sites (ICOMOS), given on 28 March 1990, by Angus Stirling, Director-General of the National Trust, from which I have taken the following passages:

> In the Lake District, in the Peak District and in Snowdonia tourism is now creating problems of huge complexity, eroding the ancient trackways, and generating more traffic, roads, hotels, time-share complexes, marinas, leisure facilities, signs, car parks – in short an ever-increasing incursion into the countryside of urban amenities which tend to conflict with the very qualities which draw people to travel in the first place.
>
> Conservation must be twinned with tourism. They should be two sides of the same coin, and the remit of all tourist agencies and tourist promotion schemes should reflect that marriage . . . if tourism is to fulfil its potential in buttressing, rather than undermining, local culture and heritage, then the infrastructure which supports it should be provided for the specific benefit of the residents of the area as well as for the tourists . . . Nowhere is the dichotomy clearer than in the upland moors where unrivalled scenery provides recreation for millions, but sheer numbers threaten the ability of sheep farmers to conduct their daily business.
>
> There is no object of a traveller's curiosity, be it a city, an art gallery, a church, a country house, an island, a beach, a river, a nature reserve or even a mountain range that does not have its own threshold beyond which visitor numbers will begin to take physical toll of structure, fabric, and ultimately the spirit of the place . . . Long before the threshold of destruction is reached, there is another threshold: beyond it visitor numbers will be such as to diminish the quality of experience for everyone; and, more importantly, the quality of life of the local community will begin to deteriorate. These principles apply equally to buildings and to the natural environment.

Exmoor – take note!

CHAPTER ELEVEN

Living and Working on Exmoor

When I and my family started farming at Brushford in 1947, the impact of the war was evident in all sorts of ways. No mains electricity to the farm, overgrown hedges, a chronic lack of machinery, so that we had to rely either on the 'War Ag' pool (very chancy), or on picking up worn-out items of equipment at rip-off prices at farm sales. It was the same story all over Exmoor, and much worse on some of the moorland farms, where horses and putt carts were still in use, and such things as seed barrows and stone rollers, now only to be found in rural life museums, if found at all. Only the main roads were in fair order – the by-road to Nightcott (home of the blacksmith) was as narrow and twisting as a corkscrew (it still is) and, after rain, as rough as a river bed. Brushford had several businesses – some, but not all, now gone – a market garden, a milk round supplied by a handful of cows grazing round the village, a shop, a garage, a coal depot and builder's merchant, the Carnarvon Arms Hotel, a railway station and goods yard with station master and staff, and a regular train service, which brought the newspapers, and took away our milk churns and the children to secondary school – until the line was axed by Dr. Beeching in 1966. Then there were the institutions – a well-attended primary school, village hall, parish church with resident vicar and (at one time) two teams of bell-ringers.

Local society was almost as hierarchical as it had been before the war. Most farms were occupied by long-established families, such as our two neighbours, the Hodges at Upcott, and the Yandles at Riphay. The three principal landowners were the Amorys at Hele Manor, the Herberts at Pixton, and Colonel Harrison at Combe.

The Colonel, a bachelor of means, had some 300 acres of indifferent farmland and amenity woods, with a very long drive leading up to his beautiful and historic house. Before the war, the outside staff had consisted of a bailiff and four farm workers, two gardeners, two grooms, and a chauffeur; inside the house there was a butler, cook, and at least three maids. In the 1950s the total staff was reduced to half-a-dozen, but the Colonel (who also owned a considerable acreage up on the moor) kept it all going until his death during the great freeze of 1962-3.

John Coleman-Cooke has written of life in Simonsbath in the same period, at which time he was living in the Lodge (now the Simonsbath House Hotel): of the shepherds who tied up their Exmoor ponies outside the inn where they drank rough cider.

> The same ponies carried men – and sometimes women – to weddings, funerals, near-by markets, and regularly to hounds and church. Their wilder equine cousins, free ranging and unbroken, trooped down for shelter on wild nights into the village . . . But that was before Brendon Two Gates had a cattle grid. It was also pre-mains electricity, pre-TV, pre-Lynmouth flood; there was only a trickle of motorists, the school had two teachers, and most villagers kept their fires permanently alight with peat.
>
> With no TV, no regular bus service, and with only a few families owning cars, people foregathered for communal entertainment. Amateur theatricals were popular. The plays had to be very carefully chosen. Too much emphasis on death, or on a plot that laid unhealthy stress on a son or daughter in serious trouble, or a husband or wife misbehaving with somebody else's partner – such happenings (when dramatised) could – and sometimes did – shake the very foundations of the community, and present insuperable problems in casting. The love scenes were especially tricky. If you didn't throw yourself into them with zeal they seemed wooden, and if you did the rumours began . . .
>
> Up to 1952, when TV and the Lynmouth flood happened on the same day, Simonsbath seemed a place apart, rich in community life, strengthened and not weakened by the war, with not a shadow of uncertainty on the high, encircling skylines.[1]

As the 1950s slipped into the 1960s and decade followed decade right up to the present day, the pattern of rural life on Exmoor

1. *Exmoor Review*, 1969.

began to alter, slowly at first, then gathering momentum, switching from a semi-self-supporting economy to a semi-absentee one, or something very near it. At one time you could rely on buying necessities – food, groceries, newspapers, toiletries, and much else, as well as having a post office, in settlements – some quite small – all over Exmoor. As the years passed and cars became common, many housewives got the habit of driving into their local town to stock up once a week at the local supermarket (or its predecessor, the chain store), abandoning the village shop other than for daily papers and the odd item – a packet of cigarettes or a carton of milk – when they had run out. They did not set the cost of petrol against the cheapness of convenience, and anyway it was fun to go to town, see friends, and spend more money. And where cars killed the buses, some large stores started running a bus service of their own for the convenience of customers without a car.

The extraordinary thing is how determined some village shop-keepers have been to survive. The situation is vividly illustrated in an article in the *Exmoor Review 1986* written by Michael Deering who has kept the Post Office Stores at Oldways End, East Anstey since 1974. The article is so full of first-hand information and informed comment that it deserves to be read in full, but the following will give some of the flavour:

> The private trader has very little buying power . . . The giants can buy very cheaply from the manufacturers, so much so that the private trader often has to pay more for an item than the public may pay in a giant store . . . we are insulted by the person who gives us a sound telling-off for making fantastic profits, robbing people with high prices, taking advantage of pensioners, etc. She does not, of course, understand present day trading and thinks that shops can all buy at the same price and nothing will convince her otherwise.
>
> However, we are still expected to provide when the weather is bad, after hours or at weekends when people run out, to pass messages, cash cheques, advise on this or that, distribute medicines from the local surgery and 'vet', help to fill out forms and witness documents, deliver to those ill or housebound, take in children off the school bus when mother can't meet it, quietly give extended credit to those in trouble – and there is always one – and get let down, put those looking for jobs in touch with potential employers, keep an eye on the elderly living alone, and act as father confessor to the troubled, indigent and lonely, and co-operate actively with the police and

emergency services and public authorities, all for free. But then that's part of the fun of running a village shop.

Neither the shop on its own, nor the post office on its own, could provide a living today for a single person, even assuming they owned it outright. Together they just cover the overheads or provide for one's day-to-day living, not both.

In fact Michael Deering is an established photographer, and his wife a dressmaker, and these two activities are the real source of their income. Sadly since the article was published, the shop at Oldways End has given up all lines except newspapers and the post office. Recently residents of Wootton Courtenay have combined to buy their village shop which was on the point of extinction: an admirable effort that may point the way forward for other villages on Exmoor in a similar situation, especially as it involved support from the Rural Development Commission. At first sight, however, it does not necessarily solve the problem of running the shop at a profit.

*   *   *   *   *   *   *   *   *   *   *

Even large villages, with a population in excess of 1,000 are under pressure economically and socially. The 'Spar' organisation, notably in the West Country, has helped save the general store in several places, the owner benefiting from collective buying, delivery and publicity; and there is the by-product of part-time work for villagers (ladies, mostly) serving customers. Other shops keep going because of special lines, e.g. delicatessen, or because they enjoy a reputation for quality and service, not normally available in the larger units. Even so basic businesses such as the butcher, baker, greengrocer, ironmonger, shoe shop, etc., and even the post office, are all under threat on Exmoor. Several inns have disappeared, and in the remoter places the landlord may be out all day as a 'rep' or van driver, while his wife looks after the bar.

Nor is that the end of the story. The social fabric of the village has been undermined by the loss of institutions – e.g. the closure of primary or first schools (with less than c.30 pupils), though rear-guard actions have been fought successfully here and there, as at Winsford; the conversion of chapels into houses, as at Withycombe where the congregation had withered; and, for a similar reason, the making redundant of the charming little church (now being restored) at Elworthy. At Withiel Florey, on the other hand, determined action by a handful of families in a widely scattered parish saved the day; and at Brompton Regis the chapel was likewise rescued by a combination of intense local effort and unexpected help from the outside. But these are exceptions.

The problem on Exmoor, as in other sparsely populated parts of the countryside, is essentially an *economic* one. Without remunerative work, either on the spot or within a reasonable distance of home, the viability of the village as a living cross-section of class, age and income will founder. The decline of the village economy has been going on a long time, indeed ever since the majority of rural crafts and workshops were extinguished by the Industrial Revolution: for it was the 'industrial' element in village life that provided work for those not engaged in shops or domestic service, or in the primary employments of farming and forestry. This left a vacuum that has never been adequately filled, not even by the growth of the tourist trade which poses problems of its own. Tourism – as already emphasised – is seasonal, lasting seven or eight months at best, usually less. Visitors spend their money mostly on accommodation, food, drink, souvenirs, and – hopefully – the products of local craftsmen. They spend far less proportionately on everyday merchandise and services that keep a village afloat all through the year. Reliance on tourism is not only a gamble, but by its nature encourages fashions in enterprise that often prove temporary and, not infrequently, end in bankruptcy. Antique shops, for example, flourished in the most unlikely places in the 1960s and 70s, and were jockeying basic businesses (of the kind mentioned) out of key premises in large villages and small towns. That particular fashion has now been deflated.

Another fashion has been the over-supply of estate agents, which raises the fundamental question of housing in villages. The invasion of the West Country, Exmoor included, by commuters, 'tireds' and 'retireds', and the special attractions of the National Park for holiday 'lets' and second homes unoccupied for most of the year has have reduced the stock of houses for the truly resident population. In 1975 William Rayner noted that:

> Porlock is in danger of becoming reserve for prosperous elderly couples, a middle-class enclave more concerned with dreams taken from calendar photographs than with the working life of a real community.[1]

1. *Exmoor Review, 1975.*

The invasion has also inflated property prices to a level at which it has become impossible for young couples and 'lower income groups' to find a home, even though work may be available. In addition there is a lack of rented accommodation, due partly to the purchase of Council houses by their occupants, and partly to the absence of new house building by local authorities. Speculative estates on the edge of villages, however modest the houses, have solved nothing owing to price. It has been left to Housing Associations to try to fill the gap, and a start has been made with low cost homes, built or planned, at Timberscombe, Brompton Regis, Luccombe, Luxborough, Wheddon Cross and Exford; but this falls far short of the need, especially if new village enterprises are contemplated.

A key difficulty is the price of land allotted for housing, so high that it usually prohibits the construction of affordable homes. Two solutions have been advanced by the Government. One is to increase the amount of money available to Housing Associations, which is all to the good. The other is to authorise low cost building on sites that would not normally receive planning permission. This has potential disadvantages, mainly that it might undermine planning control and damage the environment in those very areas where the expansion of villages needs to be restricted – in short it would encourage sporadic development to start all over again.

A third idea has been proposed by the CPRE which would seem to avoid this pitfall:

> Our solution is to reform the Use Classes Order and introduce a new *social use class* for housing. This would allow authorities to identify a proportion of the land they earmark for housing development to meet the needs of those unable to afford housing on the open market, and to grant separate planning permissions for affordable or open market housing, as they do for different kinds of offices and shops.
>
> A key function of the planning system is to control the use of buildings as well as their physical development, or alteration. Thus, changing an office into a newsagent's requires planning permission in the same way as constructing a house.

In short, a new new social use class for housing would allow a local authority, not only to earmark sites and control planning permissions, but once implemented:

> . . . land prices would be controlled at levels which allowed the development of affordable housing by local authorities, housing

associations and the private sector, since the more restrictive planning controls over development would exercise a key influence over the negotiations for the sale of land.[1]

*   *   *   *   *   *   *   *   *   *

A sad feature of almost all new housing on Exmoor and all over West Somerset and North Devon is its dismal design. Although the predilection for concrete boxes has at last evaporated, it has been replaced by a no less dismal return to so-called traditional architecture, which it apes and falsifies. This is not simply a matter of cost. The average new house looks mean or fussy, with 'eyebrow' dormers and plastic coated window frames; it lacks the natural proportions and textures of vernacular building, without displaying any of the balance and sensitivity of good contemporary design. It is, in short, tasteless, and that is because the average English builder – worse in Wales – simply does not recognise taste. He is like someone whose palate has been atrophied by a surfeit of chips and vinegar. This is a national disgrace, only too evident if you look at rural building abroad. A glaring example of bad taste in recent building can be found (only too obvious alas) in the houses and bungalows in Hollam Park, Dulverton, which do indeed resemble 'carbuncles on the face of an old friend'.

It is true that, here and there on Exmoor, better ideas about elevation, proportion, and the use of appropriate materials and textures are beginning to emerge, despite the lack of a consistent vernacular style, as compared, for example, with a region such as the Cotswolds. However, whereas the ENPA offers advice on design to developers, such advice, if not accepted or settled by negotiation, may lead to an appeal which is time consuming and expensive, and may end in compromise in terms of taste – unless the proposal is so unsuitable that it has to be rejected altogether. Therein lies the pith of the problem, for although good taste is subjective, it is immediately recognisable: so that a well-designed house – standing there for all to see – will be far more compelling than any collection of rules and regulations, and will breed healthy offspring. At the same time, a new design guide for Exmoor is long overdue – the last one, *Building in Exmoor National Park*, was issued in 1977 – and it should aim to raise the whole level of contempary design in the National Park. If the planners do not set their sights sufficiently

1. *Home Truths* (CPRE/CHiCL, 1990).

high, and the planning committee allows itself to be fobbed off with the second best, then we shall continue to inflict mediocre buildings on the face of Exmoor, which by its very nature, deserves the best. In essence, as a planning authority the ENPA has a double duty: first, to exercise strict control over development in open country and to ensure the individual character of each village and hamlet; secondly, to exert positive guidance which aims at nothing less than excellence as regards the structure and appearance of all new building on approved sites.

Withypool

If, as I hold, jobs are the foundation stones of local society, how can this yardstick be applied to Exmoor, which was designated in 1954 as a National Park for the beauty of its landscape and the value of its wild life? First, let us look at a typical small Exmoor village, Withypool, immortalised by Walter Raymond in his *The Book of Simple Delights*, published by Hodder & Stoughton in 1906. Raymond came from a Yeovil glove-making family but, tiring of town business, turned to writing and giving entertainments about Somerset life, found his way to Withypool in 1905 and rented a cottage there at a shilling a week for about ten years. He is remembered by Fred Milton of Weatherslade who, as a young lad, used to pass the time of day with him before going into school. Raymond was a friendly soul, had a reddish face flanked by two haystacks of white hair, and for a time ran a reading room for teenagers 'to keep them out of the pub'.

Kelly's Directory of 1910 tells us a lot about Withypool in Raymond's day. The lord-of-the-manor was a member of the Notley family. The living – held since 1881 by the Rev. Rowland Newman – was a chapelry annexed to the rectory of Hawkridge. In addition to a stipend of £400 p.a. the incumbent had the use of 605 acres of glebe. The gentry included Miss Darbyshire who lived at Holmbush and Mrs Hamilton at 'The Palace' (then a newish house near the church). Abraham Tudball was sub-post-master (letters arrived from Taunton at 10.15 am and were dispatched at 2.55 pm), and he kept a boarding house as well. Miss Edith Macdonald was mistress of the public elementary school built in 1876 (under the new Education Act) for £970 to hold 70 children, average attendance 23. Miss Macdonald had arrived in 1907, married a local farmer and stayed 32 years at the school. John Quartly was sexton and, at the

age of 90, had been written up in the popular press as 'the oldest
working sexton in England'. Under 'Commercial', John Court kept
the Royal Oak Inn, 'with good accommodation for sportsmen and
tourists', among whom must be counted R.D. Blackmore who
wrote part of *Lorna Doone* under its roof. John Court was also the
Thursday carrier to Dulverton, and William Hooper the Saturday
one to South Molton. Withypool had four harvests a year – turf,
whortleberries (thanks to the Common nearby), hay and corn. The
farming families included the Miltons, Rawles, Williams, and
Dascombes. John Brayley operated the mill at Garliscombe on
Pennycombe Water, was active as an agricultural implement agent
and ironmonger, and kept a boarding house and farm on the side.
The population, at the last census in 1901, had been 146. In all,
judging from the entries in Kelly and the reminiscences of Walter
Raymond and Fred Milton, Withypool was still a remarkably
self-contained community, though the outside world was beginning
to intrude through tourists, most of them, no doubt, sportsmen
interested in fishing and hunting. Four years later, the Great War of
1914-18 broke the mould of the whole of country life.

Since Raymond's day, and especially since the Second World War,
changes have taken place that are more profound than might be
guessed from the outward appearance of the present-day village
which, other than a handful of new houses, does not seem to have
altered a great deal. In fact the changes are deep. A private survey
made in 1990 of the ecclesiastical parish (not the civil, as that
includes Hawkridge), revealed a resident population of 121, exclusive of dependents. Of this total, 71 were 'economically active', i.e.
they were 'breadwinners'; and of these, 43 were employed in the
primary industries of farming, forestry, and related jobs (including
spouses who worked); 28 had secondary or service jobs – at the inn,
post office stores, in transport, plumbing, charity work, and various
professions. 67 of the 71 had jobs within 15-20 miles, 4 had to travel
further afield. There were 50 retired people living on pensions and
private income, some of local origin, the majority 'outsiders' who
had chosen Withypool as a nice place to live. Thus 58 per cent
'economically active', and 42 per cent retired. 'Second Home'
owners were omitted from this part of the survey. A break-down of
the dwellings showed that 30 houses and bungalows were inhabited
by the 'economically active' and their families (with at least one
breadwinner in each house); 9 by local retired people, and 22 by
outsiders in this category: thus 31 in all. There were 15 'second

homes', bought for holidays, weekends, or for future retirement, the owners having their main base elsewhere. With one empty house, it all added up to a total of 71 dwellings, of which 'second homes' accounted for about one-fifth.

How is this population pattern reflected in the social life of the village? First, the institutions. The village hall – a very plain colour-washed building, up the hill on the road towards Hawkridge and Five Crossways, is in use every week for the doctor's surgery, also for the church bazaar on May Bank Holiday, the flower show in August, and for whist drives, dances, and other occasional events. The parish church of St. Andrew (the interior was 'restored' in the 19th century) stands on rising ground at the back of the churchyard. There are 34 names on the electoral roll, a service every Sunday – the rector (who is also the rural dean) living at Halsgrove within the parish. Apart from collections and donations, income is drawn from the proceeds of the May bazaar (£726.48 in 1990), and from the Harvest Home auction held at the Royal Oak Inn, at which buyers pay generous prices for the sake of the cause (usually c.£1,000). The Methodist chapel, built in 1881, with some nice ogee mouldings over door and windows, was closed in 1967 and has now been converted into a house. The primary school also came to an end, the pupils now being bussed (by Land Rover) to Exford and Dulverton; but a new use has been found for the building as an educational activity centre. Next to the churchyard is a triangle of grass with a stone-built shelter housing a bench, dedicated to the memory of Clair Norton, a young woman killed in a car accident. Nearby is the Church Room, shabby now, and used for meetings of the Parochial Church Council and not much else, it seems.

There are three or four commercial premises. The Royal Oak inn is kept by a keen fisherman; it is well patronised and has a clientele that extends far beyond Withypool, especially in the summer; likewise Westerclose private hotel and restaurant. Stabling is also available in the village, and horses for hire. The Post Office stores stocks a wide variety of food, stationery, and much else. It plays a vital part in local life in that, as in other moorland villages, it is a centre for news and messages, and all kinds of unofficial services; but it could not survive without the summer trade. Electricity, water and telephone are now available, a community bus runs on one day in the week, and – for local government – Withypool shares the Parish Council with Hawkridge, both places falling within the West Somerset District area.

It is my impression that, as a viable community, Withypool is hanging on by its eyelashes. With such a high proportion of retired people, it is fortunate that so many of them contribute positively to village life – often the case in country districts, in contrast to the impersonality of suburbia or dormitory estates – however, retired people are too old to have children, hence the demise of the school. 'Second homes' too are always a depressing feature: not only because they are empty for so much of the year, but because when the owners do turn up they are often self-contained, bringing their own provisions rather than buying from the village shop, and have little or no time for social life outside their own circle. If, say, 10 out of the 15 'second homes' in Withypool were lived in by 'economically viable' families, it would do much to correct the imbalance of the age groups and add to the vitality of the village. 'Second homes' are the product of market forces, difficult to tamper with in our kind of democracy, so the only solution is some form of subsidised housing – provided either by the 'Council' (now at a low ebb) or by Housing Associations, as mentioned earlier, and which now seem to be gaining ground.

What Kind of Work?

New housing requires new jobs, all the year round, on the spot or within a reasonable distance if commuter traffic is not to choke the moorland roads or compete with the summer invasion of cars. Tourism, being subject to sudden changes of choice and other economic shifts, is not the cure-all – a view reinforced by some of the observations of Angus Stirling, Director General of the National Trust, quoted in Chapter 10. This poses the whole question of rural employment, for which there are two principal possibilities. One is the prospect of more work in agriculture and forestry, in which care for the landscape is playing an ever more important part – laying and building hedges; planting, thinning and felling trees; the encouragement of extensive or organic husbandry in all its forms, including the regeneration of heather and other moorland swards. Farmers in particular will have increasingly to rely on amenity grants of this kind, as financial supports for food production decline.

The second possibility is this. Leaving aside the ordinary run of shops or employment with the doctor, dentist, solicitor, bank, builder, highway depot, etc., where these occur in some of the larger villages – the bare fact is that alternative sources of work in the countryside depend on small-scale industry, ranging from the single craftsman to workshops staffed by up to c.20 persons. Above that total, industrial units of whatever kind tend to overload the resources of any village under c.1,000 population, and are best located in small towns which are able to cope. So what works in a village?

To begin at the bottom in terms of manpower, there are the individual artists and craftsmen, working single-handed or with assistants, sprinkled over North Devon and West Somerset, a representative sample of which took stalls at the Exmoor Craft and Art Fair held at the Carnarvon Arms Hotel, Brushford, on 19 September 1990. They included potters, weavers, furniture and chair makers, artists and designers, a publisher, and specialists in horn work, wrought iron, needlecraft, wood turning, sheepskin rugs and slippers, cane and rushwork, jams and preserves, et al. Products of these kinds demonstrate skill and set standards in quality and design, lightening the lump of manufacture like leaven in bread. Overall, however, they barely scratch the surface of the labour market.

Next come those businesses that directly serve the land for example, agricultural contractors, blacksmiths and engineers (often combined with a garage), sawmilling, fencing, nurseries, and merchants of feeding stuffs and other items needed by farm, forest, garden, and estate. Few of these are manufacturers; most are suppliers of goods and services, among whom must be counted specialists such as the veterinary surgeon, farrier, saddler, saw doctor, and others, without whom farming, forestry, and horse riding could not continue. And there are others – counterparts of the craftsmen already mentioned – active in localities with particular needs: for example, men skilled in dry stone walling, hedge laying and stone dyking, land drainage, and so on.

The third category contains those units, larger than the crafts-man's studio and not necessarily connected with operations on the land, but for which there is no fixed formula as to size and type. In this instance I exclude all businesses dependent on tourism – be it holiday accommodation, camping and caravan sites, the refresh-ment trade in all its aspects, souvenir and gift shops, leisure enterprises, etc., for unless the proprietors can treat these activities as no more than useful additions to their regular business, or alternatively make sufficient money during the season to allow them to hibernate or shut down altogether during the winter months, then the economic and social benefits to Exmoor are a snare. Indeed if any kind of holiday business, attached, say, to a farm, earns more money than that gained from the farm itself, then the proprietor may well find himself in a very vulnerable situation; and this is a trap inherent in the farm diversification policy.

As stated earlier, public taste is fickle and can die away almost overnight. Alternatively it can overwhelm a village or a whole area, for man quickly kills the thing he loves if he embraces it in crowds. That places great emphasis on jobs other than those governed by tourism. However, regular work in units of industry that fall outside the two categories described so far, are rare inland on Exmoor. Most are to be found in the coastal belt just outside the boundary or on the fringes of the National Park, where labour is easily available and communications, if not good, are at least not bad: though, with mounting pressure on the A.39, a great opportunity awaits the man who can work out a deal with the West Somerset Railway, once British Rail ceases its mindless obstruction to regular rail connection with Taunton. Places like Minehead, Watchet and Williton, have a range of small-to-medium sized businesses which occur in dozens of other country towns in Britain, e.g. printing, paper and carton making, building, joinery, kitchen and bathroom units, garden machinery, reproduction furniture, etc., and – in Minehead – shoemaking which rose Phoenix-like when the Clarks' factory shut down. They have no obvious connection with the National Park, other than the fact that, no doubt, some of their staff live in the moorland villages and find commuting not too burdensome.

Small Businesses

However, thanks to technological advances and the development of telecommunications, it is now possible to run a business, small in terms of space and staffing, but relatively large in terms of turnover, in out-of-the-way places or even in an office at home, equipped with a word processor, fax machine, and computer links. Already there is a handful of small sophisticated units in Exmoor villages involved in publishing, fibre glass making, the manufacture of microscopes for laboratory use, light engineering, tea and coffee blending, sheepskin products, aerosols, conservatories, and a mail order firm specialising in stock handling equipment and medical supplies for sheep.

37   Dunster on a Bank Holiday weekend

The Pressures Of Tourism

38   Erosion on the top of Dunkery

39   Young walkers near Webber's Post

40   Trekkers at the top of Grabbist Hill

41 Withypool: a typical Exmoor village

42 Dismal design in new Exmoor housing, Withypool

43 Mr and Mrs Fred Milton of Withypool: true Exmoor people

There are, of course, additional advantages for small businesses in villages – the relative cheapness of office and workshop space, employment opportunities (full or part-time) for the housebound and women with families, openings for the self-employed, savings in travel, and in some cases the avoidance of repetitive work and its replacement by individual skills. Neither is aid lacking. The area offices of the Rural Development Commission (which has absorbed the Council for Small Industries in Rural Areas or COSIRA) offer business advice and finance for small firms in both the Devon and Somerset parts of the National Park, including loans, and grants towards the conversion of redundant buildings for industrial purposes. The RDC also injects money into tourist enterprises, such as the adaptation of the former BBC Transmitting Station at Washford Cross for use as a Tropical House, and it assists social projects. I have already mentioned its support by way of loan, for the purchase of the village shop at Wootton Courtenay – a community enterprise, both economic and social.

I regard the establishment of small-scale businesses in moorland villages on Exmoor as vital to the future of the life of the rural communities within the National Park. Lessons can be learnt from the Dartington Hall estate near Totnes (see Chapter 2).

Dartington's original purpose was to rehabilitate a run-down rural area, economically and socially, starting with investment in farming and forestry, followed shortly by a range of secondary enterprises. Some of the units were directly connected with land, e.g. a sawmill and a cider factory; others not, and they included building, furniture and joinery, a textile mill, several shops, and latterly the most successful of all, decorative glass manufacture at Torrington in a plant deliberately installed there to provide opportunities for employment in a 'lost area' of North Devon. By no means all these enterprises were successful, but a fair proportion were, notably those eventually sold to outside interests; and they included the forest plantations at Moretonhampstead, the sawmill at Dartington, Staverton Builders, and Dartington Glass itself. I discussed the implications of rural industry with Leonard Elmhirst, co-founder of the estate, and Peter Sutcliffe, chief executive. We came to the uncomplicated conclusion that – provided all the necessary home-work had been done beforehand, as to supply of raw materials and labour, market research, adequacy of communications, and size of investment required – then all depended on good management: a conclusion strikingly substantiated by the way a fresh and thrusting manager had been able in more than one instance to transform a loss-making unit into a profit-making one, and all inside twelve months. There was no secret formula in the category 'rural'.

Rural Society

The other side of community life in the countryside, and on Exmoor in particular, is expressed in social activities and institutions. Socially there is a long tradition of self-support in villages, despite the mounting pressures and attractions of the outside world. I have already written about field sports and revels in earlier chapters, but there are of course many other activities at village level – football, cricket and other team games, drama and the arts, local and natural history, young farmers' clubs, winter lectures, summer outings, and societies of all sorts. In local government the parish council replaced the church vestry in 1894, and it is still an important source of opinion and information which higher authority is well advised to heed. Few villages are without a hall; in some there are additional meeting places, denominational and otherwise, besides the informal ones of inn and shop. As to leadership, so long as the squire and his lady were in charge, private patronage was the order of the day; but as the pattern of rural society began to break up in the 1920s and 1930s, and not only the squire but the resident parson and schoolmaster left the scene, leadership of the traditional sort weakened or vanished altogether.

Historically it fell to one man, Henry Morris, county education officer for Cambridgeshire, to found a new institution, the Village College, which in a democratic fashion was to provide much of the patronage formerly dispensed by individuals. Based on the local secondary school, it offered facilities for sports and youth clubs, classes in further education, opportunities in the arts, and much else, together with administration and a tutorial staff, who did not merely wait for the public to turn up at the new centre, but 'took the college into the villages'. Morris's concept grew and spread, and today it is incorporated into the community colleges and schools which perform broadly similar functions in their respective catchment areas. On Exmoor, the Devon part of the National Park is served by Community Colleges at South Molton and Ilfracombe; the Somerset part by Community Schools at Dulverton, and Minehead, where there is also a further education centre.

Mrs Jan Ross, the community tutor at Dulverton, publishes a

bi-monthly booklet *Exmoor News*, with a circulation of over 2,000, distributed with the local parish magazines and by children direct. By way of sample, the September-October 1990 issue included a directory of about a hundred addresses of local organisations, a diary of events, a youth section, an article on guiding, various notices, and a pull-out supplement with details of all the community education classes organised for the catchment area of Dulverton and southern Exmoor. The classes engage in a very wide range of subjects, some of them exotic – languages, cookery, word processing, poetry, English literature (one course was devoted to the life and works of Evelyn Waugh), painting, Chinese body movement, family and local history, archaeology, first aid, spinning and weaving, embroidery, wildlife, calligraphy, art history, West Country Music, and yet more – in short an Open University on its own. Mrs Ross is also in touch with other established organisations, such as the Workers' Educational Association, and the continuing education department of Bristol University, which offer classes in the area.

Nor is that the end of the list, for now there are branches or autonomous groups, generated by such bodies as Take-Art, NADFAS (National Association of Decorative and Fine Arts Societies), and the Third Age movement, well supported, which appeal particularly to retired people in need of intellectual stimulus and cultural enjoyment, not otherwise easily available. This is an indication of the influx of 'tireds' and 'retireds' into North Devon and West Somerset – elderly people not content with a menu of whist drives, bingo evenings, and jumble sales, who nonetheless support amateur activities in the villages, and for whom the community programme is also a boon. It is a comment too on the changing character, in terms of age and social tastes, of a significant proportion of the population of Exmoor.

Mrs Ross's office is situated in an extension to the Dulverton Middle and Community School, built with funds supplied by the Rural Development Commission and which, as we have seen, helps finance workshops, tourist and other business projects on Exmoor. The RDC's social aid programme is likewise very varied, pump-priming or topping-up the money needed for such things as centres for old people, sports facilities, improvements to village halls, an extension to the Rural Life Museum at Allerford, and interpretation centre at Cleeve Abbey, and – in the pipe line – a contribution to the Guildhall Heritage Centre at Dulverton, which will include a museum, art gallery, information centre, and possibly a deposit for local archives. These are large projects. For smaller needs, such as helping to finance a local arts festival, or to purchase village play equipment, the RDC draws on a Community Chest for grants up to £500.

It is not possible or appropriate in this chapter to offer more than a brief outline of the pattern of society on Exmoor. This book is not designed as a directory, though it does aim to provide clues to the nature of both the economy and the society in and around the National Park. From my own studies and experiences over forty years of living and working on Exmoor, I have reached the conclusion that, however large the community effort, you cannot sustain the identity of a region, such as Exmoor and its environs, on social support alone. Society rests on the economy, and remunerative work is the foundation stone of it all.

Writing About Exmoor

In the introduction to this book I suggested that the literature of a region, such as Exmoor, is an essential element, indeed an integral part, of its identity. In support of this claim I refer to the latest edition of *The Exmoor Bibliography*, compiled by my friend, Roger Miles, and myself and published by the Exmoor Society in April 1989. This is the fourth and most comprehensive version of a work first issued in 1959, and is composed of about one thousand entries, listed under eighteen categories or subjects – evidence enough of identity as measured by the yardstick of literature. It would of course be excessive and unnecessary to reproduce these entries in detail, but the following paragraphs summarise the content of each category and mention some of the notable titles and authors. (Dates refer to first editions unless otherwise stated).

Archaeology and Prehistory

The upland areas of Exmoor, especially those north and west of The Chains, but elsewhere too, are remarkable for the quantity and variety of prehistoric remains – burial mounds or barrows, stone circles, standing stones, etc, dating mostly from the Beaker period, c.2000 BC, and the Bronze Age and the years prior to the Roman occupation. Three works describe the period overall – *Ancient Exmoor* by L.V. Grinsell (David & Charles, 1970), *Ancient Exmoor* by Hazel Eardley-Wilmot (Exmoor Press, 1983), and *Antiquary's Exmoor* by Charles Whybrow (Exmoor Press, 1970).

Buildings in History, Religious Denominations

Few country houses of size were built west of Taunton, viz., Castle
Hill, Combe Sydenham, Nettlecombe Court, Orchard Wyndham, and
Dunster Castle. Apart from farmhouses and cottages and other
vernacular buildings, most of architectural merit are parish churches
and other medieval foundations (e.g. Cleeve Abbey), and dissenting
chapels, about which there are numerous publications. The standard
work before 1800 is the *History and Antiquities of the County of Somerset*
by the Rev. J. Collinson (Cruttwell, 1791). The most compact and
best written contemporary work is *Churches and Chapels of Exmoor* by
N.V. Allen (Exmoor Press, 1974). There are several titles on the
history of Nonconformity in the area, e.g. *Methodists in West Somerset,
1790-1980* by A.G. Pointon, privately published (1982).

Coast – Ships and Harbours

Several authors have written about the coast of Somerset and
North Devon, the ports and trade. Notable titles include *The Coast
Scenery of North Devon* by E.A.N. Arber (Dent, 1911), *No Gallant
Ship* by Michael Bouquet (Hollis & Carter, 1959), *Ships and Harbours
of Exmoor* by Grahame Farr (Exmoor Press, 1970), and *Tales of
Watchet Harbour* by W.H. (Ben) Norman, privately published (1985).

Country Sports and Pastimes, including Rambling

There is an extensive list of books concerning hunting (an
indication of its historical importance), and the red deer, e.g. *Notes
on the Chase of the Wild Red Deer* by C.P. Collyns (Longman, 1862)
and *The Wild Red Deer of Exmoor* by E.R. Lloyd (Exmoor Press,
1970). Tim Abbott has written half-a-dozen books on walking, a
popular subject with several other writers and publishers. Claude
Luttrell's *Sporting Recollections of a Younger Son* (Duckworth, 1925) is
an attractive account of a young man devoted to fishing, riding, and
the natural solitude of Exmoor.

The Doones – Fact, Fiction and Legend

The chief interest here is not so much R.D. Blackmore's great
work, *Lorna Doone*, first published by Sampson Low in 1869 and one
of the world's bestsellers, as the theories about the existence and

adventures of the Doones, and where they had their lair. The most fanatical of the protagonists was the late Sir Atholl Oakeley, Bart, who persuaded Ordnance Survey to conduct a site investigation in 1968, based on his 'researches', and assign the 'Doone Valley' to Lank Combe, one of the tributaries of Badgworthy Water. The Survey is wiser now! The most ingenious work in this vein is a booklet by Barry Gardner, entitled *Who Was Lorna Doone?* (Brendon Arts, 1989).

Etymology – Place Names and Dialect

There are several scholarly works on the place names and dialect of West Somerset, no less than four by F.T. Elworthy, who also edited *The Exmoor Scolding and Courtship* (Trübner, 1879) – hard going for the ordinary reader – and a collectors piece: as is the original edition credited to B. Bowering, though the real author is said to have been the Archdeacon of Barnstaple, by the name of Hole.

The Exmoor National Park

This category is valuable for more than one reason. Firstly, because of the statutory publications about the Park, including Lord Porchester's *A Study of Exmoor* (HMSO, 1977), which proved the turning point in the campaign to save the moorland. Secondly, because of several other seminal works that have exerted a powerful influence on the course of events on Exmoor. Such, for example, is Geoffrey Sinclair's *Can Exmoor Survive?* (Exmoor Society, 1966), and Anne and Malcolm MacEwen's *National Parks: Conservation or Cosmetics* (Allen & Unwin, 1982).

Fiction – Poetry, Prose, Plays and Anthologies

Exmoor has inspired a rich variety of imaginative writing. Apart from *Lorna Doone*, there is a series of popular pony books by Eleanor Helme (Eyre & Spottiswoode); an attractive children's book, *The Story of a Red Deer*, by John Fortescue (Macmillan, 1897); three excellent plays with local historical themes by Phoebe Rees, e.g. *The Miraculous Year* (based on the visit of the Wordsworths and Coleridge in 1797-8) and published by Garnett Miller (1971); also G.J. Whyte-Melville's *Katerfelto* (Chapman & Hall, 1875), and Henry Williamson's story *The Old Stag* (Putnam, 1930).

Genealogy, Biography and Autobiography

Of the published family histories and records – including those of
the Aclands, Fortescues, Stoates, Siderfins, Sydenhams, Trevelyans,
and Wyndhams – the most recent and, in my opinion, easily the
most readable is Anne Acland's *A Devon Family* (Phillimore, 1981).
There are also plenty of life stories of notable people – of R.D.
Blackmore, Parson Jack Russell, George Williams (founder of the
YMCA), Walter Raymond, Cecil Aldin, Dicky Slader, Sir Robert
Waley-Cohen, and Auberon Herbert, about whom John Jolliffe
edited a collection of essays, *Auberon Herbert. A Composite Portrait*
(Compton Russell, 1976), by friends who knew this essentially
English and Exmoor eccentric.

Geography, Geology and Mining, including Rivers and Inland Waters

Under this heading can be found technical works on rocks, soils,
and metal deposits: among them is *Soils of Exmoor Forest* (Soil
Survey of England and Wales, 1971) by Dr L.F. Curtis, former
Exmoor National Park officer. There are studies of rivers, such as
N.V. Allen's *The Waters of Exmoor* (Exmoor Press, 1978), and C.F.
Wade's *Exmoor Streams* (Chatto & Windus, 1903); also several
accounts of mining, notably R.J. Sellick's history of the *Brendon
Hills Iron Mines* (David & Charles, 1962).

Guide Books and Maps, and Rights-of-Way

There is a mixed bag of official handbooks and other publications
on waymarked walks, Nature trails, etc., and a similar run by a bevy
of authors and commercial publishers about places of interest and
pleasant routes over Exmoor (some of them in familiar series such
as the *Red Guides*). Of historical interest is T.W. Cooper's *Guide to
Lynton* (Russell Smith c.1853), which included the first reference in
print to the Doones.

Husbandry – Farming, Forestry, and Conservation

Olive Hallam's *NFU in Somerset* (NFU Taunton, 1971) is a
well-written account of the origins of farming organisation in the
County; also her study of vegetation and land use on Exmoor,

which stands beside Geoffrey Sinclair's *The Vegetation of Exmoor* (Exmoor Press, 1970). Other important works are Orwin's & Sellick's *The Reclamation of Exmoor Forest* (revised ed., David & Charles, 1970) – the story of the Knights at Simonsbath; the MacEwens' *Greenprints for the Countryside* (Allen & Unwin, 1987); and two titles by Roger Miles *Forestry in the English Landscape* (Faber, 1967) and *The Trees and Woods of Exmoor* (Exmoor Press, 1972). There is also a number of official reports issued since 1949.

Industry, Railways and Roads

Local railways round Exmoor have bred a fine crop of histories, covering the lines from Lynton-Barnstaple, Taunton-Barnstaple, Taunton-Minehead, Barnstaple-Ilfracombe, the West Somerset Mineral Railway and the Lynmouth-Lynton Cliff Railway. Robin Madge's *Railways Round Exmoor* (Exmoor Press, 1971) provides a bird's eye view. There is a valuable account of West Somerset roads and turnpikes by B.J. Murless (1985), and a study of the village engineers, W.H. Pool & Sons of Chipstable by Derrick Warren (1988) – both books published by the Somerset Industrial Archaeological Society.

Local History – Life on the Land and Pictorial

This is easily the largest class of writing about the Moor, comprising nearly 200 works. It encompasses a wide range of subjects, including short village histories, several books of old photographs with brief texts, three serious histories of Exmoor, namely *Exmoor* by S.H. Burton (4th ed.,Hale, 1984), *The Heritage of Exmoor* written and privately published (1989) by R.A. Burton (no relation of S.H.), and *Yesterday's Exmoor* by Hazel Eardley-Wilmot (Exmoor Books, 1990). There is a number of scholarly studies by C.E.H. Chadwyck-Healey, Prebendary F. Hancock, D.H. Stevens and E.F. Williams; also E.T. MacDermot's classic, *A History of the Forest of Exmoor* (Barnicott & Pearce, 1911); Jack Hurley's account of two Exmoor workhouses in *Rattle His Bones* (Exmoor Press, 1974) and of the Second World War in *Exmoor in Wartime* (Exmoor Press, 1978). Hope Bourne's *Living on Exmoor* (Galley, 1963) is an unique personal story, enlivened by her own charming drawings.

Meteorology and Climate

Most of the information in this field has appeared in contributions to professional journals rather than as book titles. However, there are at least two accounts of the Lynmouth Flood Disaster in 1952: among them a short book with that title by E.R. Delderfield and R.B. Carnegie (Raleigh, 1963).

Traditions, Folklore and Legends

Serious studies in this area form a rather random collection including R.W. Patten's *Exmoor Custom and Song* (Exmoor Press, 1974) and R.L. Tongue's *Somerset Folklore* (Folklore Society, 1965); also more light-hearted works, e.g. the four series of *Echoes of Exmoor* (1923-26), edited by the Rev. W.W. Joyce, Jack Hurley's *Legends of Exmoor* (Exmoor Press, 1973), and a semi-serious enquiry into *The Beast of Exmoor* by T. Beer (Countryside Publications, 1985).

Fauna and Flora, including Horses/Ponies

The most important work here is the *magnum opus* of the Exmoor Natural History Society, *The Fauna and Flora of Exmoor National Park* (1988), a comprehensive directory of 272 pages (since supplemented), edited by several members of the Society, some of whom have published works on their own account, notably N.V. Allen on *The Birds of Exmoor* (Exmoor Press, 1971) and *Exmoor's Wild Red Deer* (Exmoor Press, 1990); Caroline Giddens on *Flowers of Exmoor* (Alcombe Books, 1977), and the combined work of these two writers in *Exmoor Wildlife* (Exmoor Press, 1989). Mention should also be made of E.W. Hendy's *Wild Exmoor Through the Year* (Eyre & Spottiswoode, 1930), Richard Jefferies's *Red Deer* (Longman, 1884), and several books on fish and ponies (also entered under Country Sports and Pastimes).

Reminiscences – Anecdotes and Belles Lettres

Virtually all the titles in this category make easy reading. Particularly enjoyable is Walter Raymond's *A Book of Simple Delights* (Hodder & Stoughton, 1906). Cicely Cooper's various *Memoirs* of Selworthy and Minehead (Cox), A.G. Bradley's *Exmoor Memories*

(Methuen, 1926), and Anne Garnett's two autobiographical volumes *Caught from Time* (1986) and *Fields of Young Corn* (1989) published by Tabb House. Immodestly I mention my own series of essays in *Exmoor Writers* (Exmoor Press, 1987).

No Exmoor bibliography would be complete without reference to the *Exmoor Review*, published by the Exmoor Society, and which, in November 1990 reached its 32nd annual volume. In the course of its life its contributors have touched on all the categories contained in the Bibliography and thus is a treasure house of information about Exmoor.

One last word. In 1969, S.H. Burton and I decided to launch, as a private venture, a small publishing house, The Exmoor Press. Our aim was to try to fill a gap in Exmoor literature – at that time overloaded with books on hunting and 'Lorna Doonery' – with serious but attractive titles of limited length on subjects that had either been omitted or inadequately treated in the past. Such subjects as birds, fish, deer, and other wild life, archaeology, legends, local railways, rivers, places of worship, the Exmoor pony, Exmoor workhouses, *et al:* in all nearly 30 titles published over a span of twenty years until the firm passed into other hands. All the Exmoor Press titles are to be found in *The Exmoor Bibliography*, and they do indeed fill a large gap. My colleagues and I are proud of that.

INDEX

ABBREVIATIONS

SUBJECTS

PLACES AND PERSONS: A SELECTION FROM THE TEXT